INVESTIGATIVE JOURNALISM IN CHINA

For China's professional journalists

INVESTIGATIVE JOURNALISM IN CHINA

Eight cases in Chinese watchdog journalism

Edited by **David Bandurski** and **Martin Hala**
With an introduction by **Ying Chan**

香港大學出版社
Hong Kong University Press

Hong Kong University Press
14/F Hing Wai Centre
7 Tin Wan Praya Road
Aberdeen
Hong Kong

Hardback ISBN 978-962-209-173-3
Paperback ISBN 978-962-209-174-0

Secure On-line Ordering
http://www.hkupress.org

British Library Cataloguing-in-Publication Data
A catalogue record for this book is available from the British Library.

Printed and bound by Caritas Printing Training Centre, Hong Kong, China

Contents

Introduction

The Journalism Tradition

By Ying Chan

On May 12, 2008, an 8.0-magnitude earthquake hit Sichuan Province in southwest China, claiming at least 69,000 lives. In the ensuing weeks, Chinese reporters roamed the ruins of the devastated towns to interview traumatized parents, villagers, and rescue workers, sending the public gripping images and stories of destruction, death, and heroism. For a few short weeks, the Chinese Communist Party eased its controls on the media, allowing journalists, both Chinese and foreign, to do the kind of fact-finding and reporting the tragedy demanded. For the first time in the history of the People's Republic of China, the destructive power of a disaster was broadcast live on the television screens of the homes of millions of citizens across the country. And for the first time in the history of the Republic, Chinese journalists were allowed to compete against each other and with international media on a relatively equal footing. It was a cathartic experience for the reporters, many of whom were covering a disaster of such magnitude for the first time in their careers.

The response to the disaster surprised and impressed the international community. The *New York Times* called the Sichuan events the Chinese Glasnost.[1] Others in the international media noted the extraordinary performance of their Chinese counterparts, whose reporting was cited worldwide.[2] For weeks, networks such as BBC and CNN used extensive footage from Chinese television stations, whose logos were displayed prominently on screens around the world. It was an unprecedented feat for the Chinese media. Most pundits credited the party with allowing journalists, even for a brief period, to do their job with relatively fewer restrictions.[3]

But the earthquake coverage did not happen solely because of the sudden kindness of the party. The poignant reporting and the images on television and in print also represented an eruption of the suppressed passion of Chinese journalists, who had long aspired for an opportunity to practice real journalism. The tragedy of Sichuan was an opportunity to report and to write the news precisely as it was.

Myths and oversimplifications about China's news media abound. Many in the international community are under the impression that the party gags, intimidates, and censors Chinese journalists under its authoritarian rule, or, sometimes even throw them into jail. At the very least, many regard Chinese journalists as mere tools of the party, bound to its propaganda.

The reality is much more nuanced and complicated.

Control is only one part of the Chinese media's story. The other part is the momentous economic changes taking place in China over the past thirty years that have opened a space for the practice of good journalism. Since 1978, when China adopted the "reform and openness" policy, a generation of Chinese journalists has come of age in spite of the harassment, the firings, and the jailings. By highlighting eight investigative stories that are of modern-classic status in China, this book is a tribute to the Chinese men and women who have kept their faith in the art of truth-telling and investigative reporting intact in spite of great personal sacrifices and hardships.

Contrary to the stereotypes abroad, Chinese journalists are pushing the envelope to uncover wrongs, sharing the same sense of mission as their counterparts elsewhere in the world. But they work in a challenging, even hostile, environment. The Chinese Communist Party continues to maintain strict controls on its news media through legal, administrative, and extralegal means. All newspapers and magazines are property of the state, whose officials at the central or the provincial levels can, and have, fired offending editors or reporters at will. They also have the authority to shut down publications without cause. Through a licensing system of reporters, the party-state regulates journalists' credentials, which amounts to rationing the freedom of expression to the selected. The idea of an independent media is anathema to the party, since it would pose a direct challenge to its authority.

The best Chinese journalists, exemplified by those whose work this book profiles, are survivors who have mastered the high art of navigating the Chinese media control system. They have pushed their luck, on paths fraught with setbacks and disappointments. This book is about them, their hopes and desires in the ever-evolving, brave new world of Chinese journalism. In telling their stories, this book also explores the limitations and fragile state of Chinese journalism today.

The Genesis of the Stories in This Book

This collection grew out of a fellowship program at the Journalism and Media Studies Centre (JMSC), a teaching and research unit at the University of Hong Kong. Beginning in 2001, the JMSC has hosted journalists from mainland China who spend anywhere from a week to a semester at the university, depending on the length of time they can spend away from their jobs. During their time at the university, the fellows typically give public talks and seminars. They also have time to reflect, write, and share their experiences with faculty, students, and local journalists. In return, they are invited to contribute a "case report" on their work to the JMSC. With the exception of the chapter on the Henan AIDS epidemic, all the chapters in this book began as first-hand case studies written by journalists directly involved in the stories.

The raw drafts underwent initial fact-checking and organization by veteran journalist Zhai Minglei of Shanghai. Writer and JMSC researcher David Bandurski then translated the cases into English and rewrote them as third-person narratives. He also provided additional fact-checking, context, and research on critical journalistic issues, with assistance from Martin Hala, a China scholar and media analyst. It was a long and arduous process, a collaborative effort between some of the most devoted reporters from mainland China and Hong Kong–based writers trained in the traditions of Western journalism. With their first-hand experience, the Chinese journalists offered an intimate, inside view of the complexities of working within Chinese newsrooms and juggling the myriad demands of party "eyes" while trying to execute good journalism. The Chinese journalists also gave rich and poignant details on how they had risked firings and libel suits to expose injustices and to give voice to people at the lowest strata of society — peasants, cabdrivers, mine workers. They are courageous crusaders who go after the rich and powerful.

The result of this rigorous fact-checking, rewriting, and editing is the present volume entitled *Investigative Journalism in China*, a collection of case studies of the best journalism from modern China. This is also the first book that provides a comprehensive, first-hand perspective on investigative journalism in China. The selections range from reporting that started in the late 1990s up to 2003, the year SARS struck China. Also in 2003, President Hu Jintao and Premier Wen Jiabao took over as top leaders of the country at the Sixteenth National Congress of the Communist Party of China, marking the first ever peaceful transfer of party-state power in China. As it turned out, the year 2003 would also mark a critical point for the news media in China, as this chapter will explain.

How the Book Is Organized

The eight chapters of this book are presented in chronological order. In Chapter 1, "Wu Fang's Search for Justice," a *China Youth Daily* senior reporter, Lu Yuegang, doggedly pursues the saga of Wu Fang, a village woman who was disfigured and abused by powerful local officials and her husband's family. For his exposé, Lu was sued for libel and spent four years fighting a doomed legal battle.

Chapter 2, "The Untold Story of the Henan AIDS Epidemic," tells the story behind the notorious AIDS epidemic in Henan in central China, in which hundreds of thousands of peasants became infected with the HIV virus after receiving blood sold to illegal blood collection stations set up by local officials and intermediaries known as "bloodsheads." The chapter traces how reporters from various local newspapers broke the story at a time when the party regarded AIDS as a sensitive, taboo subject.

In Chapter 3, "Unmasking the Demons of Charity," a young reporter from Guangzhou's *Southern Weekend*, China's feistiest weekly, is tipped off by an inquiry from a Shanghai company about the possible rip-off of funds donated for school children by one of the country's largest charity organizations. The reporter launches a wild-goose chase that eventually succeeds in documenting an important case of local corruption with national implications.

Chapter 4, "Ah Wen's Nightmare," tells the story of a reporter, Zhao Shilong, who investigates officials at an inner-city drug rehabilitation center who have sold women under their care into prostitution. Going undercover to present himself as a businessman interested in buying one of the women, Zhao, using a hidden camera, catches corrupt officials in the act.

In Chapter 5, Wang Keqin, the dean of investigative reporters in China, spends a year using good old-fashioned shoe-leather reporting and documentary research to expose the widespread exploitation of drivers by taxi companies in Beijing. He discovers that transportation officials in the Beijing municipal government, which was well aware of the problem, had given the unscrupulous companies their tacit approval.

In Chapter 6, reporters at *China Youth Daily* turn their investigative tools on their own profession, exposing corrupt journalists at Xinhua, the state news agency, who had taken bribes in exchange for covering up a tragic mine explosion in which many workers were killed.

Chapter 7 gives an account of how Li Honggu, editor of *Lifeweek*, a leading Chinese newsweekly, directed his reporters to uncover the web of relationships that enabled a lowly provincial official to pocket more than a million U.S. dollars, an astronomical amount by local standards. The story is a rare example of strong political reporting in a system in which officials have little expectation of accountability.

Finally, Chapter 8 recounts how Hu Shuli, noted journalist and founding editor of *Caijing*, China's most respected business weekly, rallied her troops to report on the SARS killer-epidemic even while the government covered up the fact that people were dying of the disease in city hospitals.

Each chapter is followed by a postscript written by Bandurski and Hala, who offer context and background information to the stories, as well as perspectives on pertinent critical issues. Each of the cases raises fundamental ethical and professional questions for journalists, including the piece-rate compensation system for reporters, the use of classified internal materials, and the ethics of media collaboration with police and government officials. In China, as in the West, there are no ready answers to these questions.

Since 1987, the party has adopted a policy that suggests that investigative journalism, or watchdog journalism, could be mandated for the news media. To provide background for this particular example of state-sanctioned investigative journalism, this book includes an additional chapter on the origins of the party-state policy known as *yulun jiandu*, literally meaning "supervision by public opinion." Written by Dr. Li-Fung Cho of the University of Hong Kong, the chapter traces the ideological and historical roots of *yulun jiandu*, and the way it is supposed to work. Cho's research offers readers an additional theoretical framework for the specific investigative cases covered in the first eight chapters.

Cho explains that the government uses *yulun jiandu* as an administrative tool since it mandates that the media serve as monitors of societal and governmental problems. Her chapter also explains how, even while China's watchdog journalism remains under the direct guidance and management of the party, journalists have continued to push the boundaries of acceptable reporting.

The Promises and Limitations of Chinese Journalism

Taken together, the case studies and the postscripts give a portrait of the state of Chinese journalism thirty years into the reform era and on the eve of the sixtieth anniversary of the founding of the People's Republic. It is a picture of remarkable progress and opportunities, as well as setbacks and draconian control. A few themes emerge from this picture.

First, all the reporters in this volume targeted the abuse of power and corruption in their investigations, two of which focused on local officials: a middle-rank provincial official and a drug rehabilitation center operated by the local public security bureau. Other reporters went after private and public institutions: a powerful national charity organization; the taxi cartel in Beijing and the news media itself; as well as local officials who profited from illegal blood sales.

Second, it is notable that party media, especially the national media, have played a central and pioneering role in investigative journalism. Party newspapers represented in this series include *China Youth Daily*, the flagship newspaper of the Chinese Communist Youth League, and the *China Economic Times*, published by a policy think-tank of China's State Council. *China Youth Daily* is credited with two investigations which pursued local authorities and the local bureau of Xinhua. Increasingly, party media have become bolder in their reporting as they compete with the market-oriented media for readers and advertising money. Some of the best for-profit publications — *Lifeweek*, a newsweekly founded in 2003, and *Southern Weekend*, a feisty weekly newspaper published in Guangzhou by the Southern Media Group — conducted the other investigations.

Third, the cases show the intransigence of local power, which often overrides policies and laws promulgated by national leaders in Beijing. Entrenched local power, which often acts in concert with criminal elements, poses one of the biggest challenges to the central government's efforts to reform and enforce the laws.

Finally, the stories have opened a window into an inner world, in particular the enterprising spirit of Chinese investigative reporters. An outstanding example is Zhao Shilong, the staff writer at *Yangcheng Evening News*, a leading daily in Guangzhou under the municipal government. He scooped his rivals in tracking down a story about a drug rehabilitation center that sold the women in its charge into prostitution. Concerned that the story would offend powerful local officials, the *News*'s editors trimmed his lengthy exposé into a three-hundred-word squib. Undaunted, Zhao turned to *News Probe*, a weekly investigative news magazine on China Central Television (CCTV). Working with a young CCTV producer who happened to be in Guangzhou for another story, Zhao led the television crew in re-reporting the story for a national audience. CCTV is the premier national television station owned, controlled, and managed by the central government.

Meanwhile, the stories show the limitations of investigative journalism of the period. These journalists work very much as "loners" without institutional support from their own media organizations or supervisors, who are afraid of rocking the boat and straying too far from the party line. At these media organizations, reporters are generally paid a piece rate according to the number of words published in addition to the base salary. Such a system discourages risk-taking as reporters opt to pursue "safe" stories that run no risk of being censored. Also, no incentive exists for reporters to invest their time in detailed investigative work since compensation is pegged to quantity rather than quality.

The Evolution of Investigative Journalism in China: The Precursors

The cases in this collection took place from around 1996 to 2003, starting with Lu's investigation of a brutal attack on a peasant woman, and ending with *Caijing*'s enterprising reporting on the SARS epidemic. But the seeds of investigative journalism were planted in the early years of Communist rule, when the party still tightly controlled the news media in a command economy. To underscore the significance of the stories in this book, it is helpful to give an overview of the development of investigative journalism in China.

As is the case outside China, investigative reporting is considered journalism's most challenging and valued genre. Its rise and development in China coincide with the four periods of political and economic development of China and the Chinese party-state: the first one dates from the founding of the Republic in 1949 to 1978. At the end of 1978, China's then supreme leader, Deng Xiaoping, launched economic reforms to open up the country to the world. The first reform period ground to an abrupt halt in 1989, with the Tiananmen crackdown on student protests. From 1989 to 1992, China was isolated internationally as Western countries imposed trade sanctions in an effort to pressure Beijing into reversing course. In 1992, Deng Xiaoping visited Guangzhou, stopping in Shenzhen, one of the first Special Economic Zones created in the 1980s. There, he announced to the world that China's economic reforms would continue. There would be no turning back. The period of development inaugurated by Deng's so-called "southern tour" in 1992 drew to a close in 2003, a seminal year marked both by SARS and the Sixteenth

Party Congress at which the current general secretary of the CCP, Hu Jintao, and Premier Wen Jiabao took over the reins of the party-state. Unfortunately, 2003 also witnessed the beginning of new forms of government crackdowns on the news media even while the economy surged forward.

The Pre-Reform Era

Modern journalism in China under the Chinese Communist Party dates from 1979 when the party launched the "reform and openness" era. But even before 1979, journalists chronicled the dislocations and the contradictions within the communist system. Unable to write honestly, the early generation of Chinese journalists composed their exposés of the system in a form known as *baogao wenxue*, or reportage literature, a hybrid style of writing that, at its best, involved detailed reporting and various levels of compilation of facts. Presented as literature, *baogao wenxue* was based on true incidents and characters, whose story the reporter learned through extensive in-depth interviews and observation. A pioneer of the genre was the noted author and reporter Liu Binyan. In 1956, Liu Binyan, then a reporter for *China Youth Daily*, published several important articles, including "On the Bridge Construction Site" and "The Inside Story of the Newspaper" and the sequel which explored how workers or reporters faced the dilemma between pursuing their own sense of justice and following the party leadership slavishly. The impact of the articles was electrifying. In the following year, 1957, Liu was labeled a "rightist," expelled from the party, and packed off to the countryside for hard labor. A year after the completion of his rehabilitation in 1978, Liu published his best-known work, "People or Monsters," a lengthy exposé of the corruption of a middle-aged female official in a small county in Heilongjiang Province in northeast China. Leo Lee, professor emeritus in Chinese literature, explains how Liu gave primacy to the content of the story rather than to style or the form of delivery:

> Like a detective, Liu finds himself uncovering layer upon layer of bribery, corruption, backdoor-ism, and abuse of power, with seemingly no end in sight. And he has presented himself as an over-zealous raconteur telling his readers what he has discovered with impetuous tempo and a seeming disregard for the narrative art . . . Such a somber tone and devastating exposure of the "dark side" of contemporary Chinese society is unprecedented in the entire corpus of post-Liberation Chinese literature . . . [4]

Other *baogao wenxue* writers of Liu's ilk began exploring taboo subjects, especially after Mao Zedong's death and the overthrow of the Gang of Four in 1976. Meanwhile, a new generation of reporters was coming of age in the 1980s, the first decade of the reform era. In 1987, investigative reporting received official support when then premier Zhao Ziyang for the first time incorporated the term *yulun jiandu* in his report to the annual meeting of party leaders. This report made it a party mandate that the media must play a watchdog role in monitoring the party and the government by practicing *yulun jiandu*, literally meaning "supervision by public opinion." As Li-Fung Cho explains in the chapter on *yulun jiandu*, every Party Congress report from 1987 to 2007 has included the term in its official documents.

Almost immediately, reporters read the action as a call for a more active media. When a huge forest fire raged on both sides of China's border with Russia in May 2006, more than one hundred reporters defied bans to race to Heilong River, the site of the fire, and reported on a disaster that, in the end, destroyed 10 percent of the world's conifer reserves. They reported not only on the carnage but also its ecological ramifications, such as desertification. The Communist Youth League of China newspaper *China Youth Daily* published three extensive stories criticizing officials for violating standard operating procedures.

The first reform era ended in 1989 with the government's June Fourth crackdown on student protesters, which drew worldwide condemnation. China became more isolated and insular as party diehards took over and sought to restore order. Many journalists were purged from their positions for the slightest connection with student protesters. Once again, the media retreated to their propaganda role. The period of silence lasted until 1992, when Deng Xiaoping brought reform in China back to life again with his historic visit to Shenzhen.

The Second Reform Era: 1992 to 2003

In her excellent analysis of China's watchdog journalism from 1992 to 2000, media scholar Zhao Yuezhi lauds the rise of investigative reporting as one of the most significant developments in Chinese journalism during the 1990s.[5] While earlier journalists like Liu Binyan wrote probing stories, they often did so against the wishes or policies of their employers. In the 1990s, investigative journalism became institutionalized at major media organizations as the national party media took the lead in setting up special units to pursue *yulun jiandu*. In 1992, CCTV launched *Focus*, a thirteen-minute daily news feature broadcast after the main newscast. Every evening, the show featured hard-hitting reports on corruption and government wrongdoing. *Focus* soon became one of the most popular programs on CCTV, attracting 300 million viewers every night. Li Xiaoping, executive producer at CCTV, explains:

> The program symbolizes an attempt to test public opinion and the receptivity of the government to criticism in a more open society and in a more economically competitive environment. It shows that the media can act as more than just a government mouthpiece and can play a role, albeit a limited one, in matters such as the fight against corruption.[6]

Finding the thirteen-minute format too confining, CCTV in 1996 created *News Probe*, a forty-minute weekly program dedicated to investigative news features.

China Youth Daily, the flagship newspaper of the Chinese Communist Youth League, in 1995 established another notable investigative venture, *Freezing Point*, a weekly supplement edited by veteran journalist Li Datong and Lu Yuegang, one of the contributors to this collection.

In 1998, business and finance reporter Hu Shuli launched *Caijing*, a biweekly business and financial magazine. Over the years, the magazine has earned a reputation for in-depth exposés of abuses in China's stock market and public funds. Its most noted cover stories included reports on the massive misuse of social security funds by the Shanghai municipal government. It reported on a price manipulation scam involving ten leading fund management firms, and on how the privatization of a public utility company led to the siphoning of public assets into personal coffers. Hu, who is also featured in this collection, has earned a reputation as "the most dangerous woman in China."

The stories in this collection were born against this backdrop, featuring the new breed of investigative reporters who broke new ground in content, method, and style. While they still took pains to craft a stylish story, the reporters no longer couched their writing in lengthy, literary prose as the generation before them had. They named the people and places, and told the stories directly. They also conducted extensive fact-checking. Wang Keqin pored through piles of receipts and other documents and hit the pavement with old-fashioned shoe-leather reporting, interviewing hundreds of taxi drivers in Beijing, to produce his investigative report on the city's taxi industry. *Lifeweek* editor Li Honggu plowed through classified internal reports for clues that might shed light on official corruption and its causes. Reporter Zhai Minglei spent two weeks trekking in the mountains of Sichuan in a dangerous search for a paper trail that might offer evidence of the pilfering of charity money.

Many Chinese journalists gobbled up whatever information on Western journalism they could get their hands on. In preparation for the start of *News Probe*, the founders of the investigative news show asked friends in Shenzhen to record episodes of the CBS News show *60 Minutes*, carried on Hong Kong television and accessible only in Shenzhen. They viewed and analyzed the tapes closely and took pride in using *60 Minutes* as their model.

For a long time, investigative journalists could "hunt down" only "dead tigers," corrupt officials who had already been arrested, or sent to jail by the police or the prosecutor's office. In the second reform era, reporters began to go after "live tigers," corrupt officials who were still in high positions, instead. Until the 1990s, reporters' "exposés" were limited to cases that had already been brought into the open, as was the case with Liu Binyan's extensive report on the Heilongjiang official. Despite the widespread impact of the article, Liu Binyan did not break the story. A year before "Monsters" was published, the local provincial press as well as

People's Daily, the national newspaper under the control of the Central Committee of the Chinese Communist Party, had already reported the story in detail, based on information obtained from the government.

While the odds of taking down "live tigers" was limited, there were small victories worthy of celebration. A more active corps of investigative journalists spurred changes in heavy-handed laws and brought down government officials. Even when SARS hit, the reporters remained undaunted. Veteran journalist Hu Shuli mobilized her troops to deliver extensive coverage of the crisis, despite an official cover-up. Later, she explained that the government never overtly ordered a ban on coverage of the epidemic.

In 2003, Hu Jintao and Wen Jintao came to power, in a government the Chinese media dubbed "the Hu-Wen New Deal." Its turnaround on SARS raised hopes that it had learned that suppression of the news media and of reporting the truth could be detrimental to public welfare. After four months of covering up the extent of the epidemic, the government conceded that SARS was ravaging the country and that it still had yet to find a way to bring it under control. In a high-profile live broadcast of a nationally televised press conference, the government announced the dismissal of the minister of public health and his deputy. The stunning news sent a signal to editors around the country that reporting on the matter would no longer be considered taboo.

The same year, the Sun Zhigang case also reinforced the belief that the media could bring about social change and that the party-state would allow more aggressive reporting. On April 25, 2003, *Southern Metropolis Daily*, a news tabloid of Guangdong's Southern Daily Group, a publishing group known for its hard-hitting reporting, broke the story of the death of Sun Zhigang. Sun, a young college graduate visiting Guangzhou looking for work, was picked up by police, and died a month later in police custody. The report, which created a national uproar, eventually led to the arrests and convictions of twelve city police officers. In response to petitions from the legal community, the Chinese parliament later repealed a law that allowed city police to place an alleged unemployed person in custody without due process. Fu Hualing, a professor of law at the University of Hong Kong, credited the reform as "one of the most drastic changes (in policing) since the establishment of the People's Republic."[7]

Tightening the Screws in the Hu-Wen Era

The optimism was short-lived. As it turned out, the party-state stepped up its control of the news media from 2003 onward using legal, administrative, and extralegal means, even while burgeoning grassroots networks were emboldened. Qian Gang, a noted journalist and media researcher, described the plight of the media during the five years between the Sixteenth and the Seventeenth Party Congresses in these terms:

> (During the five years,) the Chinese news media's struggle for press freedom has resulted in both advances and setbacks. The sophisticated defense mechanism by various levels of the party-state has effectively suppressed *yulun jiandu*, especially independent investigative journalism. The quality of the fact-based truths provided by the news media was seriously compromised.[8]

The "defense" of the party-state took the form of arrests, newspaper shutdowns, and the establishment of a web of laws and regulations that ensured the party's further controls on the media's ability to report and publish. The Southern Daily Group, which had taken the lead in aggressive investigative reporting on the SARS epidemic and the death of Sun Zhigang, bore the brunt of the attack.

On March 19, 2004, Cheng Yizhong, the feisty editor of *Southern Metropolis Daily* in Guangzhou, was arrested for alleged corruption in connection with bonuses that he accepted and distributed to more junior editors. The day before his arrest, Yu Huafeng, the newspaper's general manager and deputy editor, was sentenced to twelve years in prison on similar corruption charges. Li Minying, a former director of the Southern Daily Group, the newspaper's parent company, also received an eleven-year sentence. The journalistic community was stunned by the arrests. Cheng, the country's most successful editor, had turned his publication into a top-selling newspaper in the country. In an unusually bold show of solidarity, journalists, academics, and writers signed a public petition calling for his release. Cheng was released in August 2004, after spending five months in jail. He was never charged. The arrests marked the darkest days of the young newspaper, which retreated from aggressive reporting to avoid further retaliation.

In late 2004, the CCP's Central Propaganda Department ordered the media to refrain from criticizing party officials. It also banned the media from conducting *yidi jiandu*, the practice of reporting on the alleged wrongdoings of officials in other provinces. Other harassment followed. In December 2005, the chief editor of *Beijing News*, a joint venture of the Southern Daily Group and *Guangming Daily*, a party newspaper under the propaganda department, was sacked. A month later, *Freezing Point*, a supplement of *China Youth Daily*, was shut down for publishing an article by a history professor who reinterpreted the invasion of China by Western powers in the late Qing dynasty. Editor Li Datong and his deputy Lu Yuegang were removed from their respective editorial positions and banished to the newspaper's research department. Once again, the sackings sent shock waves throughout the country. And once again, both the domestic and the international journalistic communities raced to their defense.

Legal Straitjackets since 2003

In 2001, China entered the World Trade Organization, raising hopes that its new international status would usher in an era of greater openness. Instead, the Chinese government has systematically stepped up regulation of the news media since the turn of the century. Media law scholar Wei Yongzheng summarized the party-state's position as revealed in the legal changes in two simple sentences: "The people have freedom; the media belong to the country."[9] While the government pledged to allow broader participation of private capital in the cultural and media industry, it has tightened its control of news content, ensuring that the party maintains close supervision over news production. As if to dampen expectations of openness, the party-state announced, through the state-run Xinhua News Agency in late 2001, that the functioning of the news media — publishing, radio, and television — must always follow the leadership of the party. Speaking through an unnamed "spokesperson," authorities reiterated the old dictum "The party must govern the media" (*dang guan meiti*). Since then, the party-state has promulgated a series of laws and regulations governing the ownership of newspapers, magazines, radio, and television. Taken together, the laws give only official bodies the right to own and produce news content.

Dozens of laws and regulations were also enacted to step up control of the Internet, making China's the most regulated in the world. Under the new regulations, only a handful of state-owned websites, including the official one of the Xinhua News Agency, are allowed to conduct their own original reporting. "Second-tier" sites are permitted to re-post news from top-tier sites while all other sites are barred from posting anything related to current events. In 2004, the government also put into force a new licensing system for reporters. Every reporter must undergo training conducted by official bodies and apply for a license.

Investigative Journalism since 2003

Since 2003, investigative journalism has lost some of its glamor even though many regional newspapers have created investigative units, underlying the industry's acceptance of the genre. Reporters are digging up more local investigative stories, turning their investigative techniques to safer issues such as business and the environment, which have much less severe restrictions than political ones. *Caijing* has taken the lead in in-depth reporting. In 2006, the magazine published a series of exclusive, comprehensive reports that sent shockwaves through government and the business community. Notable ones have included: "Social security in Shanghai, the dangerous investment," a piece about how Shanghai's Labor and Security Bureau invested social security funds in high-risk real estate, jeopardizing billions of citizens' retirement money; "Alliance of the oligarchs," a report on how banks collaborated with developers to manipulate mortgage loans; "Tang Wanxin the dark hero," a story on the boss of a securities firm that swindled tens of millions of clients' investment money; and "The defeat of micro hard drive," an account of the collapse of a high-tech firm and the loss of a three million U.S. dollar investment, most of it loans backed by a provincial government.

In the January 8, 2007 issue, *Caijing* delivered another bombshell report entitled "Who is the owner of Lu Energy?", which traced in meticulous detail how a private company attempted to take over a state-owned energy enterprise by paying seven percent of the enterprise's ten billion U.S. dollar asset value. The company aborted the purchase as a result of *Caijing*'s exposé. This series of in-depth reports showed the maturity of the magazine as well as its ability to probe the looting of public money, while China's economy undergoes the transformation to become more market-oriented. *Caijing*, unfortunately, now faces its own problems. In late 2009, veteran journalist Hu Shuli resigned as editor-in-chief of *Caijing* owing to a row with the magazine's publisher over ownership and editorial independence.

Environmental reporting is another area where reporters have turned out exclusive coverage on topics including the adverse impact of dam construction on the environment, industrial pollution, and grassroots resistance to chemical plants.

A Survey of Chinese Peasants

As newspapers and magazines are reined in, writers are turning their investigations into books, an area of publishing that is, so far, less regulated. In 2001, Wu Chuntao and Chen Guidi, a writer-couple, began work on a monumental piece of literary reportage entitled an *An Investigation of China's Peasants* (*Zhongguo Nongmin Diaocha*), translated into English in 2006 as *Will the Boat Sink the Water?*.[10] Over a three-year period, the couple traveled to more than fifty towns throughout Anhui Province in central China and interviewed thousands of peasants. *An Investigation of China's Peasants* exposes the inequality and injustice forced upon the Chinese peasantry, who face unjust taxes, arbitrary authorities, and even extreme violence. The literary magazine *Dangdai* (Modern Magazine) first published the exposé at the end of 2003, which quickly sold 100,000 copies. Later, the article was published in book form, becoming an overnight bestseller. Though the book was subsequently banned, pirated copies have circulated widely throughout China.

Other notable books of the period include *Democracy in Zhejiang*, which explores how grassroots democracy has evolved in local towns;[11] and *City Notes*, a chronicle of the destruction of old Beijing in order to make room for modern development.[12]

The Rise of Citizen Journalism

While investigative journalism in traditional media has stalled, citizen journalists are, by contrast, taking a more active role in exposing wrongdoings. By July 2008, China had 250 million Internet users, surpassing the United States as the country with the largest Internet population in the world.

Ordinary citizens and self-styled reporters are increasingly taking reporting into their own hands. They are using Web technologies and cyber-networking to fact-check bogus claims. A small but growing number of them have traveled in pursuit of stories to cover for their personal websites, navigating on the fringes of traditional journalism. In some cases they have achieved results, as did Zhou Shuguang, a peasant who is known as China's first "citizen journalist." For nine months, Zhou roamed around China, writing in his blog about the plight of peasants and migrant workers, attracting more than 20,000 readers a day. Calling himself Zola, after the French writer and activist, Zhou captured the attention and imagination of the blogosphere — and traditional media — when he reported on the struggle of a couple against property developers in the central Chinese city of Chongqing. The couple had refused to leave their house even when buildings around them were demolished to make room for new developments. Zhou was partly credited for turning this local issue into a national sensation with his blog entries, videos, and photographs — although traditional media also reported the story.

Citizens also used the Internet to network and to conduct their own investigations of alleged wrongdoing. In June 2007, in a scandal that shook the nation's conscience, some 400 workers, many of them teenagers, were rescued from harsh conditions working in illegal brick kilns in Shanxi Province. Many had been snatched from their hometowns in neighboring provinces by black market labor brokers. Held against their will and separated from their families, these young men were forced to work in the brick kilns, toiling up to twenty hours a day. Anguished parents, who posted a letter on the popular online forum Tianya club, first brought the matter to public attention. A sharp-eyed journalist spotted their letter and reported the story for local television. The labor racket, which had been going on for many years, was then catapulted to the front pages of international newspapers. Local officials, who had until then resisted the rescue efforts urged by the parents, were forced to take action, freeing the children and returning them to their homes.

The case of the South China tiger in 2007 became another classic example of collective intelligence and investigative power. In October of that year, the official Xinhua News Agency reported that a local peasant in Shaanxi Province had sighted a South China tiger, a species long thought to be extinct. A photograph of the tiger sitting in the forest, reportedly snapped by the peasant, accompanied the Xinhua story, which ran in newspapers across the country. Responding with skepticism, netizens almost immediately raised doubts about the picture, which they suspected to be a computer-generated composite. The Shaanxi Forestry Department defended the peasant and the authenticity of the photograph. Controversy ensued as netizens jumped into the fray. The stakes were high as a genuine tiger sighting might drive an upsurge in local tourism. Meanwhile, the public mobilized on the Internet to search for the source of the suspect image. The puzzle was solved within days. One citizen posted a snapshot of a mass-produced calendar with an image bearing a close resemblance to the tiger depicted in the Xinhua photograph. It was exactly the result Internet users had hoped to achieve through collective investigation. Once again, citizen journalists had taken the lead in amassing facts and standing up to greed and deception.

Where Are They Now?

What have the reporters been up to since they braved the odds to tell the stories in this book?

Zhai Minglei quit *Southern Weekend* in August 2003, having grown frustrated and restless as editors kept him on a short leash while the propaganda department stepped up internal censorship. He turned instead to non-profit work, organizing training sessions for grassroots activists on educational and environmental issues. At the same time, he launched *Minjian* (Civil Society), a monthly magazine of essays and reportage, which did not technically require government approval owing to its not-for-sale nature. Nevertheless, in August 2007, authorities forced the magazine to shut down even though it had not broken any laws. Police entered Zhai's home in Shanghai, and seized his computer and hard drive. Undaunted, Zhai created a personal website called "1bao," literally meaning "A one-person newspaper." He continued to write on a variety of topics, including critiques of relief work for Sichuan earthquake survivors, the untold stories of wartime sex slaves under the Japanese occupation, and the environmental threats facing Inner Mongolian grasslands. Although it has been blocked in China on several occasions, the site is generally accessible both in China and overseas.

The deputy editor of *China Youth Daily*, Lu Yuegang, whose story begins this book, has also moved on. In December 2005, he and his colleague, editor Li Datong, were removed from their senior positions, while their weekly supplement, *Freezing Point*, was ordered to cease publication. Officially, Lu was transferred to the newspaper's research department, but he has since traveled, including to Taiwan, for his own research on Chinese history.

Wang Keqin has continued his investigative reporting for *China Economic Times*. He has since written other in-depth exposés about the continuing hardships facing China's taxi drivers, investigative sequels to the work featured in this volume. He has produced important follow-up reporting on China's AIDS epidemic, the issue addressed in Chapter 2, and he has written the most extensive report on the enslavement of hundreds of young workers in Shanxi's brick kilns. He has also traveled to the United States and spoken at college campuses there.

Zhao Shilong left *Yangcheng Evening News* shortly after working on the Ah Wen story. Frustrated at the lack of support he received from his own newspaper, he quit, and China Central Television quickly hired him. Before long, he was invited to start a new daily newspaper. It was a short-lived adventure. The newspaper was shut down four months after its inauguration for publishing an article advocating a government with separation of legislative, executive, and judicial powers. He returned to Guangzhou, where he taught at a local university before returning to *Yangcheng Evening News* for a reporting position.

Zhang Jicheng has continued reporting and writing on environmental and health issues as a freelancer. His articles have appeared in his blogs and in leading mainland newspapers. In 2007 he joined the staff at *Caijing*, writing about politics and social issues. He later moved on to Guangzhou's *Southern Metropolis Daily*.

Both Li Honggu and Liu Chang have continued to work for their respective publications, *Lifeweek* and *China Youth Daily*. One of Liu's more recent investigative reports concerned an informant jailed by local officials for more than two years after blowing the whistle on a major corruption case. For his part, Li actively organized *Lifeweek*'s on-the-scene coverage of the Sichuan earthquake.

Caijing founder and editor-in-chief Hu Shuli left the publication in late 2009 following a conflict with the publisher, Wang Boming, over ownership and editorial independence. Feeling it was no longer possible for her to maintain her professional journalistic goals under continuing pressure from the magazine's owners, Hu decided to leave the magazine she had turned into one of China's best and take up a teaching position at Guangzhou's Sun Yat-sen University. But the veteran editor, whose core editorial staff also resigned from *Caijing* to follow on her next venture, was not out of the game for long. News came by the end of 2009 that she would now be at the helm of *Century Weekly* magazine, where she would carry on *Caijing*'s tradition of muckraking journalism. Hu's first issue of *Century Weekly* hit newsstands in early January 2010.

The reporters featured in this book have not just survived — they are blazing ahead, each in their own way. They have suffered setbacks, but have also achieved small victories. They soldier on, finding ways to tell true stories about today's ever-changing China. All of them are in some way instilled with a passion that would win the admiration of Western reporters. They have broken stories about official corruption and institutionalized brutality, drawn public attention to critical problems, and, in some cases, forced change. In a media environment that hardly rewards such efforts, their good work owes itself largely to the initiative of individual editors or reporters. Direct acts of civil disobedience among journalists have been on the rise too, as a small but growing segment of journalists identify more with the ideals of social responsibility than with party platitudes. In 2002, after copies of *Southern Weekend* were confiscated and destroyed to remove a second sensitive report about corruption at the government-run charity Project Hope — following Zhai Minglei's story told in Chapter 3 — the newspaper's deputy editor-in-chief posted the full text of the story on the Internet under his own name. Many more examples of this kind of courage abound.

The Limitations of Investigative Journalism in China

In China, investigative journalism plays a dual role as an arm of the government and a watchdog press struggling to be free. Hugo de Burgh, a scholar on the media in China, concluded that Chinese investigative journalism "appears to be striving to realize roles traditional to Chinese culture rather than adopting foreign models or an instance of 'westernization'."[13] But maybe this is a false dichotomy. Chinese investigative journalism has strived to incorporate the best from Western journalism while adapting their practices to the realities of China. Situated within one of the most far-reaching political and economic transformations of the modern era, Chinese journalism has evolved under strengthened market forces and a defensive authoritarian state. The case studies in this book illustrate that the professional aspirations and practices of journalists constitute a third force that has played, and will continue to play, a critical role in shaping the future of Chinese journalism. In our globalized world of interlocking economies and social networks, Chinese investigative journalism will no doubt impact the world at large.

Notes

1. Nicholas Kristof. 2008. "China's Glasnost." *New York Times*, May 23.
2. Howard French. 2007. "Killing puts focus on corruption in Chinese news media." *International Herald Tribune*, January 31.
3. Andrew Jacobs. 2008. "A rescue in China, uncensored." *New York Times*, May 14.
4. Liu Binyan. 1983. *People or Monsters*. Bloomington: Indiana University Press.
5. Zhao Yuezhi. 2000. "Watchdogs on party leashes? Contexts and implications of investigative journalism in post-Deng China." *Journalism Studies* 1 (2), November: 577–97.
6. Li Xiaoping. 2001. *Significant Changes in the Chinese Television Industry and Their Impact in the PRC: An Insider's Perspective*. Center for Northeast Asian Policy Studies, Brookings Institution.
7. Fu Hualing. 2004. "Zhou Yongkang, Sun Zhigang and new policing in China." Paper presented at the annual meeting of The Law and Society Association, Renaissance Hotel, Chicago, Illinois, May 27.
8. Qian Gang. 2008. *Zhongguo chuanmei yu zhengzhi gaige* (Chinese Media and Political Reform). Hong Kong: Cosmos Books, 326.
9. Wei Yongzheng. 2008. "Thirty year's of media law development." In *China's Media in the Reform Era*, edited by Qian Gang and Ying Chan. Hong Kong: Cosmos Books, 224.
10. Chen Guidi and Wu Chuntao. 2006. *Will the Boat Sink the Water?: The Life of China's Peasants*. Public Affairs: Perseus. Translated from Chinese by Zhu Hung.
11. Zhang Jingping. 2006. *Zhejiang fa sheng le shen me?* (What Happened in Zhejiang? or Democracy in Zhejiang). Shanghai: Eastern Publishing Center, January.
12. Wang Jun. 2008. *Cai fang ben shang de cheng shi* (City Notes). Beijing: Joint Publishing, June.
13. Hugo de Burgh. 2003. "Kings without crowns? The re-emergence of investigative journalism in China." *Media, Culture & Society*, Vol. 25, No. 6: 801–20.

1 *The Danger of Libel*
Wu Fang's Search for Justice

When *China Youth Daily* reporter Lu Yuegang saw Wu Fang for the first time, she was bathing beside the Yellow River. She removed a wig of straight black hair, and he saw that her scalp was covered with scabs and scars. The area from her nose down to her shoulders had been severely burned. The skin across her chest was scabbed and raw. He understood that it had been eight years since her attack, but it looked as though her wounds had been inflicted yesterday. "When I first saw Wu Fang, I thought nothing of such things as justice or fairness. To be perfectly honest, I felt only horror," Lu Yuegang later said.[1]

Lu Yuegang had first learned of Wu Fang's story from a friend in Beijing, a film director, who spoke of a woman from northern China's Shaanxi Province who had been attacked by her own villagers. He suspected there were much deeper layers to the story, so he decided to go and see Wu Fang for himself.

Wu Fang came from a farming family in a village called Fenghuo. When she was twenty-four years old, she was married off to a young man named Wang Maoxin. The marriage never went well. She gave birth to a son, but she and her husband fought constantly. He grew more and more abusive until finally, in 1987, she ran away from Fenghuo in search of a new life, leaving her son behind.

Roughly a year after her escape, authorities from Fenghuo tracked her down and returned her forcibly to the village, locking her up in an office that belonged to the local army unit. On the night of April 26, 1988, several men rushed into the office. They wrestled Wu Fang to the ground and fought her onto her back. The village's top party leader stepped in and turned off the lights. Then, as one man pressed the full weight of his body against her and another pinned her hands down, she felt something wet splash across her face. The liquid burned as it flowed into her eyes and ears. "Mother, help me! It hurts! It hurts!" she screamed. She could hear a crowd of villagers gathered outside the door, but no one so much as lifted a finger to help her. Finally, her assailants pulled up her sweater, splashing the awful liquid over her chest and stomach.

A court medical examiner later determined that Wu Fang had been attacked with concentrated sulfuric acid. She had third-degree burns across 23 percent of her body. Though Wu Fang clearly identified her assailants, her case languished for more than three years in the local courts until finally a National People's Congress representative in the nearby city of Xianyang intervened on her behalf. Several suspects were arrested, tried, and sentenced.

But for Wu Fang, the case was far from closed. The men whom she knew were chiefly responsible for her attack escaped prosecution. She went on with her life, eventually remarrying and giving birth to a daughter. Still, she never lost hope that one day her case might see justice. Her unyielding spirit amazed Lu Yuegang. The more he learned about her story, the more he became personally invested in her cause. "We, all of us, breathe the same air as Wu Fang and other victims of injustice," he later wrote. "We might all meet some day with the same misfortune. By safeguarding their rights we tend to our own. So this was as much about rescuing me as it was about rescuing Wu Fang."[2]

The Cruel Village

Wu Fang had told investigators repeatedly that she knew the man who had turned out the lights in the office was Wang Nongye, the top party leader in Fenghuo. They refused to hear her testimony. "The investigators didn't even write it down," Wu Fang recalled. "When I asked why they were not writing it down, they would not answer. After that, they told me never to mention Wang Nongye's name again. My case would never go anywhere unless I cooperated, they said."

Despite Wu Fang's testimony, the court recorded the name of the man who had turned out the lights as Wang Maozhang, the younger brother of Wu Fang's first husband, Wang Maoxin.

As Lu Yuegang delved further into the local and regional politics in this corner of Shaanxi, he began to see patterns in the lies surrounding Wu Fang's case. Wang Nongye was an important piece of the puzzle. He was powerful as secretary of the Fenghuo Party Committee. But more importantly, he was the son of Wang Baojing, a cadre, or *ganbu*, with a long-established legacy in the province dating back to the earliest days of the People's Republic of China. Wang Baojing had risen as high as deputy mayor of Xiangyang, a prefectural capital, making him one of the province's most powerful officials. He had been forced into formal retirement at the age of sixty, but remained an active figure in local politics. The elder Wang's legacy proved crucial to understanding the violence the village unleashed on Wu Fang.

With the help of a team of researchers at *China Youth Daily*, Lu Yuegang spent a week digging up as much information as he could about the history of Fenghuo. They pored over reference materials available in Beijing libraries, and sifted through hundreds of issues of *People's Daily* and *Shaanxi Daily* from the 1950s to the 1990s. Lu Yuegang also interviewed top provincial officials, including a former provincial party secretary, and more than twenty peasants from around Fenghuo.

Shaanxi had its own special legacy dating back to the years of Communist Party resistance against the ruling Kuomintang (KMT) before 1949. The Shaanxi city of Yan'an had been the terminus of the Long March of 1934–1935, in which an estimated 100,000 communist soldiers retreated roughly 8,000 miles from their base in the southern province of Jiangxi to escape annihilation by KMT forces. By the time the Red Army finally reached Shaanxi, it had been reduced to some 30,000 fighters, but the prestige of the party soared, as did recruitment. Shaanxi became a strategic and symbolic base of Communist Party resistance.

After the Communist Party seized control of China in 1949, top leaders continued the ancient tradition of posting outside officials to regional positions of power, which they saw as an effective way of limiting regional power networks and consolidating power at the center. Exceptions were made for Shaanxi, however, which had been so instrumental in the party's rise; there, the policy was "Shaanxi governed by its own." This meant that while the central leadership had the final say in appointments, the provincial power network retained a strong local identity.

Wang Baojing was something of a permanent fixture in Shaanxi's local party apparatus, with deep political roots that made him almost unassailable. Wu Fang's native village of Fenghuo was at the heart of his mysterious power. In the 1950s, as a crafty political upstart, Wang fashioned the village as a Communist Party exemplar, a resplendent symbol of the promise of the "new China." In 1958, the first year of Chairman Mao's so-called "Great Leap Forward," in which China sought to surpass its industrial rivals in the West through the miracle of central planning, Fenghuo was celebrated for its productivity. That year, the village reported a total wheat output of 750 metric tons. Rumor had it that the grain grew so tall and thick that you could leap out of a fifth-story window and the fields would break your fall. In the 1950s and 1960s, as narrow political one-upmanship won out over realism, such lies were common currency — and Wang Baojing was a quick study. By crafting Fenghuo into the kind of exemplary village the Communist Party needed to push its economic program, Wang was able to garner official support and funding. As Lu Yuegang sifted through the news archives, he was astonished at the level of resources Fenghuo had managed to siphon off by virtue of what it represented to party leaders.

The reality of the Great Leap Forward was of course far grimmer. Nationwide grain shortages led eventually to the starvation of perhaps as many as twenty million Chinese. When Wang Baojing's fabricated crop yields of 1958 sparked outrage among farmers in the region in 1959, the unrest prompted a direct visit from the province's top leader, Zhang Desheng. This was the first of numerous complaints against Wang over the years, but he had already established himself within Shaanxi's internal politics. The all-important principle of "Shaanxi governed by its own" meant that party leaders in Shaanxi had to aggressively protect their own province.

The villagers attacked Wu Fang because she had sinned against the unassailable myth of Fenghuo, one that ensured the village's power and prestige. The village's top leader, Wang Nongye — the man who had turned out the lights — was shielded from prosecution because it meant protecting the legacy of Wang Baojing and that of provincial politics in Shaanxi.

Lu Yuegang's Report Stirs Up a Dragon

On August 8, 1996, Lu Yuegang's story about Wu Fang's attack and local politics in Shaanxi ran on the front page of *China Youth Daily*. It was called "The Strange Affair of the Destroyed Face." The next day, a directive from the Central Propaganda Department instructed other media not to reprint or excerpt the story, and *China Youth Daily* was forced to scrap its plans for a series of follow-ups.

On August 12, Wang Baojing circulated an open letter saying *China Youth Daily* had set out to destroy his reputation. He denied the accusations in Lu Yuegang's report, saying that neither he himself nor Fenghuo had ever been showered with political favors. On August 26, Wang Baojing, Wang Nongye, and the secretary of the Fenghuo Village Committee Lu Wen filed a libel suit with the Xi'an Municipal People's Court against both Lu Yuegang and *China Youth Daily*, seeking 4.8 million yuan ($693,000 US) in damages.

Several months later, as Lu Yuegang awaited news of the trial proceedings, Shaanxi Provincial Party Secretary An Qiyuan and other provincial leaders signaled their support for Wang Baojing by arranging a Christmas Day trip to Fenghuo. Secretary An delivered a speech, broadcast throughout the province and printed in official newspapers, in which he said that an "exemplary group" ran the village. On March 4, 1997, An delivered another speech that appeared on the front page of the official *Shaanxi Daily*, defending the need for "advanced models" like Fenghuo.

Even before the case against Lu Yuegang and *China Youth Daily* went to trial, legal scholars watched carefully and wondered whether Shaanxi's legal system would be capable of rendering an impartial verdict. Lu Yuegang's counsel was Zhang Sizhi, a well-known Chinese lawyer who had represented many high-profile defendants, including Jiang Qing, the infamous third wife of Mao Zedong and Gang of Four member, and Chinese dissident Wei Jingsheng.

The question of jurisdiction emerged early on as a key issue. According to one reading of Chinese libel law, cases had to be tried in a court either where the alleged crime took place — in this case, in Beijing, the location of the offices of *China Youth Daily* — or in a court where the "act had effect."[3] The latter would have meant trying the case in Xianyang, the plaintiff Wang Baojing's residence. But the case against Lu Yuegang and *China Youth Daily* was to be held in Xi'an, Shaanxi's provincial capital. In a demurral, the lawyers for *China Youth Daily* questioned the jurisdiction of the Xi'an court, but this was rejected without explanation. When the newspaper appealed this decision, the Shaanxi Supreme People's Court upheld the lower court's decision. The higher court reasoned that because *China Youth Daily* was a nationally circulated newspaper, the "act" could happen anywhere: "Are there not copies in Xi'an?" the decision read.

In truth, the question of jurisdiction had never been a matter for the courts. An inside source at the Xi'an Intermediate People's Court told Lu Yuegang they had received explicit instructions from top provincial officials. "You see?" he said, holding out a memo for the reporter. "We had refused to accept the case. After all, what does all this have to do with Xi'an? But what can we do? This has come all the way from the top."

As it happened, Wang Baojing had pulled some strings in the provincial court, whose director, Wang Farong, had instructed the lower court in Xi'an to accept the libel case. Why did Wang Baojing oppose trying the case in Xianyang, which had clear jurisdiction? Ren Wei, the chief judge running the court in Xianyang, who, as Lu Yuegang later said, had a "very keen sense of justice," was unlikely to render a verdict in Wang Baojing's favor. In fact, Ren had already contacted China's highest court, the Supreme People's Court, to appeal for a reopening of the original criminal trial against Wu Fang's assailants.

During the first week of May, just days before the trial was to begin in Xi'an, Lu Yuegang paid a visit to Ren Wei hoping to find out why the court held Wu Fang's former brother-in-law Wang Maozhang responsible, contrary to her testimony. Ren was candid about the case, saying that it had been rigged to "protect certain criminals."

"Is it possible for me to see the original case files? This is really important," Lu Yuegang said.

"Really, there is nothing to see," Ren answered. "The files are perfectly clean."

"But you just said you had to dig under the surface to arrive at the truth. If I want to back up my facts, I've got to see the original case files."

"Ok," Ren said finally.

They reviewed both the police and prosecution files, and it was clear that Wu Fang's original testimony had been tampered with. But Lu Yuegang wanted more proof.

"Would it be possible to look at the *fujuan*?" he asked.

These were the court's "auxiliary files," highly classified documents that recorded contacts between party officials and the court. These "black boxes," as Lu Yuegang called them, were the clearest proof of party manipulation of the court system.

"I'm sorry, but that's impossible," said Ren.

While Lu Yuegang understood Ren's reticence, and his need to protect himself in a system more political than legal, his failure to get his hands on the "auxiliary files" became one of his deepest regrets. On May 27, 1997, just three weeks after their meeting, Ren was found dead in a highway accident. Although he could not prove Wang Baojing's involvement, Lu felt sure this had been an assassination designed to put an end to Ren's appeal for the reopening of Wu Fang's case.

It would not have been the first time Fenghuo thugs were sent to do Wang Baojing's bidding. On October 20, 1996, not long after the Xi'an Intermediate People's Court had accepted the libel case against Lu Yuegang and *China Youth Daily*, an unknown visitor offered Wu Fang 100,000 yuan if she would keep her mouth shut. She refused the offer outright, and six weeks later two men appeared at the home of Wu Fang's mother in Beidun Village.

"Tell Wu Fang she had better shut her mouth. Anyone who talks, dies," said one of the men.

"Where do you think you are? This is China!" Wu's mother screamed back.

"I'll dig your grave with my own hands!" shouted the thinner of the two — a man Wu's mother said had a slightly jaundiced-looking face. He slapped the old woman and shoved her to the ground. "If anyone so much as whispers, they're done for!" The incident terrified Wu Fang's mother, and for days she would not eat a thing.

The man who struck Wu Fang's mother was most probably Wang Aishe, a villager from Fenghuo wanted for murder in an unrelated case. On June 1, 1996, a contingent of local police raided Fenghuo in an attempt to arrest Wang. Before they could track down the suspect, a mob of villagers descended upon them. Several officers were hospitalized for bone fractures and head trauma. Three days after the skirmish, one of the injured officers, Liu Zhiquan, sat upright in his hospital bed, his pistol at his side. "I've been a policeman for eight years, and I've been stabbed while apprehending suspects before," he sobbed. "But I can't understand these villagers in Fenghuo. Why would they act this way?"

After the suspicious death of Xianyang's top judge, Lu Yuegang was determined to investigate the scene of the car accident. At this point, his efforts to spur a fresh investigation into Wu Fang's attack were beginning to consume him. He wrote scores of letters to top party and government leaders in both Beijing and Shaanxi. His editors at *China Youth Daily* did more than encourage him. The newspaper's deputy editor-in-chief Zhou Zhichun volunteered to accompany Lu Yuegang on his renewed investigations in Shaanxi after the reporter's wife expressed fears for his safety. "If they want Yuegang, they'll have to go through me," Zhou said.

Their preparations might have seemed almost ridiculous. Zhou Zhichun dyed his graying hair, bought a pair of sunglasses, and swapped his boardroom black loafers for a pair of athletic shoes. Lu Yuegang shaved off the curly beard he had been growing for several years. But the dangers they faced were very real.

Before their departure for Shaanxi, they sat down with officials at the Supreme People's Court, briefing them on their specific plans in Xianyang. They went next to the Public Security Bureau, where they put a record of their plans on file and informed a top police official of the evidence they had gathered up to that point.

"Would it be possible for you to leak the word out that we've already filed our case materials with you?" Lu Yuegang asked the police official. Word would, the journalists hoped, get to Wang Baojing that they were untouchable.

"That's not a problem," the official said.

When they were on the road in Shaanxi, Zhou Zhichun turned to Lu Yuegang and said: "You know, the world doesn't need just one Don Quixote; it needs a whole band of Don Quixotes."

Lu Yuegang instantly understood Zhou's reference to the Spanish classic. Like many investigative reporters in China, Lu Yuegang saw Quixote's fictional attack against a group of windmills as somehow emblematic of his own quest. The image of Quixote and his windmills cropped up again one year later in his work of reportage on Wu Fang's story:

> Often, the opponent we face is like an army, or like a monster with countless arms. If one person, or a few people, face off against something as vast as this, something webbed with self-interest, we are like Don Quixote, or at best like a band of Don Quixotes. We stand for the public. Our legitimacy comes from the common good. We are, in other words, what has been called "the Fourth Estate." We are armed with truth and the law. But our opponent cares nothing about the truth. He does not recognize the law. Whether he enforces the law or breaks it, the only real law is that which benefits himself and his cronies. In such a battle, our weapons are so often of little avail . . . [4]

The two Quixotes returned to Beijing with material that would prove important to Lu Yuegang's reportage.

But the ongoing battle in the Xi'an Intermediate People's Court, a restaging of Quixote's charge against the windmills, most immediately concerned Lu Yuegang and *China Youth Daily*. Before his death, Judge Ren Wei had told Lu Yuegang that the odds were stacked against the newspaper in the libel trial. Ren had received a direct visit from representatives of the Xi'an court, who wanted to know particulars about the Wu Fang case, an unusual departure from general protocol, according to which prosecutors handled the gathering of evidence on their own. "Yuegang, you cannot possibly win this case," the judge had told him. "It is not a question of evidence. There are much bigger factors at work."

The Xi'an Intermediate People's Court began hearing the case on May 8, 1997. Almost immediately, the judge turned to Lu Yuegang and asked: "Can you inform us which official office supports your contention that Fenghuo is not an exemplary village? Was an official statement to this effect issued by any organization?" The facts and the law were apparently of no consequence to the court; the only admissible "evidence" would have been a statement of political support for the facts in the *China Youth Daily* article, something they did not have.

China Youth Daily's lawyer, Fu Kexin, said early on that three separate factors would shape the outcome of the trial: first, rule of law; second, media coverage (which might put both the plaintiffs and the court under greater pressure); and third, regional politics. As media already on the scene had been muzzled with a propaganda directive from the Central Propaganda Department against covering the court proceedings, the balance seemed to be shifting in favor of regional politics.

But it was not long before the political dynamics in Shaanxi shifted as well. In August 1997, roughly three months into the libel case against Lu Yuegang and

China Youth Daily, Provincial Party Secretary An Qiyuan resigned as Shaanxi's top leader. Li Jianguo, a senior party official previously posted to the city of Tianjin, filled his position. Within just a few weeks, the libel case was temporarily suspended under the legal principle of "criminal precedence," which states that questions of criminal responsibility must be settled first when they arise in civil cases.[5] Although it is not clear exactly what happened behind the scenes, this new line of legal argument suggested that real doubts existed about the possible involvement of Wang Baojing's son — one of the plaintiffs in the libel case — in the attack on Wu Fang. "Criminal precedence" offered a convenient legal pretext for dropping a case that was becoming a political liability.

As Wang Baojing's libel case was suspended, Lu Yuegang was quietly putting the final touches on *Big Country Small People*, his non-fiction work about Wu Fang and politics in Shaanxi. In January 1998, Wang Baojing somehow managed to get wind of the book and wrote a letter of protest to top officials at the Chinese Communist Youth League, the publishers of *China Youth Daily*. Top officials from the League pressured the newspaper, telling Lu Yuegang not to publish the book — otherwise, the newspaper, already locked in an uncertain case with Wang Baojing, might be held responsible.

Lu Yuegang, who had already delivered his final draft to the publisher, had no intention of complying with the order. But he did decide to work with the publisher to postpone the book's release for a couple of months. They decided to publish it over Chinese New Year in late February, when official business slowed down and people tended to be in better spirits. The book hit the shelves in early March, right on the heels of the holiday. Censors immediately ordered major bookstores, including the state-operated Xinhua Bookstore, not to carry the book. But it was too late. The ban served only to stimulate demand, and those who could not get their hands on authorized copies of the book could find it on the black market.

On September 18, 1998, more than a year after the suspension of Wang Baojing's libel case, the Shaanxi Supreme People's Court unexpectedly revisited the question of jurisdiction. This time, they remanded the case to the Xianyang Intermediate People's Court, a political decision that now made sense for Wang Baojing because the opened-minded judge, Ren Wei, was now out of the picture.

When trial proceedings opened on February 4, 2000, *China Youth Daily* refused to appear on the grounds that the court would be unable to yield an impartial verdict. The argument, which *China Youth Daily* lawyer Fu Kexin made in a formal letter, held that the Xianyang court had a clear conflict of interest because the newspaper article concerned had also called into question the court's verdict in Wu Fang's 1988 criminal case. Fu Kexin's letter also questioned the legality of the provincial court's suspicious change in venue. Why did they decide to move the case to Xianyang after the provincial court had twice denied challenges to the jurisdiction of the Xi'an court? The newspaper's defense team also contended that holding proceedings in Xianyang put the defendants in a dangerous position, as they had evidence that Wang Baojing had brandished a firearm at a village meeting in Fenghuo, threatening anyone who dared testify against him. Finally, Fu Kexin argued, the lingering question of "criminal precedence," which had resulted in the suspension of the Xi'an trial in the first place, still remained. All questions about the Wu Fang criminal case had to be resolved before the libel case could go forward.

The court disregarded all those objections, and the trial went ahead in the newspaper's absence. Lu Yuegang was there, and he later recalled that throughout the entire proceedings, a mysterious man walked over to the bench from the seats and passed notes to the presiding judge.

The local court was in fact taking its cues from the Shaanxi Supreme People's Court, which was acting in an advisory role at the lower court's request. Lower courts generally made this arrangement when they felt they lacked sufficient expertise and appealed to higher courts for guidance. The Supreme Court had already instructed Xianyang, where the proceedings were merely a formality. They ruled that *China Youth Daily* had indeed violated the rights of the plaintiffs, that proceedings could go ahead in the newspaper's absence, and that Lu Yuegang and the newspaper could be treated as one defendant. *China Youth Daily* should be ordered to cease all attacks on the plaintiffs, issue a public apology, and pay damages. The only question left open to the court was the exact amount of damages, to be determined by the degree to which the defendants expressed remorse.

On June 22, 2000, the Xianyang Intermediate People's Court ordered *China Youth Daily* to pay 90,000 yuan in damages in addition to legal fees. The text of the court's decision made no legal arguments whatsoever. There was no record of evidence presented to the court, nor was there any mention of how Chinese libel law had been interpreted in light of the facts. After the verdict was rendered, *China Youth Daily* lawyer Fu Kexin read the following prepared statement from the newspaper:

> Today we have appeared in this courtroom in Xianyang in a spirit of respect for the law. What we have witnessed, however, is a rueful trampling of justice and self-evident truth. Twelve years ago (1988), in the village of Fenghuo in Liquan County, Wu Fang was the victim of a vicious acid attack that left her with third-degree burns across twenty-three percent of her body — her head, face, shoulders, chest, and back. Her right ear was destroyed, her auditory passage closed off. Her right hand was severely burned. She nearly lost sight in both eyes. Many villagers participated in the attack. Many more looked on as it happened. And so a young woman's life became a ghost's life. Such cruelty, with such a consequence! But for three years no one looked into the matter. Here, on this very stretch of earth, justice and truth were trampled by savagery.

> Nine years ago (1991), in this very building, a verdict was finally announced in this terrible case. But the plaintiff, knowing in her heart that some of those responsible for the crime had escaped justice, was unsatisfied with the court's decision. Many of the plaintiff's accusations and doubtful points in the case are still on record in this very court. Ren Wei, the deputy director at that time, who later became the court's director, wrote clearly as a formal witness for the Xi'an Intermediate People's Court that there were "serious problems" with the Wu Fang case. And to sit here in the same court to hear a verdict passed down like this one we have heard today! What can one even say? Once again, justice and conscience are crushed.
>
> Everyone here today, from the city of Xianyang and across Shaanxi, is clear about the actions of the Fenghuo village leadership over the last half-century. They know about the lies and exaggeration, the undeserved reputation — all at the expense of the province as a whole. Tens of thousands of words have been written on the topic. Everyone from top provincial leaders to ordinary peasants has borne witness to these facts. And here, to have a decision like this! Justice and conscience sold to the highest bidder!
>
> We solemnly express our intention to fight on to protect the sanctity of the law, safeguard justice, support watchdog journalism, and preserve the dignity of this newspaper. We will mobilize the strength and conscience of society to open a route to justice for Wu Fang. We will fight tirelessly to record and reflect back on history for the greater good of generations that come!
>
> We are confident time and history will make a sober judgment of the decision of this court today. We are confident light will prevail over darkness, justice over injustice.

China Youth Daily's appeal was granted and the case moved on to the Shaanxi Supreme People's Court, the very same court that had just advised the lower court during the proceedings. Concerned for witness safety, *China Youth Daily* had previously presented only one witness during the Xianyang trial. They were now prepared to call seven witnesses.

The verdict in the lower Shaanxi court sparked fierce discussion within China's legal community. On August 8, 2000, on the eve of the Supreme Court trial, Beijing University's Research Center on Administrative Law held a discussion forum on the libel case and its implications for China's judicial system. Zhang Cheng, a professor at the Tsinghua University School of Law in Beijing, wrote that Xianyang court's failure to yield an independent verdict, in particular its request for assistance from the higher court, was the most serious problem in the case. "These decisions [made by the Shaanxi Supreme People's Court] were hidden from everyone's eyes, from the eyes of all society," Zhang said. "The failure to yield verdicts according to civil law, and the lack of independence among courts at various levels, are urgent problems. If you are seeking justice, if you want to win your case, you must take this route. But this means you must walk a road of injustice. This is what happens when politics and law become entangled."

Many leaders from China's legal community stepped out to support *China Youth Daily*. The newspaper accepted an offer from Wang Weiguo, a well-known professor of law from the China University of Politics and Law, to serve as the newspaper's legal counsel for the higher court trial.

Chinese media widely anticipated that the trial would go public, so newspaper reporters and television crews were already on the ground. But on September 4, 2000, the day before court proceedings were to begin, the Shaanxi Supreme People's Court announced it would be a closed trial. Cries of protest rang out among the journalists gathered outside the courthouse. "What is the reason for the court's decision?" shouted one reporter.

"Reviewing the evidence presented by both parties, we determined that some facts not presented at the previous trial . . . were matters of state secrecy," said the court's chief justice, Zhang Junzheng. "Upon consultation, our collegial panel decided the trial could not be held openly on the basis of national secrecy laws and Article 66 of the Civil Procedure Law. This will allow both sides to present evidence to the court with ample opportunity for cross-examination."[6]

When one reporter objected to this interpretation of Article 66, Zhang turned to the following portion of the Civil Procedure Law and invited the reporter to read it for himself.[7] The reporter read aloud: "Evidence shall be presented in the court and be cross-examined by the parties. However, evidence that involves State secrets, trade secrets or personal privacy of individuals shall be kept confidential, if it is necessary to be presented in the court, it may not be presented in an open court session."[8]

There was a brief pause, as everyone seemed to process the words. Then the reporter said: "It's cut and dried, is it not? It says nothing about not holding open court sessions. All it says is that anything involving state secrets cannot be presented during an open session."[9]

The objections of the media notwithstanding, court proceedings began the next day behind closed doors. *China Youth Daily* called, as its first witness, Wu Fang, who arrived by car with her husband and sister. Lu Yuegang met her outside the courthouse and they entered hand in hand. Wang Baojing, absent on the first day of proceedings, never heard Wu Fang's testimony.

The next day, September 6, as Lu Yuegang waited outside the courtroom for his turn to testify, Wang Weiguo came over with bad news. The court had decided that he could not take the stand because his newspaper report had triggered the libel claim.

The court seemed to be closing the doors one at a time. Media from across China had crowded into Xi'an, but were barred from attending the court proceedings. Party leaders in Xianyang had even taken the extreme measure of locally jamming news broadcasts from Hong Kong's Phoenix Television, which had a reputation for more open coverage.

While traditional media sat on their hands, unable to cover the proceedings, a group of journalists set up a website called FM 365 to offer up-to-date commentary on the libel case. Working from a small Internet bar down the street from the courthouse, they solicited contributions from some of China's leading editorial writers, including Yan Lieshan, Zhao Mu, Ma Shaohua, Pan Duola, and Zhang Tianwei. FM 365 played an important role in drawing the attention of international media to the case. On October 9, 2000, the Asian edition of *Time* magazine ran a cover story on Wu Fang and the case against Lu Yuegang and *China Youth Daily*. The issue included a profile of Lu Yuegang called "The journalist who won't give up."[10]

Late at night on September 9, after nine straight hours of deliberation, the trial finally came to a close. Defense lawyer Wang Weiguo stepped out to greet a throng of reporters and said they expected a verdict to be announced within several weeks, but, in fact, it ended up taking almost seven months. Finally, on March 26, 2001, four and a half years after Lu Yuegang's report, the Shaanxi Supreme People's Court ruled that it would uphold the lower court verdict against *China Youth Daily*.

Wang Weiguo said the case had been doomed from the outset: "Under the current climate, it is nearly impossible for media in China to win libel cases. Media are at an acute disadvantage from start to finish."[11] He Weifang, a law professor at Beijing University and one of the country's top legal experts, said the *China Youth Daily* case had underscored "the problem of regionalized power":

> I think it is critical that we work to separate our civil justice system from regional power as quickly as possible . . . If we agree that the law should take precedence over local political influence, we should not accept verdicts like this. If the whole fabric of our court system is regionalized, then we cannot have the comprehensive system of law on which the people depend. Having a comprehensive legal system does not just mean that all courts read from the same Civil Procedure Law; it means, more importantly, that they share an understanding of the Civil Procedure Law. Centralizing China's legal system is a far more pressing concern than centralizing China's banking system. This is a problem we must solve.[12]

China Youth Daily issued a statement criticizing the court's verdict, saying it had made a mockery of Chinese law. But the newspaper had run out of options. In June 2001, the newspaper wired 900,000 yuan in damages and legal fees to the Shaanxi Supreme People's Court.

When news of the court verdict reached the village of Fenghuo, Wang Baojing "opened his pockets" and declared a three-day festival of celebration. There were lion dances and fireworks displays. There was even an outdoor screening of the communist movie classic, *The Decisive Battle*, in which China's ideological enemies scattered before Mao Zedong and the fearless soldiers of the revolution.

Postscript

The debate over libel in the West is about striking a balance between the right to free speech and the individual's right to safeguard his or her reputation. In China, however, the interests of party and the state continue to define the media's role, and political considerations often override the truth. In a climate of state media control, and as the term "freedom of speech" itself is still regarded as moderately sensitive, one of the most important concepts around which investigative reporters rally is "supervision by public opinion," or *yulun jiandu*.

Seen from the vantage point of party leaders, "supervision by public opinion" — which we might also call "watchdog journalism" — consists of using the media as a tool to expose corruption and other crimes at the local or regional level. But with the advent of more professional, commercially-oriented media in the mid to late 1990s, "supervision by public opinion" became associated with the media's right to monitor officials on the public's behalf, and, in this sense, came much closer to the ideal of investigative reporting, and other more critical forms of news coverage, as an exercise of freedom of speech.

The debate over libel in China, therefore, is often couched in terms of the need to balance the prerogatives of "supervision by public opinion" with the rights of the citizen. Media cannot, in other words, argue that they are exercising freedom of speech. They can, however, talk about the importance of "supervision by public opinion" as one of several forms of power-monitoring.

This debate has surfaced as an issue ever since China's first libel case against the news media in 1983, in which a Shanghai-based engineer named Du Rong sued two reporters from the city's *Democracy and Law* magazine for an article alleging that Du had abused his wife since the 1960s, based entirely on interviews with the wife. In 1987, Shanghai's Changning District Court ruled in the plaintiff's favor. While some Chinese hailed the case, saying it had fostered a more acute legal consciousness in the general public, others were concerned it might discourage media from tackling tougher political or social issues: "What about supervision by public opinion?" they asked.[13]

As we discuss elsewhere in the book, poor ethics and lack of professionalism are serious problems in China's media, and undoubtedly cases exist where media make accusations without sufficient facts. But given China's imperfect legal system, in which party officials often control the courts in order to protect their own vested interests, "supervision by public opinion" can be a dangerous enterprise. The lack of legal protections for "supervision by public opinion," the reporter's right to interview, and the public's right to know, heighten these dangers. This has led many journalists and scholars in China to call for a press law that would protect the media, resulting in its greater independence.

Given the weak political and legal position of China's media, libel suits have become a convenient way for corrupt officials to combat charges brought by media carrying out watchdog journalism. Wang Baojing's libel action against Lu Yuegang and *China Youth Daily* offers a classic case in point. Bringing a libel case against the newspaper on his home turf, with the backing of top leaders in Shaanxi, Wang Baojing was able not only to defend his reputation, but also to protect his political standing and to fight off attempts to try him in criminal cases, like Wu Fang's.

Most probably, Wang Baojing had also leveraged his political contacts to influence the original criminal case stemming from Wu Fang's attack. This is why Lu Yuegang so forcefully insisted on seeing the case's "auxiliary files," which might contain actual proof of Wang's behind-the-scenes involvement.

These auxiliary files are, as Lu Yuegang has called them, the "black boxes" of China's legal system. They contain not only a record of closed consultations among court judges and decisions by the judicial committee, but also those of contacts between party officials and the court. Strictly speaking, the auxiliary files are a direct violation of judicial independence as mandated by Article 126 of China's Constitution, which reads: "The people's courts shall, in accordance with the law exercise judicial power independently and are not subject to interference by administrative organs, public organizations, or individuals."[14]

In the clearest reflection of how ordinary people in China view the law, there is a popular saying that it takes two things to win a lawsuit — power and money. The auxiliary files, viewed as matters of state secrecy, most clearly confirm the truth of this statement.

Notes

1. Lu Yuegang. 2004. Case study on his personal experiences reporting the Wu Fang case. Hong Kong: Journalism and Media Studies Centre at the University of Hong Kong. Case study on file with the China Media Project.
2. Ibid.
3. Criminal Litigation Law of the People's Republic of China, Article 2, Clause 29, amended October 28, 2007, Xinhua News Agency release of full text, October 29, 2007. Available at http://www.china.com.cn/policy/txt/2007-10/29/content_9139262.htm.
4. Lu Yuegang. 1998. *Da guo gua min*. Beijing: Zhongguo Dianying Chubanshe.
5. *Lanzhou Morning Post*. 2007. "*Xian xing hou min: sifa shijian de biran xuanze*" (Criminal precedence: a necessary choice in judicial practice), November 12. Available at http://news.sina.com.cn/o/2007-11-12/095012889170s.shtml.
6. *Beijing Youth Daily*. 2000. "*Zhong Qing Bao 'Shaanxi guansi' zhui fang ji*" (Notes from the *China Youth Daily* case in Shaanxi), September 19.
7. Civil Procedure Law of the People's Republic of China (1991, amended October 28, 2007). Available at China.org.cn, http://www.china.org.cn/government/laws/2007-04/16/

content_1207343.htm. Article 66 of the Law states that: "Evidence shall be presented in court and cross-examined by the parties concerned. But evidence that involves State secrets, trade secrets and personal privacy shall be kept confidential. If it needs to be presented in court, such evidence shall not be presented in an open court session."

8. *Beijing Youth Daily*. 2000. "*Zhong Qing Bao*" (Notes from the *China Youth Daily* case), September 19.
9. Ibid.
10. *Time* (Asian ed.). 2000. "China: when things go wrong," October 9, 156.
11. *Zhongguo Funu Bao*. 2000. "*Yulun jiandu neng zou duo yuan?*" (How far can watchdog journalism go?), September 9.
12. *Southern Weekend*. 2000. "*Zhongguo xuyao you liangzhi de ren*" (China needs more people of conscience), August 9.
13. Wei Yongzheng. 2000. *Yulun jiandu yu xinwen jiufen* (Supervision by public opinion and news media disputes). Shanghai: Fudan University Press, 65.
14. Constitution of the People's Republic of China (1982). Available at People's Daily Online, http://english.peopledaily.com.cn/consitiution/constitution.html.

2 *Breaking through the Silence*
The Untold Story of the Henan AIDS Epidemic

In January 2000, almost a full year before Western readers learned of the AIDS epidemic in Henan, an inland Chinese province south of Beijing, a detailed exposé from an unknown reporter in Henan, undertaken at great personal risk, might have blown the whole story wide open had it sufficiently captured the popular imagination or attracted the government interest it warranted.

The facts in Zhang Jicheng's report suggested HIV infection in the rural villages of Henan had reached epidemic proportions, and that infection was linked to blood collection centers, which had pooled blood by-products and re-injected them into donors.[1] However, too few people at the national level took notice of Zhang's story, which had run in *Huaxi Dushibao*, a market-oriented metropolitan newspaper in China's western Sichuan Province. The newspaper had a considerably larger circulation than Zhang's own publication, *Henan Science and Technology Daily*, a newspaper run by the Henan Association for Science and Technology, but was apparently not influential enough at the time to make major ripples. The article did not go unnoticed, though, and Dr. Wang Shuping, whose actions this chapter discusses in some detail below, later recalled having received a copy of Zhang's report in Beijing that January from a colleague working in Sichuan.[2]

In the months following Zhang's report, Chinese media continued to cover HIV-AIDS despite strong opposition from local governments. Much of the coverage dealt only with infected blood products and the legal cases arising from infections through blood transfusions. Others, however, were bolder.

To give just a few examples: in February 2000, several weeks after the *Huaxi Dushibao* article, the *Chinese Journal of Epidemiology* published the first scientific study of the spread of AIDS among blood donors in China.[3] On March 31, 2000, a *Southern Metropolis Daily* report said that police in Shanxi Province had arrested eighteen people involved in the operation of an illegal blood collection center and confiscated two tons of blood products. It also said that eleven of the eighteen donors arrested were HIV-positive, sixteen had hepatitis and seven had syphilis.[4] Other national and regional newspapers excerpted the report. In April 2000, *Southern Metropolis Daily* and others reported on the case of a nine-year-old boy infected with HIV through a blood transfusion, whose family was now suing a Henan County health office.[5] *Legal Daily* also followed the case closely, providing with their coverage the information many Western reports used.[6]

Notably, on May 11, *Dahe Daily*, a commercial newspaper under the control of the province's principal official newspaper *Henan Daily*, faced great political risk locally by running a special series called "AIDS in Henan."

Quite contrary to the general perception that the Western media broke the story of AIDS in Henan, international media were quiet at this point. Large numbers of reports covered AIDS in China, while much of the overseas media quoted Chinese experts who believed the rate of HIV infection in China far surpassed official figures. As early as November 1999, Reuters cited Xu Hua, a specialist in the study of AIDS from Beijing, as saying that domestic health experts had put HIV infections at over 800,000 for that year, as opposed to the 15,088 confirmed cases reported by the Ministry of Health.[7] International coverage, though, still focused on intravenous drug use and the sex trade as the principal means of infection.

While overseas media had not apparently connected the dots between AIDS in Henan and the practice of illegal blood collection, Western governments were clearly aware of the problem. A series of reports from the U.S. embassy in Beijing had kept close tabs on Chinese media coverage of AIDS in China, and particularly Henan, and posted these on the official embassy website, www.usembassy-china.org.cn. A full translation of Zhang Jicheng's initial news report had been available since March, along with the article from the *Chinese Journal of Epidemiology*, which said 25 percent of plasma donors tested in one Chinese village were HIV-positive.[8]

An April 2000 report from the U.S. embassy stated that an ESTOFF, or officer of the Environment, Science and Technology section of the embassy in Beijing, had made a one-day tour in March to Henan's Shangcai County, where, the report said, "according to a Chinese press report [by Zhang Jicheng], the transmission of HIV among blood donors has become a serious problem in Wenlou Village, several kilometers to the south of the county seat of Shangcai City."[9]

Editors at *Dahe Daily* noted later that year that an official at the French embassy had contacted them to express his appreciation for their May series on AIDS in Henan, and had volunteered educational materials on HIV-AIDS.[10]

By August 2000, international media recognized the link between HIV-AIDS and illegal blood collection in China's hinterlands, as a result of the efforts of Chinese health experts to publicize their concerns. On August 2, 2000, the *New York Times* ran Elisabeth Rosenthal's "Scientists warn of inaction as AIDS spreads in China," the first English-language media report to establish the link between HIV-AIDS and black-market blood collection. It detailed the process of separation and re-transfusion, and the repeated warnings by Chinese health experts that the country's HIV-AIDS figures were vastly underreported. It also quoted Zeng Yi, a renowned professor of medicine credited with diagnosing China's first domestic AIDS case in 1987, who said "a survey in Henan found rates as high as 16 percent in locales where illegal blood selling was common . . ."[11]

On August 18, the next breakthrough in the Henan story came in *China Newsweekly*, then an upstart current affairs magazine. It brought the Henan AIDS story to a more national Chinese audience, exposing the AIDS epidemic in the countryside, and calling it a "national disaster." Media across China ran or excerpted the *China Newsweekly* report. One possible explanation for the failure of Henan's AIDS crisis to turn into an international story at that point was that *China Newsweekly* was just eight months old, having been launched in January 2000, with the stated goal of becoming China's *Time* magazine. Its influence had not yet become decisive.[12]

On August 30, 2000, *South China Morning Post* edged closer to the larger Henan story while following up on China's campaign against illegal blood sales. Jasper Becker wrote: "Henan is a center for the illegal blood plasma market and many villagers have become infected through careless blood transfusion technology. In some areas, five per cent of blood donors have been infected with HIV. Blood from numerous donors is combined in a centrifuge to extract plasma and the unused red cells are returned to donors. Often the machinery is not cleaned between donations."[13]

On September 1, 2000, Taiwan's Central News Agency (TCNA) and others quoted Zeng Yi, the Beijing health expert, as saying China's AIDS problem would become "a national disaster" if not dealt with aggressively and that, "according to conservative estimates by mainland experts," at least 500,000 Chinese were already infected with HIV.[14] The TCNA report relied heavily on mainland media, specifically the *China Newsweekly* report, which had been the first to call AIDS a "national disaster."

By October 2000, the trail had been blazed. It led directly to Henan's Wenlou Village. On October 28, the *New York Times* stepped in and reported the story to the world, instantly making Wenlou emblematic worldwide of China's AIDS crisis.

This October 28 story marked a watershed moment in the battle against the spread of AIDS in China. It galvanized international attention and activism and put Chinese officials under greater pressure. But something else happened too — the fuller story behind the story vanished. In the outside world, even as civilians, such as Gao Yaojie were praised for their efforts, Western sources perpetuated the widespread myth that the Chinese media had been silent on AIDS in Henan until after Western reports began appearing.

Western coverage, in some cases, fueled this misperception. The *New York Times* reported on December 17, 2000, that "although many earlier articles suggested that the [AIDS] problem was growing in urban areas, they made little mention of the staggering problem in the countryside, hinting that the disease was almost exclusively a problem of addicts and prostitutes." "But that bubble has been burst in the last month," the report went on, "as a few relatively high-profile newspapers and magazines have described a raging AIDS epidemic in rural China that local officials had tried to cover up."[15]

The contention that the Chinese media had made "little mention" of the AIDS problem in the countryside was entirely inaccurate, as the brief summary above makes clear. The Zhang Jicheng and *China Newsweekly* reports alone, which dealt in depth with Henan's Shangcai County, totaled more than 14,000 words, while the *New York Times* article in October ran to just over 1,600. Though much Chinese coverage of AIDS did emphasize the link to drug use and prostitution, still, scores of reports also covered HIV transmission through blood transfusions as well as the high rates of infection among blood donors.

The suggestion that Chinese media had previously "mostly cited official statistics" in its reporting on HIV-AIDS was also misleading. Although many Chinese newspapers continued to cite the low infection figures from the Ministry of Health right up to 2001, not all of them did so. In fact, the August feature in *China Newsweekly* had stated clearly in its opening lines that "conservative estimates by experts suggest the number is over 500,000, and that infection will increase by a rate of 30 percent a year."[16]

By the time the Asia Society, an international nonprofit organization, awarded Elisabeth Rosenthal the first Osborn Elliott Prize for Excellence in Asian Journalism in May 2003, the myth was fully formed. Announcing the award, the Asia Society said: "[Ms. Rosenthal's] dispatches brought the crisis [in Henan] to the attention of health officials in Beijing where after a delay of several months, its seriousness was finally acknowledged. Her reports also inspired coverage by newly emboldened Chinese journalists."[17] While it is impossible to deny that foreign news reports can bring pressure to bear on China's domestic politics, the suggestion that Rosenthal's report awakened Beijing officials to the crisis in Henan is plainly erroneous. Rosenthal's own coverage in August 2000 made it clear that health experts, including the tireless Zeng Yi, had already filed reports with national officials in 2000.[18] Nor was Zeng Yi's report the first of its kind.

In point of fact, Western news reports had a negligible impact on Chinese media, not simply because few Chinese journalists read English-language newspapers, but also because foreign news reports generally do not take into account what is and is not safe or permissible in Chinese news coverage. It is only fair to say that the *China Newsweekly* and *Southern Weekend* reports (August 18, 2000, and November 30, 2000, respectively) had influenced domestic media the most decisively.

The true story behind the reporting of the Henan AIDS crisis represents a far more complicated version than the one that took shape in the West. It was about the dedication, courage, and continued frustration of Chinese doctors, journalists, and citizens — and, of course, the essential role of the foreign media in raising international awareness of the epidemic. That story follows.

HIV-AIDS with Chinese Characteristics

On June 3, 1985, when the Beijing Friendship Hospital admitted an American tourist for treatment of acute respiratory problems, Chinese doctors came into contact with their first case of AIDS.[19] After routine treatments proved ineffective, a Chinese doctor called the patient's general practitioner in Los Angeles. "We think he might — " the doctor on the Beijing side, Wang Aixia, began. The American doctor cut in before he had finished: "You've guessed right. He has AIDS."

The news spread like wildfire among hospital staff. AIDS was a foreign menace, terrible and unknown. When the patient died three days after being admitted, the hospital sent everything he had touched straight off for incineration.[20]

This story defined Chinese media coverage of HIV and AIDS for the next decade. AIDS was an American disease, an African disease, a European disease. The mere mention of AIDS elicited loathing for the behavior of foreigners. The Chinese media reinforced the sense of alien-ness by referring to AIDS as a form of "heart disease" caused by a dissipated lifestyle, a just punishment facing drug abusers, prostitutes, and homosexuals.[21] The Chinese could rest assured that AIDS remained a distant concern. If one believed the official figures, the total number of HIV infections totaled just 15,088, as late as September 1999, with the vast majority of these cases linked to intravenous drug use.[22]

But in the central Chinese province of Henan, officials had already laid the foundation for what has since been called "AIDS with Chinese characteristics," an epidemic rooted in greed and official corruption.

In 1992, China buzzed with the excitement of accelerated reforms. That spring, Deng Xiaoping, the country's top leader, toured key cities in southern China, including Shanghai, Guangzhou, Zhuhai, and Shenzhen, emphasizing the need for rapid economic development. In the midst of this national fervor, Henan's newly appointed top health official, Liu Quanxi, proposed a modest policy change: the province would create a network of blood collection centers, giving poor peasants a leg up by paying them for donating blood, and exporting these valuable blood products to ready markets in South Korea as well as major Chinese cities.

During an internal meeting of top health officials, the minister laid his figures out on the table. More than 80 percent of the province's 70 million people were poor peasants. If they could convince just one to three percent of this population to sell blood once or twice a year, the resulting blood supplies would bring in annual revenues of around 100 million yuan ($1.7 million US).

The blood market sprang up almost overnight in Henan. More than 200 government-run blood collection centers — advertised as "legal blood collection centers" — opened their doors for business in 1992. Hundreds of illegal ones flourished in their shadows, many of which were mobile units rigged atop garbage haulers or other vehicles.[23] A new slogan became popular among the farmers of

Henan: "Extend your arm, expose a vein, make a fist, and it's fifty yuan."[24] One blood collection center in Shangcai County recorded more than 5,500 registered donors at its height, and received between 444 and 500 per day.[25]

In the early days of this blood economy, collection centers used centrifuges to isolate the more desirable proteins. But soon a common question arose: what should be done with unwanted blood proteins after separation, which could not be sold to medical supply companies? Someone then suggested blood cells from donors of the same blood type be combined after isolation and re-transfused into donors. This way, blood collection centers could justify paying five yuan less per donor (because, after all, they were removing fewer proteins). At the same time, they could lessen the effects of anemia. It was not long before re-transfusion became standard practice at blood collection centers across Henan.[26]

At the time, apparently no one within Henan's health infrastructure considered the dangers of re-transfusion, which were astronomical, in the spreading of infectious diseases between donors. All if took was one person in the donor pool to be HIV-positive for everyone to incur a risk of infection. By 1994, when a blood products company in Lanzhou found HIV-infected samples in a shipment bound for the South Korean market, originating in Henan, provincial health officials were almost certainly aware of the problem.[27]

Before long, health workers became aware of HIV infection among blood donors in Henan. One former doctor from the area has since told media that out of the ten patients he tested in 1995, three were HIV-positive. A few doctors sent samples for verification to laboratories in Shanghai, Beijing, Nanjing, and Wuhan. The results alarmed health experts, and some, including the renowned professor of medicine Zeng Yi, of the Chinese Academy of Preventive Medicine, pressed officials to investigate the situation.[28]

A thirty-two-year-old doctor named Wang Shuping, who ran a medical lab in Zhoukou City, alerted Zeng Yi to the HIV problem in Henan. She discovered her first case of HIV infection in 1994 and, in May 2005, found large numbers of HIV-infected blood samples among the 404 she had collected from donors. She and four other health workers filed a handwritten report with the provincial health department in November that year. Fearing reprimand, they did not detail their laboratory findings in the report, but instead proposed prevention methods. The health department did nothing. "I knew they simply wanted to keep this thing under wraps," Wang later said, "so I went to Beijing myself." She took sixty-two blood samples along with her.[29]

On December 16, 1995, Wang Shuping walked into the Institute of Environmental Health and Engineering (IEHE) in Beijing hoping to get more definitive results for her sixty-two samples.[30] She was told testing would cost 700 yuan per sample, totaling over 40,000 yuan ($5,780 US). Wang, who had just enough money to travel, left IEHE, planning on returning home. As she was walking out the door, she bumped into Zeng Yi. "What on earth have you come here for?" he asked. When Wang explained her concerns, he suggested they begin by testing fifteen samples. When the results came back, thirteen had tested HIV-positive. Zeng Yi and Wang Shuping sent a report to the Ministry of Health on January 10, 1996, underscoring the dangers of blood separation and re-transfusion, citing high rates of HIV infection in the countryside.

According to Zeng Yi's account, the Ministry of Health telephoned provincial health officials in Henan for details the day after they received the report. By the time Wang Shuping made it back to Henan, officials awaited her. "You're flirting with disaster," one health official reportedly said to her.[31] They told Wang and her team of nurses to stop nosing around and making trouble. Early the next year, a senior Henan health official circulated rumors that Wang was HIV-positive and had hepatitis, and advised that her credentials be revoked. Her clinic was shut down.[32]

The report by Wang and Zeng put pressure on the provincial government in Henan, but officials there still fought to keep the full extent of the epidemic under wraps. To throw Beijing off the trail, Henan's provincial health department organized its own campaign of HIV-testing for blood donors in thirteen Henan counties in 1996.[33] Six testing crews fanned out over the area, eventually testing more than 100,000 people. But provincial leaders carefully controlled the release of the results. They did not allow crews to exchange data or make them available to anyone outside the provincial health department, while they required each team to report its results independently so they could not be tabulated. When Zeng Yi made his own inspection visit to Henan, local officials kept him at bay, and prevented him from entering the countryside.[34]

A member of a testing crew covering Henan's Shenqiu County later said that his crew had found an HIV infection rate as high as 84 percent among donors there. In Weishi, Xiping, Shangcai, and Taikang Counties, the results were similar, with the lowest rate at 67 percent.[35]

After results came back from the testing crews, the officials from Henan stated that cases of HIV infection had been found, but with no evidence of widespread infection. Efforts to put a lid on the crisis went into high gear. First, officials moved preemptively against journalists likely to attempt to file news reports on HIV-AIDS. Wang Yanheng, a veteran health reporter for *Dahe Daily*, was transferred to a post outside Henan.[36]

In late 1998, when officials got wind that *Dahe Daily* was planning an AIDS feature, they sent over a negotiator who knew the editors at the newspaper well. The negotiator, known only to the newspaper as "Mr. Hang," asked *Dahe Daily* to accept 80,000 yuan in cash ($11,500 US) for a large "advertisement" that would fill the void left after the newspaper killed the AIDS report it had in the works. The editors took the hint and stopped the story, but the hardheaded Mr. Hang took the further step of having several *Dahe Daily* reporters on the health beat removed for trumped-up offenses, including disobeying the department's line on AIDS reporting.[37]

At this point, Gui Xien, a retired doctor from Hubei College of Traditional Chinese Medicine in neighboring Hubei Province, stepped quietly into the fray. In November 1999, Gui visited Henan and, assisted by a former pupil working at the local TCM hospital in Shangcai County, obtained samples from blood donors, which he tested upon returning to Wuhan. The rate of HIV infection shocked Gui. On his second trip to Shangcai, he analyzed samples from 155 donors and recorded an infection rate of 61.9 percent.[38] Gui submitted a report with supporting data to health officials in Beijing, including, once again, Zeng Yi.[39]

Zhang Ke, an epidemiologist from Beijing's You'an Hospital, also played a key role in fighting AIDS. In August 1999, Zhang traveled to Donghu, a village southeast of Wenlou, where he trained health professionals to deal with HIV-AIDS and treated many patients.[40]

While Zeng Yi and Gui Xien struggled to force action through governmental channels, Gao Yaojie, a gynecologist at a hospital affiliated with the Henan School of Traditional Chinese Medicine, placed her hopes in media coverage.

In April 1996, Gao discovered her first AIDS case — a patient who had contracted the virus through a blood transfusion. That year, she set out to educate the general public about the dangers of HIV-AIDS. To commemorate International AIDS Day that December, she printed up pamphlets and handed them out at bus and train stations in Henan.

In August 1999, Gao Yaojie later recounted, Chinese reporters started telling her about the severity of AIDS in the countryside. That November, she contacted twelve villagers infected with HIV. Nine had contracted the virus through selling their blood, three through blood transfusions. She began making regular trips to the countryside to educate and treat peasants with HIV-AIDS, and her efforts caught the attention of local media. *Dahe Daily*, *Zhengzhou Evening Post*, and *Metro Morning Post* all reported on Gao Yaojie's personal efforts to fight the disease, but they played it safe by focusing on prevention and avoiding mention of an epidemic. On International AIDS Day, December 1, 1999, Zhengzhou television station, the local broadcaster for Henan's capital city, invited Gao for a special segment on HIV-AIDS prevention. She told media later that an official sought her out repeatedly that day, insisting her claims were dangerous nonsense, and that no confirmed cases of AIDS existed in Henan.[41]

The provincial office of the propaganda department responded to the spate of press coverage by issuing an informal warning to the media under its supervision, banning additional stories. They would confiscate and destroy the notebooks and film of any reporters caught entering the countryside.[42]

Though Henan's AIDS crisis had not yet become common knowledge, a storm was brewing on the horizon. Reporters from local and national media could sense a big story, and they were searching for a way inside.

AIDS Creeps Closer to Home

Zhang Jicheng, a young reporter with *Henan Science and Technology Daily*, was on a train from Xinyang City bound for the provincial capital of Zhengzhou in October 1999 when he met two fellow passengers who said they were going to Beijing with their wives to seek medical help. They told Zhang they had contracted a strange illness. Many people in their village had fallen ill, and several had already died, they said.[43]

"It's not just our village," one of the men said. "Many villages and towns [in our area] are the same way. County doctors tell us treatments for this illness outside China have been ineffective, but they won't even tell us what it is."[44]

They had decided to pool their money together with members of their extended family, some of whom were also sick, and chose four of them to travel to Beijing by train to see if doctors there could help. They said they came from Wenlou Village in Henan's Shangcai County. After first asking a friend who was a trained doctor to inject him with an antiviral agent, Zhang Jicheng traveled to Wenlou Village. He spent eight hours there, meeting with eight villagers who had contracted HIV through selling plasma at local blood collection centers.[45] Sources said that in one extended family with fifty or sixty people, nearly everyone was HIV-positive.

Zhang returned home to Zhengzhou and wrote his news report, understanding only too well that it would infuriate local officials and pose great danger. His editor suggested they play it safe by running the report as an internal reference rather than as an article in the newspaper. Zhang declined, deciding instead to send his report to *Huaxi Dushibao*, a more commercial metropolitan newspaper in China's western Sichuan Province, with a much wider circulation. As officials in Henan did not control *Huaxi Dushibao*, this offered a safer alternative for the article, if not for Zhang himself.

On January 18, 2000, shortly after the Chinese New Year holiday, *Huaxi Dushibao* ran Zhang's report, "'Mystery illness' in Henan villages shocks top leadership."[46] It was the first story, in either the domestic or the international media, to report in-depth on AIDS in Henan:

> January 18, 2000/Zhang Jicheng — In the summer of 1999, a doctor in Henan's Shangcai County made an unnerving discovery: one of his patients had contracted AIDS! He reported this immediately to his [former] teacher, professor Gui of an unspecified university in [neighboring] Hubei province [this is Gui Xien, who is quoted further down].

> Ten of the first eleven blood samples Professor Gui studied from patients in Wenlou Village tested positive [for HIV]; of the next 140 samples, eighty tested positive.
>
> Professor Gui was shocked by the rate of infection he found.
>
> After learning this news, the reporter went to the area to investigate on December 12 [1999].[47]
>
> Henan's Shangcai County is home to an agricultural population of 1.3 million people. While it does not suffer from abject poverty, the area has been nationally designated as a "poor county." When the reporter arrived at Wenlou Village, he found it covered in a pall of terror. A middle-aged woman named He Ling had died of AIDS in June 1999, and since then more than ten young people had died . . . [The story of He Ling's illness as told to Zhang Jicheng by He's husband follows in four paragraphs. A description of symptoms suffered by sick villagers, as given to Zhang by the secretary of the village party branch, follows]. "This was the curse brought down on those who sold their blood years ago," the secretary told me, revealing that Wenlou was well known as a "blood-selling village."
>
> In the early 1990s selling blood for money reached new heights of popularity in the village. The administrative village had a population of around 3,000, and about 1,000 of these residents sold blood, from teenagers all the way up to sixty and older. Some even gave gifts [to blood collection center operators] so they could give blood more than once in a single day ...
>
> Visiting Wenlou Village, my heart was heavy. On the road back to Zhengzhou, the words of the secretary of the village party branch pounded in my head: "People outside [the village] only know about Wenlou. Actually, the villages on all sides of us are even worse off!" In order to confirm what he had said, I went to the county health office and disease prevention center. But the two people on duty denied the charges: "Who says we have AIDS here? Other villages haven't been inspected so it's not clear," they said. At the health office they avoided the question altogether, saying it "couldn't be explained."
>
> On December 13, 1999, I interviewed by telephone Doctor Gui [Xien], who had just returned to Wuhan from Beijing. "Based on what I've seen, many people in Shangcai County have been infected. This will be clear to everyone some day . . . I believe this is just the tip of the iceberg."

Henan's provincial propaganda office moved swiftly against Zhang Jicheng, sending out an order that he be removed from his position.[48] The newspaper protected Zhang surreptitiously by telling propaganda officials that they had already removed Zhang. In fact, they had simply shifted him to a new position, while Zhang continued with the AIDS story, popping in and out of various villages in Henan.

Some regional media, as for example, Hunan Province's *Changsha Evening News*, ran Zhang Jicheng's report after it appeared in Sichuan, whereas official state media, such as *China Daily* and the Xinhua News Agency, and most national media, either failed to see the story or feared the political consequences of pursuing it.[49]

The next report to tackle AIDS in Henan, more directly and openly, came on May 11, 2000, four months after Zhang Jicheng's initial story.[50] It was a ten-page feature entitled "AIDS in Henan," appearing in *Dahe Daily*, whose first AIDS article the provincial propaganda department had suppressed two years earlier. The newspaper had originally planned the story as a series, but Ma Yunlong, the editor, decided to run the entire 25,000-word article at one time to ensure propaganda officials could not kill the following segments of the report. "AIDS in Henan" took an in-depth look at the life of one AIDS patient who had contracted HIV through a blood transfusion, and criticized the government for its negligence in dealing with contaminated blood supplies. The story's tone was ominous, driving home the point that HIV-AIDS was now everyone's problem:

> May 14, 2000 — Entering the countryside during the growing heat of April, we came at last to a world that was strange to us, a world of desperate and lonely people. It was as though we had stepped onto a lonely and uninhabited island. There we faced a child who was about to vanish — Zhang Chengshuai.
>
> We listened to the helpless cry of this unfortunate child, who like others in his family is shackled with AIDS, and must endure a life under fearful and hateful eyes. Some infected like this child no longer dare show their faces in public. The prejudices of the healthy drive them into hiding . . .
>
> In Henan, 200 milliliters of blood infected with HIV changed Zhang Chengshuai's life. It might similarly transform the lives of others. Today, the unfortunate one is Zhang Chengshuai — tomorrow, it might be you, or me, or anyone else.
>
> Most people in Henan still believe HIV-AIDS is a distant concern, but the facts ruthlessly confirm that this demon is among us, in our bustling cities and our quiet countryside. It wears a cruel grin and hides in every corner around us, waiting for an opportunity to strike . . .[51]

The day after the *Dahe Daily* report, Henan issued its first formal ban on news coverage of AIDS. Less than a year later, Ma was removed from his position for running "AIDS in Henan" and another hard-hitting story on a fire in the city of Luoyang.[52] Henan's press fell silent on AIDS in the months following the ban.

It took two non-journalists, Kong Yunxing and Du Huazu, to break the silence. These were small-time officials in Shangcai County, where Wenlou and other AIDS-racked villages were located. Kong oversaw the implementation of family planning policy in Lugang, one of several administrative townships in Shangcai. Though not from the area, he kept his home in Wenlou. Du was a procurator in Shangcai who had gone to Wenlou to pursue a corruption charge against a village official.[53] In Henan's bureaucracy, these men held minor positions, but the devastation AIDS had wrought in Wenlou deeply concerned them. They had also earned the trust of villagers there.

Du and Kong had been among Dr. Gao Yaojie's first contacts when she visited Wenlou back in August 1999, and had helped her approach the villagers and gain their confidence. Du, Kong, and Gao provided a vital information pipeline at this key stage. Du and Kong would obtain from Gao lists of reporters outside Henan working on the story, then, they put the reporters in touch with the sources they needed.[54]

Zhang Jingping and Zhang Jie, reporters from *China Newsweekly*, a magazine published by China News Service, one of China's two official state news agencies, were among the first to visit Henan's AIDS villages. For their story, which appeared in the magazine on August 18, 2000, Kong and Du provided key background about the blood collection centers that had dotted the countryside throughout the 1990s. The *China Newsweekly* story, "AIDS: the new national calamity," gave a full account of HIV's spread through the province, and went further than Zhang Jicheng and the *Dahe Daily* stories in reinforcing the point that AIDS was not confined to Wenlou. This described not the tragedy of one village, or of Henan, but of an entire nation. The first one-third of the *China Newsweekly* report, written by Zhang Jie, dealt generally with the history of AIDS in China and contrasted estimates by health experts with those of the Ministry of Health. The lead and portions that deal with the spread of HIV through homegrown blood collection centers follow:

> August 18, 2000 — Fifteen years ago China was a pure land. Now, look anywhere and you will find AIDS. Fifteen years ago, when people talked about AIDS, they smiled with embarrassment. Now when people talk about AIDS it is as though they are talking about what to have for dinner.
>
> According to a government report, China had just over 15,000 confirmed cases of HIV-AIDS by 1999. Conservative estimates by experts say that number was probably 500,000, with cases growing by a rate of thirty percent a year. Experts say categorically that AIDS in China has already entered a period of rapid growth.
>
> Already HIV-AIDS is giving China precious little time. In the year 2000, the number of HIV-AIDS patients in China is expected to reach between 600,000 and one million, costing the country between 460 and 770 billion yuan ($66–111 billion US). This will make AIDS a national disaster.
>
> There is still time for prevention and control [of the disease]. But the most frightening thing is cold denial and inaction. Unfortunately this is exactly what many officials and government agencies are doing right now . . . [A portion that follows compares Zeng Yi's estimates with those of the health bureau, and then discusses the spread of HIV-AIDS to all areas of China].

> Beginning in 1993, more than ten provinces discovered there were large numbers of HIV-positive people in the blood donating pool. One inside source revealed that one important reason for contamination was the operation of grass-roots blood collection stations. These stations took excess blood of the same type and mixed it together in a centrifuge, isolating the more valuable components and then re-transfusing the remaining blood cells into the donors, in order to ensure they could quickly produce blood again. In this way, the rate of HIV infection rose dramatically . . .[55]

The latter two-thirds of the *China Newsweekly* report, written by Zhang Jingping and Zhao Fei, detailed the spread of HIV-AIDS in Henan's "AIDS villages":

> In order to avenge themselves for the county government's inaction on AIDS, the peasants injected melons with their own [contaminated] blood. This rumor has spread throughout Shangcai County in Henan Province this summer, and is still going strong.
>
> The origin of the rumor lies in Wenlou Village in Lugang Township. In this village not more than three miles from the county seat, close to 3,000 people live under the shadow of AIDS, and scores of people are dying one after the other.
>
> On August 17, *China Newsweekly* reporters went to see for themselves this village, which has shocked high-level leaders and will shock the world. It surpassed our expectations . . .[56]

The *China Newsweekly* report unflinchingly criticized government leaders, whom it said had buried information about the epidemic out of fear for their own political hides. *China Newsweekly* had run a huge risk in printing the story. The absence of explicit bans on the topic of AIDS did not mean a green light for media coverage, and the magazine had stepped into a huge gray area. The idea of self-discipline, or the media taking initiative in safeguarding the political interests of the state, is more critical in China than the orders and bans issued by propaganda officials. Officials essentially want to ensure that concern about possible government reprisal is strong enough to make directors and editors at Chinese media think twice before running sensitive reports. But, most surprisingly, in the report's wake, officials took no disciplinary action against Zhang Jingping or others at the magazine. This seemed to tacitly approve coverage of HIV-AIDS in the countryside, even if local leaders in Henan did their utmost to stop it. The *China Newsweekly* feature did not receive the attention it deserved domestically or internationally, in large part because the magazine had launched just eight months earlier and had not yet gained a definitive national audience. The article did, however, bring the interest of other media to the AIDS crisis in the countryside.

International media did not move immediately on the *China Newsweekly* coverage. As noted earlier, stories in the *New York Times* and *South China Morning*

Post that ran on August 2 and August 30, 2000, respectively, mentioned blood collection in the countryside as among the key causes of HIV infection there. But the real bombshell came in late October, more than two months after the *China Newsweekly* report. Elisabeth Rosenthal's story, "In rural China, a steep price of poverty: dying of AIDS," appeared in the *New York Times* on October 28, totaling just over 1,600 words. It began with a portrait of the AIDS crusader Gao Yaojie:

> To celebrate the Moon Festival last month, a frail retired doctor named Gao Yaojie scraped together money to hire a taxi, packed it full of medicines, brochures, sweet drinks and cakes — and slipped off, once again, from this provincial capital to see patients in remote mud-brick villages where countless farmers are silently dying of AIDS.
>
> Chinese officials here generally deny there is AIDS in rural parts of Henan Province, a farming region in central China south of Beijing. They have forbidden the local news media and government health workers to discuss the topic and blocked outside researchers from studying it. Dr. Gao, a small serious woman of 76 in dark hand-me-down clothes, is regularly chased out of the villages she goes to help. But Dr. Gao and a few others familiar with the area say small towns here and scattered elsewhere in central China are experiencing an unreported, unrecognized AIDS epidemic. A few covert studies suggest some of the towns have some of the highest localized rates of H.I.V. infection in the world; some say 20 percent.
>
> The problem is that for many years large numbers of poor farmers have illegally sold their blood to people known as blood heads, whose unsterile collection methods have left many infected with the virus that causes AIDS. The blood donors get the virus not only because blood heads reuse contaminated needles but also because donated blood is often pooled and, after the desired elements are removed, the remainder divided and returned to donors . . .[57]

Rosenthal's story shocked the world by revealing the sinister nature of China's AIDS epidemic and HIV infection through blood collection. It also put a great deal of international pressure on China to face its HIV-AIDS problem. The sources for the story were Gao Yaojie, Kong Yunxing, Du Huazu, and Gui Xien, the same cluster of concerned physicians that *China Newsweekly* had used for its August feature. In fact, Rosenthal's story made reference to the *China Newsweekly* report to give a sense of the epidemic's scale: "In Shangcai County, more than a dozen families in one village of 2,000 people included individuals who had died from AIDS — and rates are similar in all the surrounding villages, a local cadre told a small Beijing magazine called *China Newsweekly*, one of the few publications to broach the subject."[58] Rosenthal's story lacked the direct interviews with patients in the AIDS villages that made the Chinese articles, going back to Zhang Jicheng's, so vivid.

Other international media followed up on the *New York Times* story that November, and Wenlou became world news. Here, for example, is a November 30 story from Agence France-Presse:

> Nov 30 (AFP) — The village of Wenlou has been devoured by AIDS, but the authorities have abandoned the sick to a painful death and tried to cover up a phenomenon which has terrifying implications for China. Nobody knows how many people in Wenlou have AIDS or the HIV virus.
>
> In the past two years thirty of the 800 residents have died from the disease, while at least ten others are dying. A sample of 155 villagers tested found ninety-five were HIV-positive, a staggering sixty-five percent.
>
> But while the poor lettuce and onion growing community in the central province of Henan was being ripped apart by the disease, the government ordered locals to keep quiet and villagers have been ostracised.
>
> They cannot sell their vegetables, a Wenlou stamp on an ID card can lose a job, young women cannot find husbands and ladies from other villages refuse to touch Wenlou's men.
>
> Doctors at the local Shangcai county hospital, lacking basic understanding of the disease, turned away AIDS patients and even refused treatment to a villager who had injured his leg.
>
> "This is not a major problem, there are just a few cases," an angry official at the Shangcai county health department told AFP.
>
> The villagers feel they have been left to die by petty local officials fearful of a scandal in their neighborhood and complain they have received no medical help from the government . . .[59]

Although Rosenthal's story gave the impression that coverage of the AIDS epidemic in the countryside was "taboo," the *China Newsweekly* feature had in fact set a precedent for national coverage. While *China Newsweekly* may have qualified as "a small Beijing magazine" in terms of circulation, China's number two official newswire published it. Chinese journalists widely acknowledged the magazine's AIDS feature, even if the magazine did not have the national audience that it has today. Moreover, the fact that the AIDS report had sailed through without political opposition suggested the epidemic in Henan was an admissible subject.

Entrenched local power posed the real problem in getting the story out, an all-too-common issue in China, where the old saying goes, "Even the mighty dragon cannot flush the snakes out of their holes." Officials in Henan were still trying their best to stonewall reporters and keep them out of HIV-infected areas.

While the *New York Times* story was making ripples overseas, and international and domestic media were rushing to Wenlou Village, *Southern Weekend*, at that time the most influential domestic newspaper in China, was working on its own investigative story about the AIDS epidemic in Henan. The process had not gone smoothly. Reporter Li Yuxiao spent two discouraging weeks traveling alone through eastern and southern Henan. While he saw signs everywhere advertising treatment of unexplained fevers, he failed to turn up conclusive evidence of an HIV-AIDS epidemic. Finally, a reporter from Henan's *Chengshi Zaobao* newspaper helped Li track down Gao Yaojie. From Gao, the trail went to Du Huazu and thence to Kong Yunxing.

By this time, local officials had drawn a cordon around Wenlou. When Gui Xien, the retired doctor from Hubei, tried to enter the village with a stock of medicines, local police attacked him and his students. Even under such circumstances, Kong Yunxing agreed to help Li Yuxiao and his photographer, Fang Yingzhong, gain access to other villages. In two villages, Dong and Xincaixiong, they found the AIDS situation there as dire as it was in Wenlou. They also tracked down a former party branch secretary who had kept a careful log of those who had fallen ill in his village.[60]

Police were dispatched to deal with Li, but he continued to report on the run, sleeping in public bathhouses rather than hotels to make sure he remained invisible. He interviewed Wang Zhe, a health inspection official in Henan, as well as the provincial director for disease control and prevention. Both men confirmed that disease inspection authorities had filed reports on the HIV-AIDS problem soon after the first signs appeared. Clearly, top officials had been aware of the gravity the situation all along.

Li Yuxiao's story, "Mystery illness," appeared in *Southern Weekend* on November 30, 2000, one month after Rosenthal's article. Based on first-hand accounts from villagers in Shangcai County, it offered the most complete, vivid picture yet of AIDS in Henan, and how the tragedy had come about. The first six paragraphs follow:

> November 30, 2000 — When a serious illness visits those who are most vulnerable, what kind of misfortune results?
>
> From the end of the 1970s through to the mid-1990s, as government offices were slack in their duties and bloodheads [operators of illegal collection centers] were blinded by the desire for personal gain, illegal blood collection centers were terribly common in eastern and southern Henan. This is the direct cause of the AIDS epidemic in this region today, and some of the villages that in those days were centers of blood collection are now AIDS villages.
>
> A strand of evening light passes into a cramped room, half falling across the body of a sleeping woman and half across a broken plastic basin. The woman, bedridden with the "mystery illness," is Sun Aijuan. The basin holds her vomit, covered over with sandy earth.

> Her husband, Zhang Junwu, 36, prematurely balding, clad in a T-shirt of murky color, huddles at her bedside and tells the story of his wife's "mystery illness," crying as he speaks.
>
> Last summer Zhang Junwu "got a cold," then a low fever that would not pass and diarrhea that would not stop. She saw doctors a few times, took some medicine, and then never again went to the hospital. The couple had no income, and besides, she knew already that she had the "mystery illness."
>
> The "mystery illness" is not easy to treat. It is a specter that, over the last three years, has taken more than 20 lives in this village that lies on the road to the Xincai County Hospital. All of these victims were young. Their sicknesses began as "colds," progressed to fevers and diarrhea. All of them had donated blood years before . . .[61]

As with Zhang Jingping's *China Newsweekly* story, officials exerted no political pressure upon Li Yuxiao when the *Southern Weekend* report hit newsstands, which was read as a second green light on AIDS coverage. Other domestic media followed suit, including local Henan papers such as *Dahe Daily* and *Zhengzhou Evening Post*.

Chinese news media covering the AIDS epidemic started breaching the embargo. A poison-pen letter that appeared on the Internet on December 1, 2000, dated November 28, made a notable contribution. "Exposing the 'mortal wound' of HIV-AIDS infection in Henan Province," published under the pseudonym He Aifang, detailed plans by Henan health officials in the early 1990s to profit by setting up a network of blood collection centers throughout the province.[62] To this day, the true identity of He Aifang remains unknown, but journalists in Henan have said a former reporter there who has now left the news business wrote the letter and posted it on the Web.

On January 11, 2001, the *Washington Post* ran a story by correspondent John Pomfret: "The high cost of selling blood: as AIDS crisis looms in China, official response is lax." Pomfret's in-depth story helped to draw further international attention to the AIDS epidemic in Henan.[63]

The next flood of international coverage came in late May 2001, as Doctor Gao Yaojie was invited to the United States to accept the Jonathan Mann Award for Health and Human Rights, awarded by the nonprofit Global Health Council. Gao was unable to attend the ceremony because she could not obtain travel documents from authorities in Henan, who were still bitter about her role in drawing attention to the epidemic. Since late 2000, local officials had severely restricted her movement, and prohibited her from lecturing in college classrooms or accepting media interviews.

China's government still seemed in no hurry to take action on the country's HIV-AIDS problem. Only in August 10, 2001, did national health officials make their first public visit to the AIDS-devastated village of Wenlou. Two weeks later, on August 23, officials held a press conference in Beijing, and publicly acknowledged the true crisis in the village. The Ministry of Health said 241 village residents, out of a total population of 3,170, had tested positive for HIV. Since 1995, they said, thirty-one villagers had died of AIDS. Yin Dakui, a top health official, said most infections occurred as a result of illegal blood collection. For the first time, the Ministry of Health brought their national numbers for HIV-AIDS more in line with estimates by health experts. China had around 600,000 cases of HIV-AIDS, they said.[64]

The Fight Continues

As Beijing slowly and reluctantly gathered the political will to deal with the disease, the true scale of the AIDS epidemic in Henan remained a mystery. Officials in the capital seemed unable to prod provincial leaders into action. On the eve of the central government's announcement in Beijing of new figures for HIV infection in China, provincial leaders moved again against their public enemy number one, reporter Zhang Jicheng. Under an order from provincial propaganda officials, Zhang was stripped of his job for the second time.[65]

Zhang had, by this time, left *Henan Science and Technology Daily* and taken a position as assistant editor-in-chief of another newspaper. Since his AIDS exposé more than two years earlier, Zhang had continued to quietly visit villages. He had spoken with scores of AIDS patients. Fearing punishment from local leaders, however, he published nothing.

If propaganda officials had intended to intimidate him with their order, it backfired miserably. Now a *persona non grata* in Henan's media circles, Zhang packed up and went to Beijing, where he quickly found a job with the *China Times*, a newspaper fronted by the China Disabled Persons' Federation. Safely out of Henan, Zhang saw little point in withholding the information on HIV-AIDS in Henan he had worked more than two years to gather. He sold his second major AIDS report, "Passing through HIV-AIDS-infected regions," to *Qi Lu Weekly*, a newspaper in China's coastal Shandong Province. It ran on September 19, 2001.

Media across China picked up Zhang's report, which said Wenlou was not the most seriously affected village in Shangcai County, and that the situation in other counties was even worse. Zhang listed scores of AIDS villages by name. "The government wants to make the people believe Henan has only one AIDS village and that it is an exceptional case. We want to make it clear to everyone that Henan has many, many AIDS villages," said the *Qi Lu Weekly* report.

Government misinformation belied overtures of greater candor. A credibility gap opened between the old-school central party media and the more localized newspapers. Stories from major party mouthpieces such as *People's Daily* and *Guangming Daily* continued to report that the AIDS situation in China had been brought under control and treatment had been arranged for those affected. A *Guangming Daily* report on December 1, 2001, said: "Recently, the pattern of life and productivity in Wenlou Village is essentially normalized, and the social fabric and mood of the people are stable. This 'AIDS village' is emerging from the shadow of horror."[66]

In September 2002, China's top health official, Zhang Wenkang, at last sent a stronger message that the government was prepared to deal with HIV-AIDS. He announced publicly that the disease no longer presented a potential danger, but a clear and present one. In recent years, HIV-AIDS cases had been increasing at a rate of around 30 percent, he said. If China did not deal urgently with its HIV-AIDS problem, the country would have 10 million people living with HIV-AIDS by 2010, giving it the unfortunate position of leading the world in HIV infections. Following Zhang's announcement, government funding for the prevention and treatment of HIV-AIDS increased substantially.[67]

It has been a long and arduous journey since Zhang Jicheng's first story on the Henan epidemic in January 2000. China has come a long way. But the truth remains constantly in contention.

In June 2004, Henan finally bowed to central government pressure and consented to comprehensive HIV-AIDS testing in the countryside. The results disappointingly replayed those of the testing campaign triggered by the Wang Shuping and Zeng Yi report back in 1996. Henan had only 25,000 HIV-AIDS cases, local officials said.[68] Numbers from independent health experts, as for example, Zhang Ke, the infectious diseases expert from Beijing, told a very different story — over a five-year period, Zhang treated 11,057 HIV-AIDS patients in one small region of Henan.

Angered by the government's report, Zhang Ke struck back later that year by publishing a scientific study on the Internet. On the basis of data collected from more than one hundred AIDS villages, he estimated that the province had around 300,000 HIV-AIDS cases, and an estimated 60,000 patients had died.[69]

In the March 2005 issue of the quarterly magazine *Min Jian*, AIDS activist and doctor Gao Yaojie wrote about the lingering "dark corners" of HIV-AIDS in China, crisis-areas local officials in the hinterland had struggled to keep secret. "In some areas, local leaders lie and cover up the epidemic to protect their own political credentials, or do not let villagers reveal the situation to the outside world. This means the unfortunate ordinary people are the ones most hurt. They cannot get government assistance, cannot get free medicine, cannot send their children to school, and when they die no one knows." While Henan has become, for Chinese and foreigners alike, symbolic of China's critical HIV-AIDS problem, pockets of HIV infection may be more common elsewhere; Gao said: "I estimate places like this are more prevalent outside Henan and account for two-thirds of affected areas in the whole country."[70]

Civilians, such as Gao Yaojie, are still under great pressure from the government at all levels. In February 2006, the prominent AIDS activist Hu Jia resigned as head of Loving Source, a nongovernmental organization (NGO) helping orphans of AIDS victims. Announcing his resignation, Hu cited unrelenting harassment from authorities.[71] In a crackdown on dissent before the 2008 Beijing Olympic Games, authorities detained Hu in December 2007. The following March, he was found guilty of "inciting subversion of state power" and sentenced to three and a half years in prison.[72]

Much more needs uncovering as Chinese reporters continue to push against official silence while navigating their way through a tough political climate. To mark International AIDS Day in 2005, Beijing's *China Economic Times* ran an investigative story on HIV-AIDS by muckraking reporter Wang Keqin. The story, a 40,000-word *tour de force*, exposed hospital doctors regularly prescribing unnecessary transfusions for profit as the chief cause of HIV infection in Henan's Xingtai City.[73] It told the heart-wrenching story of a young girl named Tian Tian, born with HIV after her mother was given repeated transfusions with infected blood while pregnant.

Unfortunately, as Wang Keqin's recent work shows, the words of Doctor Gui Xien to Zhang Jicheng in 1999 seem perhaps as fitting now as they were then: "I believe this is just the tip of the iceberg," he had said.

Postscript

Many of the cases in this book tell the stories of the persistence and ingenuity of individual reporters working in a difficult environment. But China's biggest stories, those with far-reaching political impact, can be reported only through the concerted effort of professional journalists from various media, as well as independent experts, who push relentlessly to reveal the truth, and who collectively suffer the political consequences.

Chinese reporting of the Henan AIDS crisis exemplifies how media and concerned citizens can work in an informal system to expose major public interest stories. It is often a slow, painstaking process of steadily increasing scrutiny, constantly testing the limits of party tolerance.

Investigative reporting has been on the rise in China since the 1980s, particularly during the 1990s, as the mandate for "supervision by public opinion" (or watchdog journalism) has somewhat emboldened newspapers, and as commercialization has helped create a broader market for exclusive news. One of the most important tools available to media in pursuing more sensitive stories has been cross-regional reporting, known in Chinese as *yidi jiandu*, a reference to media from a particular province or city — one controlled by local officials in that area — conducting investigative reporting in another region. In other words, by taking advantage of political decentralization, the media can minimize the risk of disciplinary action when dealing with sensitive stories.

The Henan AIDS story demonstrated the effectiveness of cross-regional reporting — a commercial newspaper in Sichuan Province printed the first major feature by Zhang Jicheng, written in defiance of local bans. As the case shows, that article kick-started a cycle of coverage extending for several months until national media, such as *China Newsweekly*, took to the story. From that point, it graduated from a local topic, reported across provincial borders, into a full-fledged one of national concern and attention.

In the past several years, cross-regional reporting has often infuriated local officials. In a recent case in June 2005, *Beijing News* broke a story about a violent clash over land requisition in Hebei Province that resulted in the deaths of at least six people.[74] The report prompted the removal of one of the newspaper's top editors that December, partly because of pressure from Henan's top leader.[75] That incident, media insiders say, factored crucially into causing local party leaders in late 2005 to press the Central Propaganda Department to place restrictions upon cross-regional reporting. The Hong Kong media reported the news, noting that seventeen provinces and municipalities had petitioned for limits on the practice.[76] While it remains uncertain that these requests were ever made formally or jointly, as the Hong Kong reports seemed to imply, the effort is very real.

Some local party leaders have also crafted their own policies to deal with cross-regional investigative reporting. In July 2005, the propaganda office of Nanjing, the capital of Jiangsu Province, said "every article of supervision by public opinion must be approved by officials concerned [in the article] before appearing in the newspapers."[77] Other local party leaders, including those in Shenzhen, followed suit. Often, these rules operated as reciprocal arrangements. For instance, Guangdong provincial leaders might issue an order to a local newspaper, such as *Southern Weekend*, prohibiting the coverage of, for example, a breaking news story in Henan, with the understanding that leaders in Henan would similarly reign in their reporters should the need arise.

It remains a constant struggle. Journalists look for loopholes in the system, and those in power do their utmost to plug these holes. With both professional and commercial interests at play, Chinese media continue to test the limits of party media control.

Over the years, Chinese reporters and editors have developed a number of metaphors to explain how journalism can survive in China's extreme, control-oriented environment. One of the most notable is Fan Jingyi's "shouldering the door theory." Fan, the former editor-in-chief of *Economic Daily* and *People's Daily*, both central-level party newspapers, is widely regarded in China as an official, scholar, and journalist. According to his metaphor, if someone forcefully kicks down the door on a prohibited news story, authorities will react with force, and they will deal with the person responsible severely. On the other hand, if enough people apply limited force to the door, the space between the frame and the door will gradually widen until the door cracks opens and light sneaks in. It minimizes the cost to each person, and the door eventually opens.

Coverage of HIV-AIDS in Henan provides a good example of this approach, and the trajectory of the story arguably fits well with Fan's "shouldering the door theory."

In late 1999, a number of smaller media in Henan and bordering provinces braved interviews with AIDS crusaders, as for example, Gao Yaojie and Gui Xien. They raised the issue of AIDS, but focused on the personal and avoided outright talk of an epidemic. In early 2000, Zhang Jicheng's report tackled the issue straight on, but the real blow came from *Huaxi Dushibao*, a newspaper in the western province of Sichuan. Officially, it cost Zhang his job — a yellow-card warning from propaganda officials in Henan. In the months that followed, a non-threatening scientific report appeared in the *Chinese Journal of Epidemiology*, as well as numerous stories about legal cases brought by the families of AIDS victims against local governments. In May, *Dahe Daily*'s risky report, "AIDS in Henan," appeared, framed as a personal story about an unfortunate child suffering from AIDS. This was a relatively safe platform from which to criticize the government for its negligence and inaction. It brought a local ban on AIDS coverage, but it did not give sufficient cause to shut down the newspaper. The precedent having been set by a major commercial newspaper in Henan, *China Newsweekly* followed. To a growing national readership, they described HIV-AIDS and the epidemic in Henan as a "national disaster." Propaganda officials stayed silent in the wake of the *China Newsweekly* story, and *Southern Weekend*, one of the country's most influential newspapers, saw an opportunity to move.

At each step in this process, individual journalists, doctors, and activists paid what they viewed as an acceptable price to advance their agendas. In some cases, as for example, Gao Yaojie's or Zhang Jicheng's, their aim could include pressing for action on HIV-AIDS. Others, such as the *Huaxi Dushibao*, might hope for a revenue-generating news exclusive. The net result, however, was a slow but relentless group assault on the door.

Another of Fan Jingyi's favorite images described the work of journalists in China as "monkey boxing under the table," a reference to a martial arts routine once performed by the legendary Beijing Opera star Gai Jiaotian under an eight-person dining table. Fan believes it is possible for journalists to excel while navigating the restrictions of China's media environment. The legs of the table might be understood as the policies and rules of the party and the propaganda regime. The table must not be upset, but journalists can continue to perform, improving their techniques and building their professional strength.

Shen Changwen, the former senior editor of *Read* magazine, provided one of the most colorful characterizations of journalism in China. He calls it "Jiao Junior" (*jiao er*), inspired by a well-known episode in Chapter 7 of the Qing dynasty literary classic, *The Dream of the Red Mansions*. A servant named Jiao Da, or Jiao Senior, has feces stuffed in his mouth as punishment for cursing his master. Chinese journalists, Shen explains, cannot follow the example of Jiao Senior because it incurs too high a price. But they can be "Jiao Junior," which means they can keep quiet until some other unfortunate soul speaks out — at which point a harsh word goes unnoticed by the master, who is too busy dealing with the unfortunate Jiao Senior. During Shen Changwen's tenure at *Read*, the magazine escaped disciplinary action on a number of occasions because other breaches of propaganda regulations distracted them.

At *Southern Weekend*, which has a reputation for braving political danger, they talk in the newsroom of "taking a half step." Moving ahead a full step means jumping the gun. Staying still does not endow a professional newspaper with a strong sense of mission. So *Southern Weekend* takes a half step. In the 1990s, when talking about introducing democratic concepts from the West posed a great danger, *Southern Weekend* answered by running a regular column called "Xichuang Fayu," in which a young legal scholar looked at key Western legal and political concepts in the past.

These colorful characterizations illustrate well how Chinese journalists attempt to define their role in society and strike a balance between duty, professionalism, and self-preservation. A handful of Chinese reporters regard themselves as solo fliers, more willing to stick out their necks. The majority of journalists in China, however, approach their work carefully, taking calculated risks.

Notes

1. Zhang Jicheng. 2000. "*Henan mocun 'guai bing' jingdong gaoceng*" ("Mystery illness" in Henan villages shocks top leadership). *Huaxi Dushibao*, January 18.
2. Yu Chen. 2005. "*Henan faxian aizibing shi nian*" (Looking back on ten years since the discovery of AIDS in Henan). *Southern Metropolis Daily*, December 16.
3. Zheng Xiwen, Mei Zhiqiang, and Wang Cunlin. 2000. "*Wo guo mou xian xieye shaixuan hou chuanbo aizibing bingdu de canyu weixian du yanjiu*" (Residual risk research of HIV infection after blood screening in one county in China). *Chinese Journal of Epidemiology*, February, Vol. 21, No. 1: 13.
4. *Southern Metropolis Daily*. 2000. "*Aizibing meidu, binggan bingdu Shanxi poqu 2 dun xiean*" (AIDS, syphilis, hepatitis: Shanxi exposes case involving 2 tons of infected blood), March 31.
5. *Southern Metropolis Daily*. 2000. "*Xuetong shuxue ran aizibing suopei 1100 wan*" (Child who contracted HIV through blood transfusion seeks 11 million yuan in compensation), April 19.
6. *Legal Daily*. 2000. "*9 lingtong touxie ranshang aizibingdu shenggao fayuan tiaojie da cheng peichang xieyi*" (Provincial court reaches compensation agreement in case of nine-year-old infected with AIDS through blood transfusion), August 19.
7. Sanny So. 1999. "Asia could top Africa with AIDS." Reuters News Agency, November 12.
8. United States Embassy Beijing. "PRC blood donors and the spread of rural AIDS." Available until January 2006 at http://www.usembassy-china.org.cn/sandt/AIDSblood.htm.
9. Ibid.

10. *Dahe Daily*. 2005. "*Henan shinian xinwen pandian: 2000 nian dashiji*" (Review of news stories in 2000), August 3. Available at http://www.hnby.com.cn/xwzx/zt/hnzt/dhbszhn/dhbshznxwpd/t20050803_199802.htm.
11. Elisabeth Rosenthal. 2000. "Scientists warn of inaction as AIDS spreads in China." *New York Times*, August 2.
12. Jin Liping. 2005. "*Women de kunjing he women de chulu*" (Our predicament and our way out). Hong Kong: Journalism and Media Studies Centre at the University of Hong Kong. Case on file with the China Media Project.
13. Jaspar Becker. 2000. "HIV fear spurs new war on blood sales." *South China Morning Post*, August 30.
14. China News Service. 2000. "*Aizibing jiang shi Zhong Guo meinian sunshi 7000 yi*" (AIDS will cost China 700 billion yuan a year), September 4.
15. Elisabeth Rosenthal. 2000. "Chinese media suddenly focus on a growing AIDS problem." *New York Times*, December 17.
16. Zhang Jie. 2000. "*Xin guonan: aizibing*" (AIDS: a new national disaster). *China Newsweekly*, August 18. Via CNKI. Available at http://www.cnki.com.cn/Article/CJFD2000-XWZK200018006.htm.
17. Asia Society. 2000. "Asia Society announces first winner of the Osborn Elliot Prize for excellence in Asian Journalism." Available at http://www.asiasociety.org/pressroom/rel-oe_award.html.
18. Rosenthal. 2000. "Scientists warn of inaction as AIDS spreads in China."
19. Panos Institute. 1997. "AIDS prevention better than no cure: China's 'last' chance"? January 20. Available at http://www.aegis.com/news/panos/1997/PS970101.html.
20. China Central Television. 2002. "*Zhongguo aizibing baogao*" (China AIDS Report). November 30. Available at http://www.cctv.com/zhuanti/newsprobe/dangan/2876.html.
21. Yu Buhui. 2002. "*Aizibing de 'matai xiaoying'*" (The "Matthew effect" of AIDs). *Lifeweek*, December 23.
22. So. "Asia could top Africa with AIDS."
23. He Aifang. 2000. "*Jiekai Henan sheng chuanbo aizibing de 'xiejia'*" (Exposing the "mortal wound" of HIV-AIDS infection in Henan Province). Aizhi.org, November 28. Available at http://www.aizhi.org/news/jkb2.htm.
24. *Beijing News*. 2004. "'*Xiejiang jingji' yinlai aizi*" ("Blood plasma economy" brings AIDS), December 1. Available at http://news.sina.com.cn/c/2004-12-01/00585084320.shtml.
25. *Jiangnan Shibao*. 2001. "*Henan you yi 'aizibingcun': ganranlu 61.9%*" (In one Henan "AIDS village": rate of infection 61.9%). March 1.
26. Zhang. "*Xin guonan: aizibing*."
27. Gao Yu and Yu Yanlin. 2001. "*Xie huo: zoufang Henan 'aizicun'*" (Blood disaster: visiting Henan's "AIDS villages"). *Lifeweek*, September 5.
28. He. "*Jiekai Henan sheng chuanbo aizibing de 'xiejia'*."
29. Yu Chen. 2005. "*Henan faxian aizibing shi nian*" (Looking back on ten years since the discovery of AIDS in Henan). *Southern Metropolis Daily*, December 16.
30. IEHE is now the Institute of Environmental Health and Engineering (IEHE) of the Chinese Center for Disease Control and Prevention.
31. Yu. "*Henan faxian aizibing shi nian.*"
32. Wan Yanhai. 2002. "*Zhongguo zhengfu he shehui dui aizibing de fanying*" (Chinese government and popular response to HIV-AIDS). Available at Aizhi.org, http://www.aizhi.org/shyx/aidsreaction.txt.
33. He. "*Jiekai Henan sheng chuanbo aizibing de 'xiejia'*."
34. Ibid.

35. Ibid.
36. Ibid.
37. Ibid.
38. *Jiangnan Shibao*. 2001. "*Henan you yi 'aizibingcun': ganranlu 61.9%.*"
39. He. "*Jiekai Henan sheng chuanbo aizibing de 'xiejia'.*"
40. Yu. "*Henan faxian aizibing shi nian.*"
41. Gao Yaojie. 2001. "*Aixin tiaozhan aizibing*" (Facing AIDS with loving care). *China Youth Daily*, July 27.
42. He. "*Jiekai Henan sheng chuanbo aizibing de 'xiejia'.*"
43. Chen Kaixiang. 2001. "*Aizibing minjian fangxian*" (The civil line of defense for HIV-AIDS). *China News Service*, November 1.
44. Ibid.
45. Ibid.
46. Zhang Jicheng. 2000. "*Henan mocun 'guai bing' jingdong gaoceng*" ("Mystery illness" in Henan villages shocks top leadership). *Huaxi Dushibao*, January 18.
47. In news reports, Chinese writers often refer to themselves in third-person, as "the reporter." Subsequent uses in this excerpt are translated as first-person "I."
48. Chen Kaixiang. "*Aizibing minjian fangxian.*"
49. The report appeared in *Changsha Wanbao* on January 21, 2000.
50. Wang Li. 2000. "*Aizibing zai Henan*" (AIDS in Henan). *Dahe Daily*, May 11.
51. Ibid.
52. Li Yuxiao. 2005. "*Ma Yunlong: wo jiushi yi Tanjihede*" (Ma Yunlong: I am a Don Quixote). *Southern People Weekly*, August 24. Available at http://www.nanfangdaily.com.cn/rwzk/20050824/gg/200509080012.asp.
53. Zhang Jingping. 2002. "*Jiuzhu Zhongguo aizibing de minjian liliang*" (Helping [fight] AIDS in China through people power). *Economic Observer*, January 17.
54. Ibid.
55. Zhang. "*Xin guonan: aizibing.*"
56. Ibid.
57. Elisabeth Rosenthal. 2000. "In rural China, a steep price of poverty: dying of AIDS." *New York Times*, October 28.
58. Ibid.
59. Agence France-Presse. 2000. "Chinese villages 'devoured' by AIDS; Locals ordered to keep silent," November 30.
60. Li Yuxiao. 2000. "*Guai bing*" (Mystery illness). *Southern Weekend*, November 30.
61. Ibid.
62. He. "*Jiekai Henan sheng chuanbo aizibing de 'xiejia'.*"
63. John Pomfret. 2001. "The high cost of selling blood: as AIDS crisis looms in China, official response is lax." *Washington Post*, January 11.
64. "HIV-positive people in China surpass 600,000 by last year end: latest statistics." Available at People's Daily Online, August 23, 2001, http://english1.peopledaily.com.cn/200108/23/eng20010823_78084.html.
65. Wan Yanhai. 2002. "*Zhongguo zhengfu he shehui dui aizibing de fanying*" (Chinese government and popular response to HIV-AIDS). Available at Aizhi.org, http://www.aizhi.org/shyx/AIDSreaction.txt.
66. Xinhua News Agency. 2001. "*Zoufang zhujian zou chu yinying de 'aizibing cun'*" (Visiting an "AIDS village" gradually emerging from the shadows), December 3. Available at http://www.people.com.cn/GB/tupian/75/20011203/617733.html.

67. Drew Thompson. 2003. "HIV/AIDS epidemic in China spreads into general population." Population Reference Bureau, April.
68. China News Service. "*Henan aizibingren 2.5 wan: quan sheng jiang jinxing 'la wang shi' diaocha*" (25,000 cases of AIDS in Henan: tests to be carried out throughout the province), September 11.
69. Zhang Ke. 2004. "*Henan aizibing wu nian diaocha baogao*" (A report on AIDS in Henan over the past five years), October 14. Archived at Universities Service Centre for China Studies, Chinese University of Hong Kong. Available at http://www.usc.cuhk.edu.hk/wk_wzdetails.asp?id=4955.
70. Gao Yaojie. 2005. "*Dakai aizi 'heidong'*" (Opening the "dark corners" of HIV-AIDS). *Min Jian*, March.
71. Reuters. 2006. "China activist quits amid crackdown on NGOs," February 8.
72. Bill Schiller. 2008. "Family of jailed Chinese activist targeted by police." *Toronto Star*, June 4. Available at http://www.thestar.com/News/World/article/436555.
73. Wang Keqin. 2005. "*Henan Xingtai aizibing zhenxiang diaocha*" (An investigation into the truth behind AIDS in Xingtai, Henan). *China Economic Times*, November 30.
74. Irene Wang. 2005. "Six killed as thugs attack holdouts in Hebei village." *South China Morning Post*, June 14.
75. Geoffrey Fowler and Juying Qin. 2005. "Editors at *Beijing News* protest efforts to tone down coverage." *Wall Street Journal*, December 31.
76. Kiu Sun Sang. 2005. "Those who govern need not fear the media." *Ta Kung Pao*, October 3, A19.
77. Kiu Sun Sang. 2005. "17 provinces and cities send written statements calling for control of the media." *Sing Pao Daily News*, September 19.

3 *The Kingdom of Lies*
Unmasking the Demons of Charity

In the 1990s, as charitable giving grew more common among China's burgeoning middle class, Project Hope, an education assistance program set up through the China Youth Development Foundation (CYDF), became a popular choice. The program offered a ray of hope for poor rural children whose families could not afford basic school fees.

The basic mission of the program, founded in October 1989, was sponsorship. Chinese individuals, companies, and even officials, including Deng Xiaoping and Jiang Zemin, sponsored children directly. The project established an account for each child, and transferred donations, which would cover tuition and other basic costs, directly from the foundation to the child's local school. Sponsors would receive photographs of the children along with personal letters of thanks. They could even chart a child's progress through regular reports on their schoolwork.

The system was direct and personal. And who could place a price tag on seeing a child prosper?

By the late 1990s, however, rumors of serious corruption at Project Hope surfaced. Though they did not sufficiently substantiate their claims, Hong Kong's *Next* magazine alleged problems with the foundation's accounts. The China Youth Development Fund launched a libel suit against *Next* in the Hong Kong courts, and on June 21, 2000, Judge Andrew Chung ruled in the foundation's favor, ordering the magazine to pay $3.5 million HK in damages.[1]

"This Is All a Misunderstanding"

During National Day celebrations in early October 2001, a letter arrived at the offices of *Southern Weekend*, a weekly newspaper that for years has been regarded as one of China's most outspoken publications. The newspaper was struggling at that time to preserve its reputation for covering hard-hitting news in the face of sustained pressure from propaganda leaders. Two of its top editors, Jiang Yiping and Qian Gang, had been forced to vacate their posts in January 2000 and June 2001 respectively after sensitive coverage angered party leaders.

The news editor Wu Xiaofeng casually opened the letter, which bore a return address from Keyon, a private company based in Shanghai. As he read through the letter, his eyes lit up. It alleged that Project Hope had deceived Keyon about its donation to support twenty-four children in Sichuan Province. The letter explained that Keyon had sponsored Project Hope school children as part of a corporate community service initiative. In return for its contribution, the company had received seventeen letters from students, who warmly thanked the company for its generosity.

Moved by the letters, Keyon's chief executive decided to make an unannounced visit to Sichuan over the National Day holiday. He wanted to see for himself what the company's donations had achieved. Much to his surprise, he found that only three of the children on his list had in fact received Project Hope funding, and most denied having ever written thank-you letters. Studying the individual letters more carefully, he found that many of the letters bore identical handwriting.

Wu Xiaofeng assigned two reporters to the story: the first, Xu Liuwen, a veteran *Southern Weekend* reporter and a native of Sichuan Province; the second, Zhai Minglei, a young reporter who had worked for less than a year at *Southern Weekend* but had worked for three years at *Cash* magazine. Xu set straight off for Sichuan to pick up where the Keyon chief executive had left off, while Zhai was given the more mundane task of speaking to Keyon representatives in Shanghai for a full account of their story.

Xu Liuwen spent roughly a week in Sichuan before returning to the office empty-handed. He said that he had spoken at length with the local secretary of the Chinese Communist Youth League (CCYL) in Xuanhan County, and had also paid visits to several local schools. Nothing seemed out of the ordinary, he said. Heavy rains unfortunately had prevented his traveling into the mountains to visit the more remote schools.

The county CCYL secretary, Li Xiaodong, presented Xu with deposit receipts for all twenty-four of the students sponsored by Keyon, bearing the signatures of parents, teachers, and local education officials. Project Hope's account books looked clean, said the secretary. Project Hope policy required the foundation to transfer all donations directly to county and district committees of the CCYL. From there, the committees then disbursed them to local education offices, where officials responsible for administering Project Hope could draw funds only with invoices issued by the local CCYL committee. No one in this process could withdraw cash, making misdirection of Hope funds impossible, he said.

Xu Liuwen had also located the author of the fake thank-you letters, Tang Chunxu, the person in charge of political and ideological education in Fengcheng District. He was responsible for disbursement of Project Hope funds to local schools. "I arranged for the writing of the fake letters," Tang told Xu matter-of-factly. "Earlier this year one of the donors came down from Shanghai to see how the money was being used. There were, of course, no problems whatsoever with the money . . . In most cases, it is the teacher in charge of the class who directly withdraws the Project Hope funds, so the students and parents don't have a clear idea where the money comes from. So when you ask the kids to write letters, they're not so keen on it. Also, the eight-cent postage is a big expense for them."

"So I had the head teacher write letters and pass them on to me. I bought the envelopes, addressed them, sealed and stamped them and sent them out myself. Of course, some of the children had no idea we were writing letters on their behalf, but our intentions were good. It is not what you think — only deception with the best of intentions," he explained.

When Xu Liuwen asked Tang why the office claimed some students attended school when, in fact, they did not, the official said this was to avoid discouraging donors. While Project Hope donations helped pay a portion of school fees, they did not cover all of them. Inevitably, some hard-luck cases could not keep up with their education. When this happened, the office continued to mark the child present in school, and sometimes even provided records of their grades, so as not to make donors feel their money had gone for nothing. Xu had asked Tang if he regretted his actions. "Not at all!" he said. "I only regret not having done a more delicate job of things. Not sending letters wasn't an option, of course. That would have been inconsiderate."

Tang seemed to have a perfectly convincing explanation for every question. Xu Liuwen said he admired the official's candor. "I'm telling you, this is all a misunderstanding," Xu told his editors. "The real reason [for the Project Hope kids not going to school] is regional poverty."

The story might have ended right there. However, Zhai Minglei remained unconvinced. He told editor Wu Xiaofeng that some facts still could not be explained. Why, for example, were some of these children totally unaware of their sponsorship? Even more to the point, where had the money earmarked for these children gone?

If the Keyon executive had given a truthful account, the rumors about mismanagement at Project Hope must have some merit. Zhai Minglei carefully wrote out a list of each point that did not seem to fit. "We should go out there and take another look," he said to Wu.

The story, unfortunately, remained in Xu Liuwen's hands. The case was put on hold while he handled some personal matters. The second Sichuan trip was postponed again and again. After two weeks had passed, Zhai Minglei grew anxious. "Why don't I just go out to Sichuan myself?" he suggested again to Wu Xiaofeng.

This time the editor relented. He was not quite ready to drop a possible story of corruption at one of China's most sacred charitable institutions.

The next day Zhai Minglei went on the road.

When he arrived in Sichuan, Zhai made no attempt to speak with Xuanhan County officials. Instead, he met with Zhou Haolan, a local Sichuan reporter who had expressed interest in working for *Southern Weekend.* Zhou would help orient

Zhai Minglei, with the assignment considered as a kind of informal job interview. They hired motorcycle drivers and traveled straight into the mountains, trying to blend in with the locals by wearing drab trousers, old shirts, and faded blue revolutionary-era caps.

It was not long, though, before Zhai began to feel he had set an impossible task for himself. Sometimes they traveled on the road for more than twelve hours at a stretch, day after day. Schools were often located four or five hours apart, and the landscape was unyieldingly monotonous. Mountain tops rose constantly ahead of them, and at the top of each agonizing climb stood another row of peaks. Rain fell every day, and the roads became mires. Seemingly, landslides and rockslides awaited them around every turn.

By the end of the first day, Zhao Haolan's buttocks were so bruised from riding that he could not lay on his back. Zhai had lost some of the feeling in his legs. They slept in roadside shops or wherever else they could find. In one place, they paid the proprietor five yuan each for their beds, from which he pulled a sleeping villager, and then pointed, "There's your bed."

It was obvious to them that in the two weeks since Xu Liuwen's visit, local education officials had launched a concerted campaign of damage control. In village after muddy village, schoolmasters and teachers kept their mouths clamped shut. Four full days into their trip left them still empty-handed.

The physical hardships could not rival the hopelessness the reporters felt in their hearts. "There is not a shred of real evidence, and suddenly it dawns on you that perhaps you are wrong," Zhai Minglei later reflected. "You think to yourself, 'You doubted a veteran journalist who came up with nothing. Maybe he was right and you're wrong. These people greet you with calm eyes and innocent smiles. Where are the lies that you've come looking for? It is you who are wrong'."

Zhai Minglei became anxious, doubting his instincts. This mood reached its peak in a mountain village so remote local people referred to it as "Outer Mongolia." It was pitch-black there, so dark the stars looked like pinpoints, right above their heads. That day, they had traveled eight agonizing hours.

For the first time in his career, Zhai resigned himself to defeat. He phoned his editor Wu Xiaofeng. "Damn it, Wu Xiaofeng! You're going to kill me for this. But we're at the end of our rope here and we haven't come up with anything."

"You have to find something, no matter how long it takes," came Wu's unsatisfactory answer. "Every *Weekend* reporter faces an impossible assignment once a year. It comes with the territory."

Zhai Minglei's entry in his notebook that night painted a picture of despair hardening into resolve: "When someone has arrived at the absolute threshold of psychic and physical endurance, can they go on? When all hope is gone, can they still go forward? A friend once shared a passage of T. S. Eliot with me. It went:

> I said to my soul, be still, and wait without hope
> For hope would be hope for the wrong thing; wait without love,
> For love would be love of the wrong thing; there is yet faith
> But the faith and the love and the hope are all in the waiting.
> Wait without thought, for you are not ready for thought:
> So the darkness shall be the light, and the stillness the dancing.[2]

These words perfectly express the feelings I now have in tackling this assignment. I won't throw up my hands, even though I have passed beyond my own limits. I'll come out of this a new person . . ."

With this, Zhai Minglei found his second wind.

A Bad Pasting Job

At dusk several days later, Zhai Minglei and Zhao Haolan came to the home of a Project Hope recipient, Zhang Qiang. They had crossed four mountain passes that day to reach the small village of Nanping.

As the reporters spoke with the boy's mother, Xiong Shengbi, Zhang Qiang looked on quietly. His big toes poked out where the soles of his shoes had worn down. Xiong insisted they had not received money from Project Hope until just a few days before, on October 31, when the schoolmaster gave them 150 yuan.

The schoolmaster in Nanping, Yuan Shuhong, explained that the executive from Keyon had misunderstood what he told him the month before about never receiving fifty yuan from Project Hope. In fact, he said, the money had been disbursed on time.

"Well then, where did this 150 yuan payment in October come from?" Zhai Minglei asked.

The schoolmaster changed tack. "At the time, I knew that Zhang Qiang's money had gone through. So we advanced the family 150 yuan, 50 yuan for each of three school terms. According to regulations, the Project Hope money and the school waivers are lumped together in one payment," he said. However, the reporters knew this statement was untrue.

"If that's the case, why did you give the 150 yuan to Zhang Qiang's mother and not to the school?" Zhai Minglei asked.

"We realized Zhang's family needed help, and we didn't need the money right then. So we offered the money to give them a leg up," said the schoolmaster.

"You're a school, not a charity organization. Why would you offer assistance to families?"

The schoolmaster paused for a moment and then said, "The 150 yuan payment came from up top," by which he seemed to be referring to the education office.

There was a long silence. The reporters waited.

"It was given to the school," the schoolmaster elaborated.

The reporters glanced across to one another. The schoolmaster's story did not add up. They asked to see the school's account ledgers.

About forty minutes later, the schoolmaster emerged from the schoolhouse across the way with the bookkeeper, carrying a stack of account books. Sure enough, there was an entry for a Project Hope disbursement back in January, almost a year earlier. "Zhang Qiang, 100 yuan," it recorded in tiny print. On another entry, dated June 10, Zhang Qiang's mother signed for fifty yuan. This was curious indeed. Had she lied to the reporters, and to the Keyon executive, about not receiving the Project Hope money?

A short time later, Xiong Shengbi herself came over to the school, apparently suspecting something was amiss. She had come over to confront the schoolmaster directly, in front of the reporters, to say that she had not received any money until October 31. The schoolmaster led her outside to talk things over.

At that time, Zhai Minglei noticed that the June 10 entry in the account ledger had just been pasted onto the page. The glue was not even dry yet. A bolt of clarity shot through his head. He turned to the bookkeeper: "This entry has just now been pasted in! Why would you do a thing like that?" Flustered, the bookkeeper could only blurt out, "The schoolmaster told me to do it!"

The game was up. They confronted the schoolmaster, and he finally confessed: "When the executive came from Shanghai we were totally mystified," he said. "We had no idea the company had made a contribution to the district office [of the Communist Youth League] the September before. We had paid Zhang Qiang's reductions out of our own pockets for three school terms. Soon after the executive's visit, Tang Chunxu (the district official who had won over the *Southern Weekend* reporter Xu Liuwen) came from the education office with 150 yuan for me to give to Zhang Qiang's mother. Tang also knew she was illiterate, so he wanted me to make up fake account slips for all three school terms and have her sign these when she collected the 150. This way, we could paste the entries in and they would bear her signature."

As for the other accounts, the schoolmaster said, Tang had asked them to lump the Project Hope funds together with the school's own tuition and fee subsidies. This way, if anyone grew suspicious, they could simply say that they had combined the funds, making it virtually impossible to carry out an audit.

They learned that, after the year 2000, the district education office, at Tang's bidding, had ended the practice of listing the individual names of Project Hope recipients when settling accounts. Instead, they simply entered the total number of children sponsored. In this fashion, they could shift funds around as they pleased, giving the schoolmasters no way of knowing which of their students were to receive aid. To further complicate efforts to conduct an audit, Tang did away with the practice of disbursing funds for each of the three school terms. Instead, he paid them in one lump sum, siphoning off a portion to pay whatever money schools owed the district education office. If, for example, new desks had been purchased for a school that year, Tang would ostensibly settle their account by slashing the Project Hope allotment.

Given the huge "debts" owed by many of these poor country schools, this practice effectively voided Project Hope. "Typically, schools owe thousands or tens of thousands of yuan each year. When accounts are handled in this way, some schools have no hope of seeing money from the foundation," said Yuan, the schoolmaster.

The payment of cash to Zhang Qiang's mother in October also appeared strange, he said. According to his understanding, Tang should not have been able to withdraw cash. How had he managed to do this? Where had the money been going all along?

That night, fear of the significance of what they had uncovered at first tinged the sweetness of their discovery. The education official, Tang Chunxu, had succeeded in luring schoolmasters and teachers throughout the county into this scheme. How could they be sure they would sleep safely through the night? They considered traveling without stopping, but eventually settled down and slept more soundly than they had for days.

The confession of Nanping's schoolmaster was the key they needed to throw the case wide open. They worked solidly for the next eleven days, traveling a total of more than 2,000 kilometers, mostly by motorcycle, interviewing more than sixty people. They rested for only one of those days.

Confronting the school children was a painful process, Zhai recalled. They had been coached and coerced into lying about the letters they had written to Project Hope donors. Zhai watched as one child struggled to recall the lies she had been pressed to commit to memory. Moments like this strengthened the reporter's resolve to overthrow what he called "The Kingdom of Lies."

The teachers always began with the same story, about how funds had come on time, as promised. When the journalists refuted these claims with their own findings, the teachers would fumble desperately for other explanations. In every case, the parents told a different version from that of the teachers, and different yet again from those given by the bookkeepers.

In some ways, this confusion benefited them. It had taken *Southern Weekend* two full weeks to organize a second trip after Xiu had come back empty-handed, giving local education officials time to orchestrate a widespread cover-up. But while Tang Chunxu had carefully coached schools and gotten them to falsify their account ledgers, the cover-up remained far from watertight, and made a powerful story in its own right.

The determination of the teachers and schoolmasters to hold this fabric of lies together baffled Zhai Minglei. Mainly, an us-versus-them suspicion of the outsider motivated them. Tang Chunxu, however questionable his intent, was still one of "them"; while the reporters were outsiders, nosing into local business. "Face" was also an important motivation to upholding the deception. As ugly as it seemed, this whole affair was theirs — no good could come from airing it out to the outside world.

Nonetheless, once the reporters had broken through the lies, these fragile loyalties crumbled. Schoolmasters and teachers shared their deepest thoughts and feelings toward Project Hope's operations.

Having succeeded in building their story, Zhai Minglei and Zhao Haolan turned more attention to examining the conditions in which the local people lived. Although most of this material never made it into the *Southern Weekend* report, the reporters nevertheless believed in its relevance. Poverty in the area was astounding. People slept on blankets blackened with filth, with no electricity when the sun went down, not even oil lamps. Schools were the only symbol of hope, but they were black and cavernous, full of crooked, unbalanced desks, with rough-hewn planks in place of blackboards.

Digging for the Deeper Story

In his article on Project Hope, Zhai Minglei exercised care not to scapegoat the local education official, Tang Chunxu. He wanted, rather, to show how gaping loopholes in the system had allowed abuses at the foundation to develop. Fearful of the political impact the report might have if it directly attacked Project Hope, a nationwide institution, *Southern Weekend*'s editorial committee redirected the story, focusing on Tang's actions in Xuanhan County.

The portions removed from Zhai Minglei's original version convey the systemic failure to make the project transparent and accountable:

> In interviews with *Southern Weekend* at least four schoolmasters and assistant schoolmasters pointed out that Project Hope had substantial loopholes.
>
> Before 1996 every Project Hope child was assigned an account number. Only when approval came from the local Chinese Communist Youth League (CCYL) could teachers access the funds. After 1996 this system changed. Funds were transferred directly from the Communist Youth Development Foundation (CYDF) to district education offices, which then distributed money to the schools. This created endless opportunities for abuse. Xuanhan County is Sichuan Province's model county for Project Hope, and it has repeatedly been given a stamp of approval by the central government and by the provincial committee of the Communist Youth League. Over the last 10 years, the county has reportedly assisted 9,800 children with their school fees, more than any other county in Sichuan. Now problems like these have come to light. But if it had not been for the extraordinary efforts of Keyon and this newspaper in getting to the bottom of the issue, these facts would have been kept in the dark.

One assistant schoolmaster said poor management of the Project Hope funds potentially enabled schoolmasters to have head teachers withdraw the funds. When a child graduated, he said, the school could continue drawing money in the child's name, applying it for the school's general use, giving it to others, or pocketing it. The failure to separate Project Hope funds and general funds from the district education office set the conditions for corruption firmly in place. The disbursing of Project Hope funds to schools from the education office in no way guaranteed they would be used for children. Schoolmasters could apply these in whatever way they wished.

Given the extreme remoteness of this region, misuse of funds by the education office, schoolmasters or head teachers was nearly impossible to detect. Parents have no way of knowing when they can expect Project Hope funds for their children. At least five parents in Xuanhan County had no idea their children were even on the list of Project Hope aid recipients until an executive from the donor company, Keyon, visited Sichuan to see the results of the program.

Three schoolmasters said the Communist Youth Development Foundation should establish accounts for Project Hope children and disburse the aid money directly, allowing access to the money only when the head teacher and the parent are present. After withdrawing the funds, parents could apply these directly to the child's tuition and fees. This, they said, would remove the potential for misapplication of funds and ensure parents did not use the school fees for household expenses.[3]

Despite the heavy editing of the article at the hands of *Southern Weekend*'s editorial committee, Zhai Minglei received hundreds of letters praising the newspaper's coverage of Project Hope. Soon after, China Central Television's (CCTV) *Eastern Horizon*, a news talk show, featured an interview with Xu Yongguang, the leading national official at Project Hope. While Xu acknowledged there had been a few hiccups with the project, he insisted that the Communist Youth Development Foundation was actively exploring nationwide changes in the program. The show also interviewed Zhai Minglei, who spoke about endemic institutional problems at Project Hope. Zhai's portion of the interview was removed before the segment aired. Party officials sought to avoid casting the story as anything other than an isolated case of corruption.

The news of Tang's public admission of guilt that came shortly after the CCTV segment had aired surprised no one. The party committee in Xuanhan County vowed that it would deal harshly with Tang, which seemed to quench the state media's thirst for blood.

But Zhai Minglei's report eventually prompted two whistleblowers, both former employees of the project, to publicly accuse the foundation of general mismanagement, and at the same time implicate the national offical Xu Yongguang. The sources were Liu Yang, former deputy head of the accounting department at Project Hope, and Yi Xiao, another former employee. In early 2002, Liu presented

Southern Weekend with evidence that the charity had been defrauded of some 12 million yuan. Based on this new information, the newspaper's editor-in-chief Fang Jinyu wrote a report that clearly implicated Xu Yongguang.

In light of the report's sensitivity, the editors agreed that printing an unedited version would be dangerous. Instead, they explored the option of running it as an "internal reference," or *neican*, where it might draw the attention of China's political elite. According to his own account, Fang offered the story to several internal references, including those of his former employer, Xinhua News Agency. But the article was too hot for anyone to handle.

Having risked their own necks, Fang's sources grew anxious, and wanted to leak information to newspapers in Hong Kong. Fang helped arrange a meeting between Liu Yang and a correspondent for *Ming Pao Daily*. Once *Ming Pao Daily* had broken the story outside China, other media followed suit, including Hong Kong's English-language *South China Morning Post*. Emboldened by international attention, Liu Yang called a press conference in Guangzhou for domestic media. On March 20, 2002, the day of the scheduled news conference, *Southern Weekend* put Fang Jinyu's four-page exposé on the front page, and sent the issue off to the printers. Xu Yongguang, meanwhile, was pulling his own strings. He characterized the allegations circulating in the Hong Kong press as "a terrorist attack on Project Hope," and successfully pressed the Central Propaganda Department to issue a directive banning the story, which the propaganda authorities in Guangdong enforced. It ordered the destruction of *Southern Weekend*'s entire print run of roughly 300,000 copies.

Fang Jinyu countered with an incredibly risky maneuver — he decided to post the article on the Internet in its entirety, putting it under his own name instead of that of the newspaper. Within hours, the story spread around the globe. Most damningly, Fang's report revealed that the Communist Youth Development Foundation had changed disbursement procedures in 1996 to enable the diversion of funds by high officials into other speculative ventures more easily.

The *Southern Weekend* reports pulled Project Hope down from its lofty perch. In the year following Zhai Minglei's report, contributions to the fund dropped more than 60 percent.

Postscript

Zhai Minglei called the hostile environment he faced in remote Sichuan Province the "Kingdom of Lies." His story underscores the challenges of reporting in the rough terrain of China's hinterland, where journalists face a range of problems — from underdeveloped infrastructure and entrenched local corruption, to the reticence of the populace.

As insurmountable as these obstacles seemed to Zhai at the time, they only marked the beginning. Once the newspaper had penetrated the "Kingdom of Lies" in Sichuan, it faced a more daunting hurdle in a system that worked to actively suppress politically dangerous facts. In this case, Xu Yongguang, the powerful official at the head of the China Youth Development Foundation, posed one of the most formidable obstacles.

Ultimately, exposing institutionalized corruption at Project Hope required two acts of desperation on the part of *Southern Weekend* editor Fang Jinyu: the first, the decision to relinquish a major, hard-earned scoop to another media organization — an idea that might seem abhorrent to journalists working in freer environments; the second, the very risky decision to post the full text of the newspaper's second Project Hope report on the Internet. In both cases, cooperation with international media and using the Internet gave him powerful ways to get the full story out.

Through most of the 1990s, the official yearly "white books" on human rights hailed Project Hope as a model and a yardstick of social progress, making it much more than simply a common charity. As such, it provided an extremely sensitive target for watchdog journalism. Government employees and party members were encouraged to contribute as part of their "ideological education." In 1994, then Premier Li Peng made a point of emphasizing the project's achievements in his Government Work Report to the National People's Congress.

Established just a few months after the crackdown on student demonstrators on Tiananmen Square in 1989, Project Hope boasted explicit political support from China's highest leadership. The project, created under the auspices of the Communist Youth League, exemplified the GONGO, or government-organized nongovernmental organization. Deng Xiaoping, Jiang Zemin, and Li Peng, at that time China's three most powerful men, all wrote ceremonial inscriptions for the project in their personal calligraphic styles. Retired high-ranking cadres from institutions such as the Secretariat of the State Council, the Ministry of Education, and the People's Political Consultative Conference staffed the organization's supervisory ranks.

Given Project Hope's strong political backing, perhaps it comes as no surprise that *Southern Weekend*'s editor-in-chief Fang Jinyu could not even publish the second exposé in a classified internal reference. Faced with no other alternative, Fang turned, with great reluctance, to international media and the Internet. "Here I am, a party news worker, meeting with a mainland correspondent [for a foreign publication] and sifting through the evidence against a corrupt mainland official; why must things turn out this way?" he later wrote.

It is important to note in this case that Fang Jinyu did not choose to post his report on the Internet before the international media coverage. To do so might have presented too great a danger, inviting trouble from propaganda authorities. By first leaking the story to Hong Kong media, and drawing international attention to problems at Project Hope, Fang found a way to minimize the risk of punishment for releasing his news report online, notwithstanding the March 21 propaganda ban. The story then traveled quickly, both domestically and internationally. By March 24, an article on the exposé's suppression at *Southern Weekend* had appeared in the *New York Times*.[4]

The Internet continues to serve as protection and an important network for journalists in China, linking them to a global professional community. This power manifested itself again in January 2006, after the Central Propaganda Department ordered the shutdown of *Freezing Point*, a weekly supplement to *China Youth Daily*. Within hours, the *Freezing Point* editor Li Datong circulated an open letter protesting the action via e-mail and the Internet. He was able to draw attention quickly to the issue, which rapidly became an international incident, prompting party leaders to announce the following month the re-launch of the supplement (although without its two top editors, including Li).

Unfortunately, even when journalists succeeded in breaking through the "Kingdom of Lies," it did not guarantee government action or a change in policy. Xu Yongguang dismissed the allegations in the second Project Hope report as "rumors" and an attempt at "news distortion" by disgruntled former employees. Xu eventually stepped down as the head of Project Hope; he remained, however, on its governing council, and advanced into another leading position in the nonprofit sector, that of vice secretary general of the China Charity Foundation.

Several official audits and investigations targeted Project Hope, but without public disclosure of the findings. The full story remains off-limits to public scrutiny, and to this day it is difficult to establish the facts among the forest of allegations and counter-allegations. According to one well-informed and impartial observer, Liu Yang's original assertions in *Ming Pao* and *Southern Weekend* were "substantially true," but might have resulted from "institutional mismanagement" rather than personal corruption of the project's leadership.

Suppression of the second exposé on the mainland made it impossible to refute or confirm the allegations convincingly. A cloud of doubt remains. But one thing at least is certain — Project Hope has not yet recovered its previous standing in the eyes of the public.

Notes

1. People's Daily Online. 2000. "HK court backs Project Hope over libel," June 22. Available at http://english.people.com.cn/english/200006/22/eng20000622_43648.html.
2. T. S. Eliot. *Four Quartets*. London: Faber and Faber, 2001.
3. Portions provided by Zhai Minglei, on file with the China Media Project, University of Hong Kong.
4. Elizabeth Rosenthal. 2002. "Beijing in a rear-guard battle against a newly spirited press." *New York Times*, September 15.

4 *Undercover Reporting*
Ah Wen's Nightmare

Close to midnight on March 13, 2002, a telephone call from his editor, Fang Hongning, jarred *Yangcheng Evening News* reporter Zhao Shilong awake. Fang said a woman had just called the newspaper's hotline saying that she had been forced into prostitution at a government-run drug rehabilitation center in Guangzhou. She had escaped from her captors that very night. Her name was Ah Wen.

Given the seriousness of the charges, the story's prospects were not good, Fang Hongning said outright. Even if he managed to report the story without any problems, it might never make it past the editorial board. Top leaders of Guangzhou controlled *Yangcheng Evening News*, one of three leading dailies in the city. Its editorial board would have to carefully consider the political ramifications of such a story, one that would certainly reflect badly on city leaders.

At the same time, there was no denying that this was potentially a great story. Fang needed to know if Zhao Shilong was interested. Zhao agreed without any hesitation. Given the seriousness of the allegations, how could he simply look the other way? He jotted down the name and telephone number, which rang to a private payphone. A male attendant answered first, and Zhao asked for Ah Wen. They talked only long enough to arrange for a meeting the next morning at nine in the offices of *Yangcheng Evening News*.

When a gaunt, sickly-looking woman stepped into the newsroom the next morning, Zhao sensed instantly that it was Ah Wen. She had the "telltale signs" of a chronic heroin user, he later said, with haggard features beyond her years.

Ah Wen explained that she had checked in and out of drug centers at least six times since her high school graduation in 1990. She was now thirty years old. During her most recent stint of compulsory drug treatment, Guangzhou police had packed her off to the Changzhou Drug Rehabilitation Center, located on an island at the center of Guangzhou's Pearl River. Soon afterwards, Ah Wen grew suspicious of the way female inmates were dragged from their rooms without warning. Other inmates began whispering that the officials in charge of the facility were selling women into the local sex trade.

Ah Wen's turn came one morning in early February 2002.

Shao Liai, a female supervisor at the rehabilitation center, whom the inmates referred to as "Ah Ding," came for Ah Wen. Shao escorted her along with several other women to a small waiting area partitioned off from a visiting room by a large glass window, with a speaker and microphone panel installed on one side, so those in the visiting room could converse with the inmates.

"Look, if this fellow offers to pay for you, you'd better do things right," Ah Ding cautioned them, motioning to a strange man eyeing them from the visiting room. "Otherwise, he'll hold you responsible for the money he's lost."

They never closed a deal that day. Ah Wen later heard that the man had been unwilling to fork over the 1,000 yuan ($144 US) that Ah Ding asked for each inmate, and the supervisor had held her ground.

A few weeks later, on March 2, the rehabilitation center's head supervisor Chen Taizhong led Ah Wen to the viewing area for a second time. There were two other young women there, surnamed Chen and Gu. On the other side of the glass, a forty-something pimp they called "Grandfather Mao" said he would purchase all three women. Ah Wen was terrified. She pleaded with Chen Taizhong to let her stay.

"At this point, you don't really have a say in the matter," he spat back at her. "We've been covering your boarding fees for five months now!"

They gave the women a few minutes to pack up their belongings, and then they drove off with Grandfather Mao to an urban village called Kangle in Guangzhou's Haizhu District. Grandfather Mao and his mistress, Ding Chuanju, herself a former prostitute, bought "work outfits" for the women. At seven o'clock that evening, he forced them to stand out in the alley and wait for customers. Mao promised that each of them would be released once they had paid back the 5,000 yuan he claimed he had paid for each of them at the rehabilitation center.

Over the next three days, eight men paid Ah Wen between thirty and fifty yuan ($4.3–7.2 US) for sex.

On March 6, her fourth day in captivity, she ran away as she was heading off to see her ninth "client."

Ah Wen could not return to her family because the drug rehabilitation center had registered her personal information, which meant Mao could easily track her down. She went instead to a friend's apartment.

She felt angry, hurt, humiliated. She was determined to do whatever she could, she said, to help *Yangcheng Evening News* bring Mao and the others to justice.

Zhao Goes Undercover

Zhao believed he had only one way to get the full story and substantiate the criminal involvement of facility administrators — he would have to go undercover. "Many aspects of the story would have remained buried had I not gone undercover," Zhao explained in 2004. "If I had chosen to report the story openly, it is very probable that I would never have discovered the deeper story about what was really going on at the rehab center."

Zhao discussed his plan briefly with his editor, and then worked out the details with Ah Wen. They decided to visit the rehabilitation center under the guise of buying female inmates. Zhao would pose as the pimp, Ah Wen as a former prostitute with an active role in the business. Ah Wen explained that it was not uncommon for former prostitutes to set up their own rackets once they had managed to buy their freedom.

Ah Wen phoned the rehabilitation center from the newsroom, and asked to speak to the director, Luo Jianwen. Luo, as it turned out, also sat on the board of the state-owned-and-operated Guangdong No. 2 Workers' Mental Hospital on nearby Changzhou Island, where he was the director of general affairs.

Ah Wen said she wanted to bring her "big brother" along to have a look at some prospective "girls." They were looking to pay a thousand yuan apiece, she said.

Luo Jianwen was obliging on the phone, but by the time they arrived at the facility, he had already left for the day. An attendant in the main waiting room said they were not permitted to release inmates without Luo's prior approval. Over Zhao's protests that they had already negotiated a price, the attendant said they would have to try again the next day.

At eight o'clock that evening, Zhao and Ah Wen scouted out Kangle, the village where she and the other women had been forced to work. The alley was only about 10 feet wide and about 150 feet from one end to the other, dimly lit with grimy yellow lamps, intersected by a series of smaller passages. Approximately ten prostitutes stood in the alley, each closely watched by a pair of thugs. Customers came by regularly, striking a price before heading off to nearby rooms. Ah Wen recognized several of the women, but refused to enter, fearing the guards might recognize her.

At about ten the next morning, March 15, Zhao Shilong and Deng Bo, one of the newspaper's photographers, rendezvoused with Ah Wen and took a taxi back to the drug rehabilitation center. Zhao and Deng had disguised themselves as pimps, and prepared for the undercover mission by enclosing a tiny camera inside the plastic casing of a mobile phone. Deng would snap photos while pretending to chat on the phone. Zhao, meanwhile, would record their conversations with a concealed digital recorder.

Luo was away again that morning. The attendant suggested that they come back after lunch. They walked to a nearby restaurant and waited there.

It was already two p.m. by the time they returned to the rehabilitation center. Several men slouched in the waiting area. One was growling on and on about Luo Jianwen, and how he had gone back on his word: "He said 1,300 at first, then he jacked it up to 1,500."

The waiting room attendant tried to engage Zhao in small talk. "You know, most of these women have worked as prostitutes before," she said dismissively. "It's a simple question of economics, really."

Ah Wen grew impatient. She waved down a supervisor she recognized from the women's ward, and said she had brought her "big brother" along for some purchases. But another full hour elapsed before Luo Jianwen finally stepped out into the waiting room. He put his hand out warmly and introduced himself as the center's director.

"1,300 each," Luo said, getting right down to business.

Zhao winced with pretended disappointment, and said they had already agreed on 1,000 yuan. Luo's smile melted into a humorless grin. He stepped out of the room and came back a minute or two later with another attendant. "How many women did you say you needed?" he asked.

Zhao had a feeling they had not finished talking. But Luo's attendant waved to a sign on the wall over her shoulder: "We will charge a viewing deposit of 500 for each patient."

"What's that?" Zhao protested. "Look, I've come to buy, not to ogle. How do you expect to get any business from me if I can't see the women first?"

Luo finally relented. "All right. Just give us ten yuan for each woman you want to see and we'll settle the rest once you've made your selections."

Zhao fished a fifty yuan note out of his pocket.

Ah Ding, the same women's ward supervisor who had dragged Ah Wen off to her first viewing, came out to greet them. She took over from there, but had her own game to play. "I'm afraid it won't be possible to show you any women until later this afternoon," she said suggestively.

"She wants a red envelope," Ah Wen whispered to Zhao. At that point, the reporter pulled out an envelope stuffed with 200 yuan in bills, and offered it to the supervisor, who flashed a grin as she pocketed the money. "Just wait for me out in the courtyard," she said. "Then I'll walk you over to the viewing room."

When they finally arrived in the viewing room ten minutes later, two women were waiting uneasily on the other side of the glass partition. Ah Wen recognized the first woman as Fan X Wen, a chronic drug user since 1989 from Guangzhou's Yuexiu District, whose name Zhao Shilong later redacted with an "x" in his news report to protect her identity. Ah Wen spoke to Fan quietly through the speakerphone. "My big brother is a decent guy," she said, indicating Zhao. "Once we've gotten you out, you won't have to work the streets. OK?"

Fan nodded.

The next woman looked miserable. She was clearly wracked by the deepest throes of addiction. Zhao used this as an opportunity to keep up his act. He balked to Ah Ding, saying he needed better material to work with. The supervisor soon returned with two more inmates. Zhao settled on a woman named Dong X Ling. Dong, a migrant from the city of Yichang in Hubei Province, had been a heroin addict for eight years.

Having made their selections, they went back to the waiting area, where an attendant scribbled out receipts that said "boarding and treatment costs" across the top. She asked Zhao to settle his bill at a small sundries shop right outside the main gate of the mental hospital — the kind that sells soft drinks, bottled water, and other basic items. He could then return to pick up the women.

A cashier at the shop wrote out four receipts, and exchanged them for Zhao's. As he walked back to the hospital, a group of men stopped him. The one in the middle, the apparent ringleader, took two of his receipts, saying nothing. When the reporter stepped back into the waiting room, Fan and Dong were already waiting with Ah Deng, Ah Wen, and their bags.

Luo Jianwen stepped out briefly to see them off. "We've got a decent supply of good-looking women here. You'll get the same price next time," he said.

"Thanks," Zhao said. "There's no doubt you'll see us again."

Back at *Yangcheng Evening News*, Zhao spoke at length with Fan and Dong, then took down their stories. Both told horrifying accounts of the so-called "treatment" they had received at the center. Fan rolled back her sleeves, and Zhao saw that bright red sores covered her arms. These came, she said, from a toxic ammonia solution they used, without gloves, while assembling pearl jewelry in twenty-hour shifts for the center.

According to their accounts, officers in the ward routinely beat inmates. They called it "getting to work." Generally, the beatings took place in the washroom. Sometimes the attacks occurred impulsively — for example, when the inmates were working too slowly. At other times, the officers planned them to the extent that they gave inmates with chronic conditions — like Dong X Ling, who suffered from asthma — injections to prepare them for the abuse. After all, patient deaths were a dangerous inconvenience.

Fan and Dong estimated that in the two to three months they had stayed there, more than thirty inmates had been sold to pimps from Kangle Village. Others were sold to pimps in Yuancun, another urban village on Guangzhou's outskirts, though they could not be sure how many.

That night, Zhao Shilong returned to Kangle Village with Ah Wen, the photographer Deng Bo, and the two women. Within minutes Fan X Wen recognized her roommate from the rehabilitation center, who had evidently been sold that same day. They spotted many others too, all under the hawk-eyed watch of hired muscle.

Zhao Shilong wanted to document the scene more closely. With Fan leaning on his arm in a display of intimacy, he strolled into the narrow alley while Deng Bo snapped photographs behind them. The alley was so dim they had to slow their steps from time to time in order that Deng could get longer exposures. They eventually drew the attention of one of the guards, who moved toward them. Deng scurried out of the alley, back the way they had come. Zhao, meanwhile, who was now too far in to make a run for it, played it cool. He slowed his step a bit, held Fan close, and whispered in her ear until they exited safely from the other end of the alley.

Hats Off to Comrade Zhao Shilong

On March 16, the day after their adventure in Kangle, the editor-in-chief of *Yangcheng Evening News* Pan Weiwen phoned the police at the Public Security Bureau (PSB) to provide a detailed account of Zhao Shilong's undercover investigation. Discussing the situation, Pan and Zhao both agreed that this was the best course of action. Zhao had already documented the rehabilitation center's involvement in the crime of selling patients.

At around eight p.m. that evening, a specially-formed police investigative squad gathered in the newsroom to meet Zhao Shilong and discuss his findings. Officer Cai, the chief of Guangzhou's 10th Police Precinct, who had been appointed to head up the team, told those gathered that it was their duty to "shed light on every corner of the case." He praised Zhao for a job well done, saying that Zhao had the "guts of an old PSB comrade."

A few hours later, Zhao Shilong and Ah Wen returned to Kangle, leading an undercover reconnaissance mission with members of the police squad. They planned a sting operation for the early hours of March 17, targeting the capture of Grandfather Mao, whom they hoped would expose the entire network in Kangle.

Shortly after midnight, Deng Bo and another *Yangcheng Evening News* photographer, Huang Xi, arrived. Everyone waited for the signal. They planned to let Deng Bo ring Grandfather Mao's doorbell, identifying himself as one of Ah Wen's friends from the rehabilitation center. Deng knocked loudly, and called out for Ah Wen. A light flashed on in the first floor window. "You're looking for Ah Wen?" came a woman's voice, saying, "She's been gone for ages. She doesn't work here anymore."

"She told me to look for her here after I got out," Deng called back. "I've brought some of her stuff."

"She ran away. It was a total loss, the 1,000 yuan we paid for her," the woman said. She held a pair of Ah Wen's shoes up to the window.

Deng changed tack. "I need a place to crash. Is it OK if I stay here tonight?"

But she refused to open the door.

This was enough conversation for the police. One of the officers stepped up, and shouted for her to open the door. The lamp was quickly extinguished, and they could hear frantic whispering on the telephone. But a full five minutes went by before they managed to rouse the building superintendent for him to open the door.

The woman identified herself as Ding Chuanju. According to Ah Wen, she was Grandfather Mao's mistress, the same woman who had bought Ah Wen's work clothes that first evening in the village. Ding refused to divulge Grandfather Mao's whereabouts, insisting that she was running a legitimate business.

After further questioning, they learned that Ding, too, had been a patient at the drug rehabilitation center on Changzhou. She had gone into business with Mao after earning back his initial investment. Combing through the apartment with the officers, Zhao discovered a ledger in which the names of prostitutes had been entered along with a careful account of their jobs and the money taken in. A number of the names on the list were former rehabilitation patients from Luo Jianwen's facility.

Later that night, the police arrested five suspected associates of Grandfather Mao, including a pimp named Gu Anle.

The police squad planned to move in on the rehabilitation center on the morning of March 19, sending in Zhao Shilong first with the photographer Deng Bo and a plain-clothes officer for another ostensible purchase of patients. Zhao, Deng Bo, and a second photographer, Huang Xi, arrived at police headquarters at nine o'clock sharp, and set off with the squad. Separated into several vehicles, they staked out a position directly across from the main entrance to the hospital.

Zhao, Deng, and the officer went inside as planned, but the waiting room attendant said they would have to wait until Director Luo returned later that afternoon. When they came back again at two p.m., Ah Ding, the supervisor, was there. She instantly recognized Zhao Shilong as a customer in good standing, treating him far more obligingly this time around. She did not ask for viewing fees, but simply pocketed the envelope Zhao gave her, and led them off to the viewing room.

As a start, Ah Ding asked for 1,500 yuan ($217 US). Zhao made a great show of irritation at this price hike. He wanted time to discuss things with his associates, he said. They returned to the waiting room, hoping to catch other buyers in the act.

A few men came in and sat next to them. They introduced themselves as former patients at the center. They wanted to know whether Zhao had bought women before, and for how much. When he said he had paid 1,000 yuan ($144 US), they were incredulous. "No way!" They shook their heads. "You shouldn't have paid anything over 600."

A few minutes later, an urgent call came from the squad posted outside. A woman they had questioned in the raid the previous day had just walked through the hospital gates. If she saw Zhao, she might blow their cover.

But it was too late. Just as the she stepped through the doorway, the woman saw them, and bolted. The undercover officer rushed after her, but she escaped on a waiting motorbike.

Afraid their operation might be compromised, the squad moved in immediately on the rehabilitation center. They arrested Chen Taizhong, the same ward supervisor who had sold Ah Wen to Grandfather Mao, and Ah Ding as they were heading home. They then divided into two teams, one raiding the shop that served as a front for the operation, the other storming the rehabilitation center itself.

They arrested ten people altogether in the raid, including Luo Jianwen, the center's director. Officers from Guangzhou's Drug Prevention and Treatment Bureau secured the center, and transferred its patients to other facilities.

Politics and the News Page

Finally, they faced the work of writing the story. Zhao paid great attention to the facts of the case, knowing for certain that many hurdles lay ahead. He wrote an 8,000-word exposé detailing criminal activity at the rehabilitation center and giving a play-by-play account of the subsequent police investigation. Just as editor Fang Hongning had anticipated from the start, the newspaper's top brass on the editorial board feared the possible political implications of the report.

One of the biggest problems was timing. The National People's Congress, one of the year's most important political events, had opened in Beijing only two weeks earlier. *Yangcheng Evening News* editor-in-chief Pan Weiwen and other members of the editorial board worried that the story might attract too much national attention, and jeopardize the long-anticipated promotion of Guangzhou's top party leader, Huang Huahua, to the post of Guangdong provincial governor, which was expected to happen any day.

To understand the editors' fears, one must remember that as high-ranking executives of a newspaper who answered ultimately to party leaders, they were as much officials themselves as news professionals. They rubbed shoulders with party dignitaries at the city and provincial levels on an almost daily basis, and were heavily invested in the bureaucracy. Running a story with such ugly truths at such an inopportune time would mean seriously rocking the boat.

At the same time, of course, the story revealed critically important information about the local abuse of power. Pan Weiwen suggested an alternative that Zhao, as a professional journalist, found completely unacceptable. Considering the risks entailed by making the story public, they could, instead, publish it as an internal reference. This would mean that party officials at the local and perhaps national level would see the story — but newspaper readers would not. In this way, officials could handle the matter internally, embarrassing no one.

Zhao fought hard against the death of his feature. In the end, however, he could only save a gutted 600-word report running on page two on March 21.

Naturally, Zhao Shilong had hoped for a different result. But the article did in fact attract enough attention to assist in the capture of Grandfather Mao. Within a few days, a twenty-six-year-old former drug patient, Little Ran, came forward. She showed up at the newsroom, looking for Zhao, saying that she could take him to

Mao's hiding place. Zhao sat her down and asked her to speak on the record about her own experiences at the Changzhou rehabilitation center.

Ran had been transferred to Changzhou with twenty-four other women from a center in Guangzhou's Baiyun District the year before. A few months into her stay, guards forced four female patients to sit all night in a pool of freezing water. Some of the women told her that a previous patient subjected to this punishment had died of hypothermia. In the guards' version of the story, this woman had died "while washing."

Another woman, Ah Ling, was pregnant when the center admitted her for treatment, Ran said. One day, the guards accused her of working too slowly. A guard the women referred to as "Dumb Elephant" beat Ah Ling with a club. When she finally collapsed, blood coursed down her thighs, and they later heard that she had miscarried.

On Christmas Day, 2001, Grandfather Mao purchased Little Ran from the center. He and several of his "guests" raped her repeatedly that night at his apartment in Kangle Village. Grandfather Mao told the men it represented a "token of friendship."

Mao forced her to have sex with at least ten "clients" in a single day. He offered her on the side to his guards at a "discounted rate." He struck her constantly, furious at her ingratitude, and threatened to sell her to another pimp. As awful as Mao behaved, the prospect of being re-sold terrified her — it would mean beginning freshly in debt again to another master, and that much further away from freedom.

She made her first escape attempt on January 8, 2002, but was dragged back to Mao's apartment. After his guards persuaded him not to break her legs, he decided instead to stab her deeply several times in each calf. Though the wounds were festering the following day, Mao still set her to work in the alley.

She appealed quietly to clients for help, and even managed to write out a message on a piece of paper that read: "I've been forced into prostitution, please help me or inform the police." Finally, one young man listened to her story, and devised an escape plan. On February 10, he came looking for her as a customer, and whisked her off to safety on his motorbike.

However, the nightmare of Ran's experience did not end there. Only a few days before she met Zhao, she had gone for a check-up at a local hospital, where doctors diagnosed her with cervical cancer and extra-uterine pregnancy. Like Ah Wen, Ran had come forward because she was angry and wanted to see justice done.

Zhao advised Ran to inform the police. Fearing the consequences, she opposed the idea. She simply wanted to show the reporter where Grandfather Mao was hiding out; then he could proceed from there. But Zhao knew Grandfather Mao provided a key link in the criminal case against Luo Jianwen and the drug rehabilitation center. Against Ran's wishes, he called police over to the newsroom, and she eventually agreed to cooperate.

Key Evidence Disappears

After the police raids on Kangle Village and the rehabilitation center, *Yangcheng Evening News* complied with a police request to hand over the materials that Zhao and the photographers had gathered undercover. These included digital recordings and photographs directly implicating the center's director, Luo Jianwen.

In the weeks that followed, Zhao continued to keep in touch with his police contacts, wanting to know when the case was likely to go to trial. They repeatedly pushed him away. The case was moving forward, they would say, but they were not at liberty to discuss the details. Clearly, Zhao was no longer in the loop.

Zhao never completely set the story aside though. More than a month after his initial report, he received an unannounced visit from a person who claimed to be an employee at the mental hospital adjacent to the drug rehabilitation center, the same hospital where Luo Jianwen served as director of general affairs. The source told Zhao that Luo had been released on bail and already returned to work in the hospital. In fact, the board had recently appointed him as director of a new psychiatric ward planned on the site of the former rehabilitation center.

Zhao went back to his police contacts with this information, but once again they rebuffed him. As 2002 came to a close, there was still no news of a criminal trial.

In March 2003, a full year after the police raid on the center, a news report appeared suddenly in *New Express*, a sister newspaper of *Yangcheng Evening News*, about a trial of the former employees of the rehabilitation center. According to the story, the local court had already rendered a verdict in the case against Chen Taizhong and Shao Liai (Ah Ding), former supervisors at the facility. The Guangzhou Intermediate People's Court held the trial proceedings on February 12, 2003, without giving prior notice to the news media.

According to the *New Express* story, the court found the defendants guilty of "disregarding national laws and engaging in the sale of people into prostitution." Chinese law stipulated that inmates undergoing compulsory drug treatment could be released from facilities only into the care of family members who could show proper documentation. Lawyers for Chen and Shao had tried to argue that the defendants simply acted on orders from their superiors, and that it would have been impossible for them to release inmates without their knowledge and authorization.

The *New Express* story went on to say court documents had revealed pressure within the rehabilitation center for employees to generate new sources of revenue, which it cited as one explanation for the conspiracy to sell inmates. According to Chen Taizhong's testimony, only about half the patient population could afford treatment expenses of more than 3,000 yuan, while the standard charges for a six-month term came to 11,000 yuan ($1,589 US). "Our bosses pressured us at progress meetings, and said everyone would go hungry if things went on this way,"

Chen had testified. Shao Liai told the court that their superiors had urged them to increase profitability by any means necessary. According to her estimates, they had sold about 200 women between May 2000 and March 2002.

The *New Express* story made no link whatsoever between the criminal behavior of the supervisors and Luo Jianwen or other members of hospital management. Nor did it mention Zhao Shilong's undercover investigation the year before. However, the *New Express* reporter had evidently sought Luo Jianwen's response. He was quoted saying: "The Public Security Bureau ordered the rehab center's closure as part of a new nationwide policy, so that is why we closed down last year."

Why had the courts not probed any further into Luo's involvement? To clear things up, Zhao sought out the *New Express* reporter, Yu Renfei, who referred him to Wang Yunsong, one of the lawyers on the case. Wang permitted Zhao to have a look through the four-inch-thick case dossier. At no point did it mention his undercover assignment or that *Yangcheng Evening News* had contacted and assisted the police. Clearly, the more important case against hospital management had been compromised for political reasons. But where had things gone off track? Had the prosecutor's office suppressed the evidence relating to Luo Jianwen, or had the police failed to turn it over in the first place?

The injustice of the court verdict made Zhao even more determined to return to the story. He began with the source from the hospital who had volunteered information. Through this source, he managed to reach other hospital employees. This time, though, he and Deng Bo, his original photographer on the case, faced staunch resistance from the newspaper's editors, who discouraged them from pursuing the story any further.

Ah Wen Resurfaces

As disappointing as it was, the *New Express* report did draw more attention to the rehabilitation center case. A few national newspapers, including *China Youth Daily*, ran their own versions of the story. But, somewhat ironically, a ban from the Central Propaganda Department issued against an unrelated news story brought Ah Wen's story into living rooms across throughout the nation.

In June 2003, news media from across China converged on Guangzhou to cover what had easily become the year's biggest news event outside of the SARS epidemic. It was the announcement of a verdict in the trial of thirteen Guangzhou police officers in the beating death of Sun Zhigang, a twenty-seven-year-old college graduate from Hubei Province working as a graphic artist. The Sun Zhigang case, which highlighted the widespread abuse rural migrants suffered under China's laws on detention and repatriation, had already developed into a sensitive political issue for the central party leadership. In order to avoid a media feeding frenzy on the Sun Zhigang story, China's Central Propaganda Department issued an order banning independent coverage. Scores of media ready with their own reporters and crews on the ground in Guangzhou lost their story — they could only sit on their hands, and wait for pre-approved releases from the official Xinhua News Agency.

China Central Television's (CCTV) *News Probe*, an investigative news program modeled after the CBS program *60 Minutes*, had previously arrived on the scene in Guangzhou. Its producers had already prepared for the possibility of a national ban by compiling a list of alternate stories in Guangzhou. No sooner had the ban taken effect than they telephoned Zhao, wondering if he was interested in re-doing his story on the Changzhou rehabilitation center, this time with his own camera crew and celebrity *News Probe* reporter Chai Jing.

Reporting the story again would not be easy. He had already handed over to the police every shred of evidence gathered in his undercover investigation. Given the pressure that local police already faced in the Sun Zhigang case, it would be unrealistic to hope for their cooperation. The first step involved tracking down Ah Wen, Little Ran, and the other sources so crucial the year before. But these women, who led unstable lives, proved nearly impossible to locate. The last time Zhao had heard from Ah Wen was a phone call to the newsroom three months earlier. She said she was staying somewhere in Guangzhou's Chigang District.

Zhao and the CCTV crew tried asking around Chigang, but no one could help. Using police records, they managed to obtain the address of Ah Wen's sister and brother-in-law who had not seen her in person for nearly two years. They last heard from her in April 2002 when Ah Wen called asking for help with bail after her arrest for petty theft, probably shortly after the police raid on the rehabilitation center. Ah Wen's sister refused to help — she had had enough of her sister's troubles.

Clearly, Ah Wen's sister knew nothing of the scandal at the drug rehabilitation center, or of Ah Wen's role in the police investigation. When Zhao Shilong shared the complete story of what she had endured, they were heartbroken and promised to do everything they could to find her. Finally, on June 15, they managed to make contact through one of Ah Wen's old friends. They arranged to meet her in the lobby of the Guangzhou Holiday Inn at eleven p.m.

It was closer to midnight when Ah Wen finally came through the carousel doors. She chided Zhao: "I never imagined you'd be so pigheaded. Spending all this time on one story."

The news of Luo Jianwen's release on bail struck her hard. "That's impossible! Luo negotiated the price for Fan and Dong himself. We even got it on tape!"

News Probe interviewed Ah Wen, who told them about her experiences at the rehabilitation center and her cooperation in the police investigation. At one point, Zhao noticed fresh needle scars tracing up her arms, but she shrugged off CCTV's question about whether she was still using drugs.

An Insider Tells His Story

Zhao's contacts at the mental hospital on Changzhou Island eventually put him in touch with a source who had once worked inside the drug rehabilitation center. He agreed to speak to CCTV only on condition of anonymity. Zhao later refers to him as Mr. X.

Mr. X told CCTV that those involved in the conspiracy at the rehabilitation center, including Luo Jianwen, had earned roughly twenty million yuan ($2.9 million US) through the sale of patients since 1992. He confirmed with several other hospital employees that guards and supervisors at the center had killed at least ten inmates, and that the patients there suffered incalculable physical and psychological damage. "It's impossible to put any kind of figure on the suffering that occurred there. Really, what is the Sun Zhigang case compared to something like this?" he said.

The sale of female inmates was a secret widely known in the hospital, Mr. X said. "I saw it with my own eyes. Some days they sold as many as thirty women," he said. He also directly implicated Zhang Yiping, the director of the mental hospital, and Liu Guohua, the associate director, saying they would often stand with Luo Jianwen, watching as the sales transpired.

The center generally bought the patients, most of whom came from places outside Guangzhou, from police and drug enforcement authorities for 800 to 1,000 yuan each. It in turn would recoup this cost by extorting "treatment" costs and other fees from the families of patients.

In October 2001, guards at the center beat a patient to death after she failed to pay her treatment fees. As soon as doctors at the hospital found out what had happened, they reported the incident to the police. The patient's family members complained loudly and protested forcefully, but the case never went to trial.

Mr. X said hospital staff members were often complicit in the cover up of unusual deaths at the rehabilitation center. Hospital administrators forced them to falsify patient records and send the body off for cremation before autopsies could be performed. After a number of such "accidents," Luo Jianwen urged his ward supervisors to exercise more caution, Mr. X said, adding that Luo would instruct: "Don't beat them quite so severely next time. We don't want any blood on our hands."

The police apparently never took criminal activity at the center seriously. The callousness of the police infuriated one of Zhao's hospital sources. They would unquestionably accept "drug overdose" as an explanation for suspicious deaths: "Overdose?" the source exclaimed. "Why didn't the police look into this further? How did drugs make their way into a drug rehab center to begin with?"

Several sources confirmed that drug use occurred commonly in the facility, smuggled in with the help of gift-wrapped flower baskets and payoffs to guards, who would then turn a blind eye. Standard bribes of between 12,000 and 14,000 yuan ($1,450 to $1,700 US) could buy a patient's early release, the legally mandated treatment term of six months notwithstanding. The center held those patients who could not afford such sums for up to ten months.

Hospital directors, including Zhang Yiping and Liu Guohua, made a point of staffing the rehabilitation center with temporary workers, usually migrants from outside the province. These employees would be far less likely to blow the whistle on illegal activity since they had much weaker social contacts in the city.

At mid-morning on June 13, Zhao Shilong arrived unannounced at the mental hospital with celebrity reporter Chai Jing and the rest of the *News Probe* crew. They marched directly into one of the conference rooms, finding Luo Jianwen seated along with an investigator from the Huangpu District Procurator's Office.

Luo apparently did not recognize Zhao. When Chai Jing asked him to comment on the rehabilitation center scandal, he dismissed the whole thing by listing his party credentials. "I'm an upstanding official now doing private sector work," he said. "I've trained with the Chinese Communist Party for many years. How could I possibly have committed such crimes?"

As for the actions of Chen Taizhong and Shao Liai, Luo denied all responsibility, saying he had had no knowledge of their criminal activities. "On March 19 last year, the police brought me in for questioning and held me for two weeks before I was released on bail. The police themselves determined that I was not responsible. Since then, I've not heard anything about the case."

The director spoke repeatedly of his unimpeachable character as a member of the Communist Party. "I've never so much as accepted a single cigarette at the expense of our patients or their family members. I've never had so much as a single cup of tea at their expense," he said.

Evidently, he was not an easy man to provoke. He turned calmly and collectedly to the question of the *Yangcheng Evening News* undercover investigation, which he characterized as a vendetta by disgruntled patients. "The entire thing was orchestrated by three former patients of ours," he said, referring apparently to Ah Wen, Fan X Wen, and Dong X Ling. "The hospital directors determined that the best policy was simply to release them from the facility."

Chai Jing pressed on with her questions. "I understand a reporter from *Yangcheng Evening News* was involved, that you personally sold inmates to the reporter, and that the entire process was recorded on video. How do you respond to that?"

Luo Jianwen kept his poker face. "I've never seen such a person. Nor have I ever had dealings of any sort with such a person."

"Well," said Chai Jing, turning to Zhao, "do you recognize this man? This is Zhao Shilong, the *Yangcheng Evening News* reporter in question."

Luo's head swiveled toward Zhao, and the color drained from his face. But he continued to dissemble. "I've never seen this man before," he said.

Zhao Shilong totally lost his cool. "You're lying! Last year, I took police on a raid of your drug rehab center. I recorded the entire process. Does that jog your memory?"

"I've never seen you before."

Zhang Yiping, the hospital's director, told *News Probe* that hospital administrators could not possibly know who actually picked up patients once they had signed off on their release forms. He also denied that he and others had pressured employees to generate new revenue sources.

After interviewing Luo Jianwen and Zhang Yiping, the television crew secretly filmed the former site of the rehabilitation center. They also went undercover in Kangle Village, where the sex trade stayed as lively as it had ever been before the police raid a year earlier.

"Ah Wen's Nightmare" Goes National

The *News Probe* segment on the rehabilitation center scandal, "Ah Wen's Nightmare," aired on July 14, 2003. The program created an instant national sensation, prompting a show of action from Guangdong's top party leader, Zhang Dejiang, who promised a thorough inquiry. Both the Guangdong provincial government and the Drug Prevention Office, the national drug enforcement arm of the Public Security Bureau, requested copies of the program from CCTV.

According to *News Probe* reporter Chai Jing and producer Xiang Xianzhong, the head of the CCTV network pressed them about the *News Probe* segment even in the final minutes leading up to the broadcast. Mindful of the same political dangers that had concerned editors at *Yangcheng Evening News*, CCTV bosses had carefully scrutinized the tapes. "Are you sure there is no connection between the rehab center and the police?" the head of CCTV wanted to know. Since the Sun Zhigang case, these relationships had become an area of great political sensitivity. They assured him that no direct connection existed, and finally he gave his approval.

The day after *News Probe* aired the segment, one of the directors at the Changzhou mental hospital, Zhang Yiping, ran away with his family. According to Guangzhou police, he had first emptied the hospital vault of tens of thousands of yuan in cash.

Despite the great show of interest Guangdong's top leadership demonstrated in the scandal, it took prosecutors in Guangzhou's Huangpu District two months before they finally issued arrest warrants for Zhang Yiping and Luo Jianwen. By that time, local police suspected that Zhang had already fled overseas.

Now that the full story had reached a national audience, re-visiting it involved less risk for *Yangcheng Evening News*. Editors grudgingly gave Zhao Shilong permission to write a story explaining the reasons why the original criminal cases against the hospital administrators had never been pursued. Zhao wanted to know why the undercover investigation had never made it into the court's dossier; why police had simply released Luo Jianwen; and finally, why Zhang Yiping had been allowed to escape while the police and prosecutors sat on their hands.

On September 26, Yuan Mingfeng, an official representative from the city procurator's office, visited Zhao Shilong at the newspaper to answer a formal complaint he had made with the office. Yuan asked Zhao about his original undercover investigation, and then explained how his office had handled the cases against Zhang Yiping and Luo Jianwen. They had not issued arrest warrants for the suspects before September 16, he said, because they had been unable to secure key evidence, including hospital records. The materials from Zhao's investigation would certainly have been helpful, said the prosecutor, but the police had never given them to his office.

Zhao Shilong and Deng Bo paid a visit to the police officer who had led the squad during the raid on the rehabilitation center. When they asked the whereabouts of the photographs and video they had taken undercover, the officer said he had no idea — it had been more than a year since the raid, after all.

"Did you include the tapes and photographs in the police report you sent to prosecutors?" Zhao asked.

"We included everything," the officer answered.

Zhao went back once more to the Huangpu District Procurator's Office. "When your office received the police report, were the tapes and photographs from our investigation included?" he asked prosecutor Yuan Mingfeng. "No, there were definitely no attachments to the report," Yuan said.

In news reports appearing in *Yangcheng Evening News* on September 27 and 30, Zhao detailed his discussions with police and prosecutors. Yuan Mingfeng reached him at the newsroom a few days later, clearly furious, due to the pressure that grew out of the reports, which reflected badly on the procurator's office.

Zhao had been receiving threats from anonymous callers since shortly after Luo Jianwen's arrest on September 16. In several instances, the callers identified themselves as lawyers wanting to arrange meetings with him, but insisting on meeting outside the courthouse. "Didn't you consider the consequences of your actions? Didn't you give any thought to your safety?" said one caller. Other callers were less subtle in their threats. While Zhao was away from the office one afternoon, a colleague reached him on his mobile telephone to inform him that a group of thugs had entered the newsroom, saying they had "business to settle with Zhao Shilong." The men caused quite a commotion before finally agreeing to leave. Since the former hospital director, Zhang Yiping, remained at large, Zhao feared constantly for his safety.

At the urging of producers at *News Probe*, Zhao posted a message on "Journalist's Home," an online bulletin board site (BBS) used widely by professional journalists. It read: "Fellow journalists take note. If anything unexpected happens to our colleague, Zhao Shilong, at the hands of those implicated in the Changzhou rehab center scandal, let us unite our strength and use whatever means possible to bring them to justice." He hoped that the looming threat of a media reprisal might stay the hand of those who wished to harm him.

Zhao also found himself increasingly at odds with the culture of *Yangcheng Evening News*. His decision to circumvent newspaper editors and cooperate with CCTV had angered the editorial board. That September, as Zhao faced pressure from all directions, the newspaper issued an internal memo, instructing all editors and reporters to seek permission from management before cooperating with other media. This was the final straw in the rapidly souring relationship between Zhao and his editors. He submitted his resignation that September and accepted a position with the news outlet that had resurrected his report, joining CCTV in Beijing.

The following November, Zhao's work on the rehabilitation center story earned him a national journalism award. It gratifyingly resulted in the publication on CCTV's international news site of his original, unexpurgated report.

Luo Jianwen Sues for Libel

In October 2003, as Zhao Shilong settled into his position at CCTV, he learned that Luo Jianwen had filed separate libel suits with courts in two Guangzhou districts, one against *Yangcheng Evening News* and the other directly against Zhao.

Luo's lawyers argued in the first case that no evidence existed to support the reporter's accusations, and that he had "defamed Luo Jianwen's character and made a mockery of justice." According to Luo's version of events, former patients of the rehabilitation center had entered into a conspiracy with the journalist to smear his reputation by falsifying documents and manufacturing photographs and video. Proceedings were held just once that October, with no concrete results. After that, the case seemed to simply evaporate.

Luo filed the case against *Yangcheng Evening News* in Tianhe, his district of residence. His lawyers argued that the newspaper had inflicted "acute emotional distress" on their client by reporting publicly on his September arrest. They demanded before the court that the newspaper cease its "attacks" on Luo and issue a public apology. The case dragged on for more than a year until the court finally ruled on December 21, 2004, that the *Yangcheng Evening News* report in question did not contain falsehoods.

In the same month that Luo filed his pair of lawsuits, Chen Taizhong and Grandfather Mao were sentenced to lifetime prison terms, with fines of 60,000 yuan ($8,600 US) and 40,000 yuan ($5,700 US), respectively; Shao Liai, ten years, with a fine of 30,000 yuan ($4,300 US); and Gu Anle, another pimp from Kangle Village, five years with the same fine.

News of the rehabilitation center case died down in 2004. The first new development only came on June 2 as the former vice-director of the mental hospital, Liu Guohua, was finally indicted and charged with "organizing and coercing acts of prostitution." He was eventually found guilty.

A few days after Liu Guohua's indictment, the Huangpu District Court finally rendered a verdict in the case against Luo Jianwen. On June 8, 2004, it ruled Luo guilty of abusing his position as an official and member of the Communist Party, and of failing to follow proper protocol in the release of drug rehabilitation patients. It made no mention whatsoever of the sale of patients into the sex trade. Luo was sentenced to two years in prison, commencing from the date of his arrest.

On November 14, 2004, only six months after Luo's sentencing, the instigator of Ah Wen's nightmare was set free.

Postscript

Western journalists generally try to avoid even the appearance of cooperation with the police when investigating criminal cases. But in China, the media's subordination to the party and the government complicates the question of collaboration with law enforcement agencies. In the Chinese system, journalists have deeply ambiguous roles. On one hand, they aspire to impartiality and independence. On the other hand, the party leadership expects them to act as obedient tools. At times, the media's official position as gatherers of information for the ruling elite is more visible, as epitomized by the notorious "internal reference" materials, or *neibu cankao*, explicitly compiled by many publications for official eyes only. At other times, the media test the limits of official control, or "guidance of public opinion," for professional and/or commercial reasons. Whatever the case, Chinese media often find it difficult to balance the goal of professional journalism with the controls and priorities of the party and government.

In this regard, Chinese media use one of the most opaque terms in their lexicon — "supervision by public opinion," or *yulun jiandu*. The term, which also translates into "media supervision" or (more equivocally) "watchdog journalism," appeared in official party documents starting in the late 1980s. In its official guise, it refers to the media acting as one among several recognized forms of supervision, a complement to party and government corruption inspectors, and the procurator's office. It might, for example, manifest itself as the powerful hand of CCTV investigating corruption in a local county government far from Beijing.

From another perspective, "supervision by public opinion" nearly equals the Western notion of "watchdog journalism," which implies monitoring by a media independent of government manipulation or control — a "fourth estate." In a Chinese context, the more independent-minded media aspire professionally to practice this sort of "watchdog journalism" against the backdrop of an institution still very much controlled by the party.

With an official mandate for "supervision by public opinion," it appears that the ambiguity of the journalist's role has been hardwired into the profession. It can sometimes be difficult to differentiate the work of reporters from that of public investigators or government regulators, while, at the same time, the press has in many ways come to be viewed as a cost-effective complement to them. Indeed, numerous government documents issued by various offices to address diverse policy objectives have mentioned the need to "strengthen supervision by public opinion" to advance these goals.

In August 2005, Zhejiang's provincial-level prosecutor's office actually moved to formalize cooperation between the media and law enforcement by promulgating regulations encouraging journalists to share news sources in criminal cases for rewards of up to 20,000 yuan. The following passage from a *Legal Daily* editorial of August 30, 2005, one of only a few responses to the Zhejiang measures, praised the idea of creating synergy between the press and police:

> Legal supervision and press supervision ("supervision by public opinion") traditionally have two ways of working in concert. In the first case, law enforcement pays close attention to media reports, which is one important way of gathering sources ... In the second case, news media ride along with police, reporting the specifics of their investigations to the outside world. These two forms work separately, with no interaction between them, so the pool of sources available to law enforcement is limited . . . A system of linkage between media and law enforcement readily solves this problem.

The editorial argued that legal supervision and press supervision share a common objective — "safeguarding social equality and justice" — even when their methods and perspectives differ.

This line of argument has, however, met with some public disapproval from the independent strand mentioned above. In an April 2003 interview, media scholar Chen Lidan criticized media cooperation with the police. "Journalists are not spies," he said.[1] "The basic responsibility of the journalist is to report facts as they occur openly. But now journalism [in China] in many ways resembles the investigative work of law enforcement, and this changes journalism's role in society."

Chen specifically objected to what he perceived as the overuse of surreptitious reporting in China, particularly by such investigative news programs as CCTV's *Focus* and *News Probe* (the program which also played a role in Zhao Shilong's story). Chen even suggested that China has now fallen victim to its own brand of "yellow journalism":

> The vivid accounts offered by some of our own journalists through surreptitious reporting might all find close corollaries in the yellow journalism of 19th century America. Is it not sad that we should revisit the shameful history of our industry peers of 100 years ago?
>
> Obviously, any discussion of the rights and wrongs of surreptitious reporting in China must take into account the extremes of China's reporting environment, and the constraints placed on journalists and media by constant meddling of the party bureaucracy. As this book should make clear, there is a growing professional community of journalists working in China despite the party's persisting media controls. But attempts to reinforce professional norms — as opposed to party norms — across the industry are limited by party control itself.

The All-China Journalists Association (ACJA), the party-approved association for journalists nominally responsible for "raising professional standards in the industry, improving the excellence of media products, and promoting media reform," issued its first ethical guidelines in January 1991, amended in 1994, and again in 1997. However, it does little to clarify the professional, as opposed to propaganda, role of journalists in China. Here is the preamble:

> Chinese journalism is an important and integral part of the cause of socialism under the leadership of the Chinese Communist Party. News workers must work hard to study and disseminate Marxism-Leninism, Mao Zedong Thought and Deng Xiaoping Theory, firmly carrying out the basic course and guidelines of the party and government, serving as staunch soldiers of scientific thinking, being leaders of correct public opinion, being noble shapers of [the public] spirit, being rousers of excellent works, firmly grasping correct guidance of public opinion, serving the people, serving Socialism, serving the overall work of the party and the country, promoting the building of the material civilization of Socialism and the building of a Socialist cultural spirit, thereby fighting toward our grand goal of a modern Socialist state.[2]

Later portions of the ACJA document speak of the need for "truthfulness of the news," and condemn the acceptance of gifts or money — a practice still rife in the Chinese media. It also called for separation of editorial and advertising. Nonetheless, ideological appeals weigh down the document, making it patently clear that the party ultimately adjudicates all press decisions, further reinforcing a relationship that has formed a key element of journalistic work in China since the Communist revolution.

Notes

1. Chen Lidan and Xu Xun. 2003. "*Guanyu jizhe anfang he toupai wenti fantan*" (A discussion about the problems of surreptitious reporting and filming). *Broadcast Studies Forum* (Chuanboxue), June. Available at http://www.people.com.cn/GB/14677/21963/22065/1933565.html.
2. *China Journalist*. 1991. "All-China Journalists Association ethical guidelines for Chinese news workers. May." Available at http://www.cnki.com.cn/Article/CJFDTotal-ZGJZ199105001.htm.

5 *The Journalist as Crusader*
The Beijing Taxi Corruption Case

On June 28, 2002, the staff of the weekly supplement of the *China Economic Times*, one of China's leading business dailies, held their Friday editorial meeting. Wang Nan, the section's editor, passed a pile of research materials over to veteran investigative reporter, Wang Keqin. They included a document from the newspaper's parent organization, the Development Research Center (DRC), a policy think-tank of China's State Council. Wang Keqin could have no idea at the time that this would mark the start of six long months of investigation, writing, and editorial wrangling.

Guo Lihong, who managed the center's economics division, had sent over the DRC document, "An investigation and petition on the plight of Beijing taxi drivers." It included statements from a few local taxi drivers. Although it was not at all uncommon for the *China Economic Times*'s reporters to cite officials from the DRC in their stories, the DRC did not generally send reports directly to the newsroom. Wang Nan suggested that Wang Keqin should explore a possible news feature about the economic difficulties that taxi drivers faced in Beijing. Wang Keqin recalled that the idea surprised him — he had always assumed taxi drivers earned a decent living in the capital.

Using the DRC report as his starting point, Wang gathered background information on the taxi industry. He quickly discovered that taxi companies, which controlled more than 98 percent of the roughly 67,000 taxis on Beijing's roads, charged drivers a whole range of ad hoc fees. One, the so-called "vehicle portion," generally entailed a driver paying several thousand yuan per month for the privilege of operating a taxi under license by the company. In almost all cases, a taxi license meant you had to use one of a number of taxi operators.

In addition to vehicle portions, companies pressured many drivers into paying "risk deposits" often as high as 100,000 yuan ($14,400 US). By paying 50,000 to 100,000 yuan when they signed their employment contracts with the taxi companies, the drivers effectively advanced the money for their vehicles without retaining any right of ownership. Clear injustices in the process allowed only those companies to which the city's Transportation Bureau granted licenses to purchase and operate taxis.

Taxi drivers had been protesting their concerns about these problems for years. In 1995, one driver tried to defend his right to own a taxi before a Beijing court. When the court refused to try the case, thousands of drivers protested at the Beijing West Railway Station, bringing traffic to a standstill for several hours. Drivers staged similar strikes in the summers of 1996 and 2000, stalling their cars outside Beijing's Capital International Airport.

These incidents brought the industry's problems to the attention of Chinese leaders, who failed to take decisive action. Wang found a 2001 article from *China Market* magazine quoting then Premier Zhu Rongji's criticism of the taxi industry nationwide before a meeting of party leaders. According to a researcher cited in the *China Market* report, Zhu Rongji had compared the tactics of taxi companies to those of the Green Gang, a Mafia-style crime group that operated in pre-Communist Shanghai. According to the article, the premier had even sent his wife on an undercover fact-finding mission in which she rode taxis and spoke at length with drivers about their plight.

By the time Wang Keqin began working on the taxi story, it was approaching two years since Zhu Rongji's criticism of taxi companies, and apparently no action had been taken. Wang Keqin learned that several newspapers had tried to assemble reports on the problem only to drop them after receiving threats from gangs that they suspected taxi companies had hired. Wang later said the media's inaction on the story angered him. "If journalists don't have a conscience, if they aren't driven by a sense of humanity, they are totally worthless," he said.[1]

Wang Keqin began to cultivate sources among Beijing taxi drivers, a much harder process than he had expected. He started with Shao Changliang, one of the few drivers listed in the DRC report, who was able to put him in touch with other drivers. But many hesitated to share their experiences. "I don't care if you're President Jiang Zemin," said one driver at a diner popular with local cabbies. "What good can possibly come from the work of one journalist? Why waste an interview?"

Wang persisted, conducting one-on-one and group interviews, paying visits to drivers' homes and their favorite hangouts. Over the course of a three-month investigation, he interviewed more than one hundred drivers. In many cases, he convinced them to sign and fingerprint their statements to make them, if necessary, admissible in court. He carried an inkpad everywhere he went. A strong believer in what he called "comprehensive, impartial, and accurate reporting," Wang sought to gather as many types of evidence as he could for his story — eyewitness accounts, expert interviews, written statements, and documentary evidence. Whenever possible, he made sure he had original documents. He also searched for multiple versions of similar documents, such as those for taxi registration, so he could compare them for accuracy and consistency.

Every driver willing to talk had a story about what his company had put him through. Deng Shaolong, a driver for Beijing Yinjian Taxi Company, told Wang Keqin that he had been hospitalized the year before for treatment of a severe perianal abscess (a work-related condition resulting from sitting for long periods in a vehicle). Although the operation took him away from work for four months, the taxi company continued to charge him the monthly vehicle portion of 5,100 yuan ($740 US). Only two hours after he had left the operating table, the company already sent someone to his bedside to collect the money.

Drivers for Beijing Wanquansi Taxi Company, one of the city's largest, provided Wang Keqin with various receipts for all the different types of penalties for which the company had charged them. They were deducted, they said, from the hefty "risk deposits" — usually between 30,000 to 80,000 yuan, but sometimes as high as 100,000 — that the drivers had to pay as a condition for their employment contracts. "The assets of the Beijing Wanquansi Taxi Company were built on fines!" many of the drivers told Wang Keqin. Every company, they said, had its own set of impossibly strict in-house rules designed with the express purpose of levying fines.

The working conditions that the drivers faced shocked and surprised Wang Keqin. Everyone seemed to know by name drivers who had died of fatigue at the wheel. On a blistering hot night in August, he visited the ninety-square-foot apartment of driver Feng Jiyou. Six family members, spanning three generations, huddled together there. Despite his early setbacks, over time, Wang eventually succeeded in building a strong rapport with his taxi driver sources. All eventually allowed him to use their real names in his story, which Wang convinced them was the best way to prove the reliability of their statements.

Wang Keqin later said self-deprecatingly that he had gone out of his way to cut an absurd figure — a small-time reporter, leading a ragged life, fighting for the equitable treatment of taxi drivers who earned about double his own salary. When assigned to the taxi story, Wang Keqin took home a monthly salary of 1,200 yuan ($173 US), just enough to cover the barest necessities in a city where a small apartment then cost about 1,500 yuan a month. Wang could ordinarily expect to supplement his salary with income from published articles — 60 yuan each. However, accepting an investigative assignment that consumed all his time meant he would have to do without.

Dealing with the Government

While Wang Keqin continued to talk to taxi drivers, he tried to secure interviews with government officials to get their side of the story, and to explain the industry's complete disarray. His investigation centered on the city's transportation bureau as the government office most directly involved. But it in fact touched on more than thirty agencies, giving Wang Keqin much ground to cover. Simply getting in the door proved a major problem.

In recent years, though a number of local governments in China have issued ordinances that call for information disclosure, beginning with Guangzhou in 2003, as a result of the government's cover up of the Severe Acute Respiratory

Syndrome, officials still maintain a monopoly on information — they decide what to release, when, and how. While these ordinances and proposed national legislation on disclosure seek to make transparency the practice and secrecy the exception, the reverse continues to predominate. No laws or regulations grant the media access to official records, and government offices can refuse requests out of hand.

All government organizations in China have publicity offices set up to disseminate information as needed and to facilitate other contacts. They cultivate close relationships with beat reporters, who in many cases, media insiders say, will not expose sensitive issues. Government offices look upon outside reporters as dangerous meddlers. If they are working away from their usual beats, or are not closely affiliated with an office, it suggests to officials that the reporters are practicing watchdog journalism, or what is called in Chinese "supervision by public opinion."

Wang Keqin called dozens of officials during his first few weeks on the taxi story. Only three agreed to meet with him, all arranged with the help of one of Wang Keqin's acquaintances, a seasoned reporter on the labor beat with good contacts in the city labor bureau.

Wang first attempted to reach officials at the transportation bureau only a few days after he started the story. Zhang Lei, an officer in the bureau's publicity office, asked the *China Economic Times* to fax over an official interview request. Thus began several weeks of back-and-forth and foot-dragging. "Our district chief is away from his desk right now," publicity officers would say, or, "Our district chief is in a meeting right now." It would follow with: "We have already forwarded your information to the Taxi Management Office and are still waiting for a response."

Before Wang's reporter friend stepped in, the city's labor bureau asked the *China Economic Times* to send over Wang Keqin's press pass, work visa, and a letter of introduction. Wang's editor faxed over the official letter, and said the press pass and work visa were on their way. No sooner had the bureau received the fax than it modified the procedure. "We will also require an official letter from your personnel department concerning the press pass," the bureau said. The newspaper's personnel office sent the letter over, as requested. The bureau then told them to wait while it consulted superiors there.

Wang Keqin had more success talking to insurance firms, which viewed taxi companies as a constant headache. They told him about repeated contract violations and illegal insurance scams by taxi companies. Two insurance firms had analysts for the passenger transport industry who briefed Wang on issues including fake insurance policies and illegal taxi permits. According to one analyst, the city's taxi industry represented a potential legitimate insurance market of over 300 million yuan ($43 million US) a year. Since current policies with licensed insurance firms totaled only one-tenth that amount, it suggested widespread abuse of regulations mandating insurance for all taxis.

But Wang Keqin had no success with city officials. Finally, he decided to circumvent the publicity office. He only managed to get the head of the transportation bureau's regulatory office to return his call. While they had a brief, unhelpful discussion, Wang Keqin tried to get a face-to-face interview after this short exchange. He showed up at the office unannounced on July 31. The secretary said her boss was out for the day, but Wang did speak briefly with another employee, who offered a few details about taxi-related regulations. Wang slipped into the publicity office on his way out, where, at last, he came face-to-face with Zhang Lei, who had stonewalled him for weeks. "I suggest you leave now and try reaching us about this later," Zhang said ominously. "We'll check and see if Mr. Liang, head of our taxi management office, will agree to meet with you." Since he saw no point in pressing the matter any further with Zhang Lei, Wang left through the main entrance as Zhang watched him go. Once outside, the reporter walked a few times around in the courtyard before darting back in and heading straight for the taxi management office.

"I'm here to see Director Liang," he said as soon as he was through the door.

"What for?"

"An interview."

"That is not possible, I'm afraid. The publicity office handles news media. We do not deal directly."

Wang Keqin could only return to his old tactic of pestering Zhang Lei.

Eventually, he located the direct line for Liang Jianwei, the head of the taxi management office. "The publicity office handles the press. I don't directly accept interviews," Liang said.

As it happened, Liang operated his own taxi company, and had been mentioned in the *China Market* article Wang Keqin had stumbled across early on in his research, the very same one that quoted Zhu Rongji's remarks on the industry.

On August 26, nearly two months into his investigation, Wang Keqin received a call from one of the taxi drivers with whom he had become close. "Didn't you say you're finding it hard to reach officials from the transportation bureau? Well, a bunch of us are going there tomorrow to meet with the director, Zhang Yansheng. Why don't you come along?"

This offered Wang Keqin his best opportunity so far. The group arrived at the bureau at nine the next morning and waited outside Zhang Yansheng's office. The staff there repeatedly told them to leave, but they refused to until they had seen the director. Two uniformed security guards paced back and forth in the hallway, keeping a close eye on them.

At about half past nine, Director Zhang emerged from a nearby office and told the drivers to wait in an empty conference room. When he returned a few minutes later, he spotted Wang Keqin immediately. "Today I'm meeting with drivers only. Are you a driver?" he asked sternly.

"I'm a friend of theirs," Wang said.

"Get out. If you're not a driver, get the hell out," Zhang growled.

When Wang refused to move, a pair of heavy-set staffers hoisted him by the arms and dragged him forcibly into the hall. They dropped him in a waiting area in an adjacent building and asked him to wait. About thirty minutes later, two white-haired cadres came in to speak with him. Government offices often retained retired officials as informal negotiators, with a softer, more sympathetic approach to problem cases. They told Wang Keqin calmly that a meeting with Director Zhang would be impossible.

Looking back at what happened in the conference room, Wang Keqin said later that he should have made a greater effort to blend in with the drivers. He could only guess that he had looked too bookish or out of place, and that staffers had alerted Director Zhang that he might be a journalist.

Dealing with the Taxi Companies

Wang found obtaining information from taxi companies at least as tough as reaching government offices. He telephoned more than twenty local taxi companies, but none of the larger ones would agree to meet with him. He tried walking directly into Wanquansi Taxi, one of Beijing's better known companies, but two guards prevented him from entering. When he pressed for a meeting with the boss, office staff taunted and threatened him. He insisted on waiting, until a man reeking of alcohol stormed out of the back office and stepped right up to his face: "What newspaper did you say you're from? We don't want an interview! Get the hell out!" The guards took him by the arms, a replay of his treatment at the transportation bureau, and tossed him out on the doorstep.

Wang continued to push, eventually speaking with office managers at a few of the smaller taxi companies. His big break came during a meeting with a low-level transportation official in Pinggu, a district of Beijing. He told Wang Keqin that the city transportation bureau's unwillingness to address the problems taxi drivers faced annoyed him. He became more and more animated as they spoke. Wang saw his opening. But he needed to gain the official's confidence before he could elicit his full cooperation. Wang chose to emphasize the *China Economic Times*'s affiliation with the Development Research Center (DRC), directly under the State Council, as a tactic. He also spoke about his earlier career in Gansu Province, where he had served briefly as a clerical secretary to a provincial official. He said the newspaper and the DRC were conducting an investigation of the taxi industry, and would appreciate any assistance he could offer.

The district official put his staff into action and requested all taxi companies in his district cooperate with Wang Keqin's investigation. A convoy of official sedans whisked Wang off to the first of several interviews. Before long, he sat comfortably in his first company conference room, at a table laid out with fresh fruit and cups of green tea.

The Pinggu official observed the meetings as company representatives explained their methods of operation to Wang Keqin. They visited several companies, where bosses spoke matter-of-factly of how they had used official regulations to start up taxi companies with little or no initial capital — all it required was knowing the bureaucratic ropes. Zhang Huiyu, a standing committee member of the People's Political Consultative Conference, a political advisory body in Pinggu District, told Wang Keqin how he had founded a taxi company with nothing: "Back in 1992 some friends of mine suggested that I could start up a taxi company without spending a cent or incurring any debt. I did all the paperwork in Xisi District in Chengguan. The village government made all the approvals and notified the [Beijing] city transportation bureau. After that, the transportation bureau issued me an instrument of ratification for the passenger transport business. I received licenses for 50 vehicles." As his next step, Zhang put out a call for drivers. Anyone with driving ability, willing to put up 50,000 yuan, could work for his company. Before long, he found twenty-five drivers and collected 1.2 million yuan in "financing funds." He used this money to buy twenty-five passenger minivans. By obtaining one approval and without spending a dime, Zhang Huibao had created a taxi company with a fleet of twenty-five vehicles and assets totaling 1.3 million yuan.

Changes in city regulations worsened the situation for drivers who felt trapped in the trade by the huge "financing funds" and "risk deposits" they had to put down to secure their contracts. When Beijing announced in June 1996 that the taxi business could no longer use minivans, the companies passed the cost of changing their fleets into sedans on to the drivers. Zhang Huiyu accomplished this by "buying" the fleet's twenty-six minivans back from his drivers for between 38,000 and 45,000 yuan each, selling them to companies outside the taxi industry, then applying the funds to the purchase of twenty-six new sedans worth 115,000 yuan each. His former minivan drivers then "purchased" the sedans for 135,000 yuan each. The licenses for these vehicles still belonged to Zhang Huiyu's company, ensuring that the drivers essentially invested in vehicle shares. Meanwhile, Zhang Huiyu increased monthly taxi portions — the right to operate the taxis — up to 1,500 yuan from 800 yuan.

Practices like these commonly occurred across the industry. They forced taxi drivers to work cruelly long hours just to scrape together enough to only get by after paying the various fees levied by the taxi companies. On average, they worked 585 full-time workdays each year, calculated on the basis of China's standard eight-hour workday. Although they worked twelve- to thirteen-hour shifts every day, they earned on average only 1,817 yuan a month, less than half of Beijing's monthly per capita income, as reported by the city government at the time.[2]

Because of regulatory loopholes, taxi companies also evaded paying their taxes. Wang estimated that if taxi companies across China paid taxes to the state of 1,500 yuan per year — less than what most companies charged their drivers for vehicle portions — state tax revenues from the industry would total about 14 billion yuan ($2 billion US). Companies routinely paid kickbacks to the city transportation officials. An accountant from one company said they paid hundreds of thousands of yuan in "gratuities" each year to officials at the transportation bureau. "This is how all the companies do it," he said.

Aside from the misery of taxi drivers and the loss of state revenues, the residents of Beijing lost out too. Wang's investigation found that unwarranted fees, taxi portions in particular, were the primary cause of higher taxi fares; if the government issued licenses directly to drivers for their own vehicles, Wang's research showed, taxi fares would drop by approximately 30 to 40 percent.

Inside the Newspaper

Wang Keqin completed his investigative report in the middle of September. Once he put the draft in the hands of his editors, the fight became one to protect the story against major changes that might lessen its impact. Editors at the *China Economic Times* had to weigh the implications of the article very carefully as it dealt with administrative corruption and mismanagement by the Beijing city government.

They first considered the issue of timing: with the inaugural session of the Sixteenth Party Congress only days away, and the heightened political sensitivities always visible in the run-up to meetings, officials worried that negative press might sabotage their prospects for advancement. News reports even mildly critical of leadership tended to evaporate during such periods.

The widespread anticipation that then President Jiang Zemin would hand the reins over to his successor, Hu Jintao, made this particular political session even more sensitive. Additional speculation also centered on the potential elevation of a high-level Beijing city official to the politburo, the elite group of about twenty-four of China's top leaders. Attacking the Beijing city government at such a time would surely make enemies. The *China Economic Times*'s board of directors — comprising the newspaper's chairman, editor-in-chief, and deputy editor-in-chief — was concerned that publishing Wang's article might put the newspaper's future and their own positions at risk.

At first, the editors suggested that the newspaper should run the report in seven sections over a week, which might soften its political impact without compromising the story itself. Wang Keqin adamantly opposed the idea. He contended that the first section would simply send up a red flag, after which officials would then make sure the other six sections never appeared. While most of the editors agreed with

Wang's argument, running the full report was simply not an option. They decided to wait for the right opportunity.

In the meantime, Wang Keqin's story had to be kept safe. The editors wanted to ensure word did not leak that they were sitting on a report about corruption in the Beijing government. They removed all records of the story from the newspaper's internal computer network, and agreed not to reveal its existence to other staff members.

Knowing that his feature, when published, would require broader support if he hoped to minimize its impact on him and the newspaper, Wang Keqin worked quietly to garner support from prominent newspaper columnists. He persuaded Xu Hui, an expert economist from the Chinese Academy of Social Sciences, to prepare a 4,000-word commentary about regulatory problems in China, using the taxi industry as a specific example. Columnists at the *China Economic Times* prepared a similar analysis. Wang also started gathering together unused material from his interviews with academics and industry experts. The piece, "What the experts say," would eventually accompany his news report.

The newspaper also considered the possibility that officials implicated in Wang's report might bring a libel suit against the paper. They wanted Wang's report as watertight as possible, so in mid-November the editorial board pored over Wang's draft with the help of a lawyer. "I don't see any legal problems here. The evidence is formidable," the lawyer said after comparing the article with Wang's impressive documentation.

The editors left the final changes to Wang Keqin, who delivered a printed, staple-bound copy to the editor-in-chief, Bao Yueyang. Some editors continued to voice concerns, however. One of the most crucial issues related to the question of whether taxi drivers might use Wang Keqin's report as an occasion to stage a large-scale demonstration like those in years past. If the newspaper's report became linked in any way to social unrest, it would guarantee disciplinary action against the paper. Officials might shut down the newspaper and demand letters of self-criticism from staff members.

Wang Keqin assured the editors that the taxi drivers would not stage demonstrations. "I know these guys well and I don't think that's how they will respond," he said. Wang even sought to allay their fears by providing signed statements from some of the taxi drivers.

After debating the report for several days, the editorial board decided to draft an "article release" signed by all seven members. The *China Economic Times* had already computerized this sign-off process, but drafting a physical release both showed support for the story, and at the same time kept it under wraps long enough to get it out safely. The final version went to Bao Yueyang's office with six signatures. Bao added his own. "The inside story on the Beijing taxi cartel" was ready to run.

As Wang's article came off the presses that night, Bao Yueyang posted a message on the *China Economic Times*'s bulletin board system (BBS): "This story, following the report on securities fraud in Lanzhou, is the second missile Wang Keqin has fired at corrupt government. For a story as truthful as this one it is only right for us to run a bit of risk."

Finally, on December 6, 2002, the *China Economic Times* delivered the issue featuring Wang's report to newsstands all over China.

The Aftermath

Wang's report turned into an instant success at newsstands. In Beijing, copies of the *China Economic Times* in some places sold for as much as 10 yuan as opposed to its one yuan cover price. In Hangzhou, Zhejiang Province, prices reached as high as 50 yuan. Within hours, the report appeared on the Web. Sina.com, one of China's top sites, logged an all-time record for readers of a single news story. Telephone calls from readers and taxi drivers wanting to thank the newspaper for a job well-done bombarded the office of the *China Economic Times*. Wang Keqin even received calls from several taxi company managers who wanted to come clean with their own stories.

City officials did not share the enthusiasm. The transportation bureau issued an order prohibiting taxi drivers from reading the *China Economic Times* while several newsstands around the city called the newsroom to tell them that government agencies were buying up copies. At least one newsstand, at Beijing's Capital International Airport, was shut down for offering copies of the newspaper. By evening, Wang's report was yanked from all major web portals, including Sina.com and Sohu.com. The Central Propaganda Department telephoned news media to ban all further coverage of the story or reprinting of the *China Economic Times* report.

Wang Keqin's preparations ensured that his was not the only voice on the issue. "It remains to be seen what impact, if any, the report will have on the city's handling of the industry. But the article will clearly go down as a historic chapter in China's effort to achieve regulatory reform," wrote Xu Hui, the Chinese Academy of Social Sciences expert, in an editorial that accompanied Wang's report. A *China Daily* editorial from the well-known columnist Ma Li called the article "a fine example of watchdog journalism."

Just over a week later, on December 14, Wen Jiabao, then vice-premier, issued an official response to Wang Keqin's report: "The problems in our taxi industry can no longer be ignored. Government agencies are instructed to review the issue and propose reforms." By the beginning of 2003, Premier Zhu Rongji received an official report describing severe problems in the taxi industry while government offices moved ahead with the drafting of reform proposals. Wang Keqin cooperated with Beijing University and the Chinese Academy of Social Sciences to help devise a new regulatory framework for the industry.

At the *China Economic Times*, editors viewed Wang's article as a major success, and Wen Jiabao's public statement seemed the surest sign of the report's impact.

But officials wanted to make it clear that the newspaper must avoid similar stunts in the future. When the *China Economic Times* submitted a request to propaganda officials for an adjustment to its publication frequency later that year, they swiftly denied the request, questioning sternly, "Who said you could do a report on Beijing's taxi industry?"

Postscript

Wang Keqin has referred to himself in the past as a "down and out Don Quixote." While this allusion to Miguel Cervantes' Spanish classic may at first seem strange, it is one familiar to investigative reporters in China. In a media environment fraught with challenges, one Quixote episode in particular came to symbolize their tenacious pursuit of the truth. In that episode, the comical Don Quixote makes a futile charge against a group of windmills he imagines to be giants. The windmills, to the Chinese investigative reporter, represent the daunting array of obstacles to the truth — the party's propaganda regime, official corruption, government secrecy, organized crime, violence against journalists, and professional ostracism. Despite insurmountable odds, a deeply held belief in justice spurs the investigative reporter into action. In the eyes of society, and in the eyes of their fellow journalists, they become ridiculous.

In Chapter 1, the *China Youth Daily* reporter Lu Yuegang — who was removed from his position at the *Freezing Point* supplement in January 2006 — recalled what his editor, Zhou Zhichuan, told him while they were investigating a story in Shaanxi in the late 1990s: "The world doesn't need just one Don Quixote. It needs a whole band of Quixotes." Lu Yuegang and Zhou Zhichuan were searching at the time for evidence in the case of Wu Fang, a woman viciously attacked on the order of a powerful local party official. Lu Yuegang had devoted months to the case, and was already embroiled in a libel suit resulting from his first investigative report on Wu Fang. But much more than simply a story remained at stake — Lu Yuegang wanted justice for Wu Fang, and by extension, he said, for all Chinese. The case had come to consume his personal and professional life.

While China's economic boom has created prosperity for some, it has compounded the misery of many others. For the millions who have had their rights and needs trampled, few means of compensation exist in a corrupt and unresponsive regime. While public awareness of China's legal system as recourse grows, the system lacks sufficient independence to balance the interests of ordinary people against those of officials who manipulate the judicial process. China's practice of *shangfang*, in which citizens can petition for an audience with the government and appeal for assistance, provides individuals with another channel to seek justice. But it entails traveling hundreds or thousands of miles to the complaints office of a regional capital or Beijing, where petitioners may wait for weeks or months without an opportunity to plead their cases.

Given the inadequacy of the legal and *shangfang* systems, many average Chinese turn to the media to air their grievances. In some instances, disfranchised rural communities or individuals view reporters as miracle workers who can take their complaints to higher authorities.

Wang Keqin recalled that one of the most pivotal moments in his journalism career — a stint as a reporter in a remote region of his native Gansu Province, where hundreds of desperate farmers dropped to the ground before him, weeping and pleading for intervention. After journalist Yang Haipeng wrote an investigative report for *Southern Weekend* about criminal gangs monopolizing a local fishing industry, regional police teams broke up the racket. Fishermen in the area expressed their gratitude by erecting a statue of Yang in their local temple.[3] In the face of such circumstances, said Zhai Minglei, another investigative reporter formerly with *Southern Weekend*, the notion of impartial reporting simply crumbles away. Affected on a deeply human level, the reporter unwittingly becomes an advocate.[4]

It is not hard to imagine that situations such as these intensify the reporter's sense of personal heroism that the experience of the dominant media culture casting them out for brazen risk-taking further compounded. Working for a government-run newspaper in Gansu's capital city, Lanzhou, Wang Keqin wrote a devastating report on questionable business practices in the local financial market that had robbed thousands of small-time investors. Criminals behind the scam put a price on Wang's head. When Wang wrote a second report that destroyed the careers of several prominent local officials, his newspaper fired him because he had become a political liability.

Apart from political and social pressures, the economic realities of the newspaper business in China place another significant obstacle in the way of quality investigative journalism. Payment systems at most Chinese media outlets employing the vast majority of journalists use a piece-rate scale that does not encourage investigative reporting. With administrative and budgetary limits placed on the hiring of essential staff, many media resort to pay in the forms of "costs" rather than "wages." These include "article payments," or *gaofei*, per-word payments based on the number of words published, and "reimbursements," or *baoxiao*, through which they pay a reporter's personal expense receipts in cash for an amount agreed upon outside the employment contract.

This system additionally creates distinct hierarchies within some media organizations between official hires, who are entitled to fixed salaries, benefits, and insurance, and those paid on the basis of output. Payment procedures vary greatly between organizations, but the vast majority of journalists receive piece-rate payment, where a lengthy reporting assignment can mean great personal sacrifice.

Even for Wang Keqin, a veteran reporter with a reasonable salary, the time-consuming reporting for the Beijing taxi story induced severe financial strain. When assigned to the taxi story, his monthly wage of 1,200 yuan barely covered the very basic necessities in a city where a small apartment costs about 1,500 yuan a month. Ordinarily, Wang could expect to supplement his salary with income from published articles — 60 yuan each. Accepting an investigative assignment would force him to give up this additional income. Moreover, the *China Economic Times* had established a policy not to reimburse interview costs, such as transportation, for stories that required only local reporting.

Considering all of the challenges together — as for example, immense social injustices to tackle, dangers to the reporter's personal safety and career prospects, and a sense of professional isolation — many investigative reporters have developed what Zhai Minglei calls "hero's sickness." "Deviant times and needs have made for deviant heroes," Zhai said.

Looking back on Wang's report several years later, it can be said, unfortunately, that it has had little impact on policy making. Wang Keqin continued to research the taxi industry nationwide, but said in late 2004 that he had made little progress in addressing the regulatory origins of the injustices drivers face.

Notes

1. Wang Keqin. 2004. Case study on reporting on the Beijing taxi corruption case. Hong Kong: Journalism and Media Studies Centre at the University of Hong Kong. On file with the China Media Project.
2. Wang Keqin. 2002. "*Beijing chuzuche ye longduan heimu*" (Exposing the Beijing taxi oligopoly). *China Economic Times*, December 6.
3. *Y Weekend.* 2007. "*Quanguo shi wei ming ji tan jizhe xiagui caifang*" (Ten journalists from around the country talk about being bowed to while reporting stories), February 16. Available at http://news.163.com/07/0216/14/37F7AVGL00011SM9.html.
4. Zhai Minglei. 2004. Case study on the Project Hope corruption scandal. Hong Kong: Journalism and Media Studies Centre at the University of Hong Kong. On file with the China Media Project.

6 *Media Corruption*
Cashing in on Silence

At ten a.m. on June 25, 2002, a caller, clearly distressed, rang the editor's desk at *China Youth Daily*. He said his close friend had died three days earlier in an explosion at a gold mine in Shahe, a remote town in northwestern China's Shanxi Province. According to the caller, more than fifty miners had died in the explosion. "I contacted you because I trust you guys at *China Youth Daily*," he said. "I hope you can send someone out here to Shanxi."

"Shouldn't a story like this have made the front pages?" asked a puzzled Fan Yongsheng, the newspaper's associate editor, as several staff members discussed the story. Why had they not gotten wind of this sooner? Xie Xiang, director of the newspaper's news desk, sensed a much bigger story. "If something like this has been covered up, someone's hiding a pretty nasty secret," he said.

"Well, let's send someone out there to see what's going on," Fan decided.

The newspaper assigned senior reporter Liu Chang and photographer Chai Jijun to the story, then told them to set off for Shanxi as soon as possible. Liu Chang first telephoned the source, a Mr. Hu, whose mobile number had been scrawled on a manila envelope. He answered on the first ring. "The explosion was three days ago, but we still haven't seen the bodies," he said hurriedly.

"Ok. I'll get there as soon as I can. Can you give me any more contact numbers?" Liu Chang feared the trail might grow cold if they somehow lost contact with this Mr. Hu.

A few minutes later, Hu called back, rattling off another four telephone numbers. "Things are really difficult here right now," he said. "Guys from the mining company are everywhere, keeping an eye on us. Don't call unless it's an emergency."

The bus ride from Beijing was grueling, and they arrived only by early afternoon, on June 27, in Shahe Town. They stopped first at a roadside diner and dialed Hu's number. "We're staying at a traveler's motel out toward Daying," Hu said. "You guys can come, but whatever you do, don't go in. The company has posted strongmen everywhere. It could be dangerous. When you [go] to the gate someone wearing camouflage will make contact."

Liu Chang flagged down a small van and worked out a price with the driver, nervously aware of his out-of-town accent. As the truck rumbled down the backcountry road, they kept their eyes peeled for the motel. They spoke as little as possible. When they had gone about six or seven miles up the road and passed a thicket of trees, they saw a compound looming up ahead. No other buildings stood around it.

They asked the driver to pull up to the gate, but before he could completely stop the truck, a young man in camouflage threw open the side door and hoisted himself into the seat next to Liu Chang.

"Hey, what's the idea?" said the driver, turning. Then Liu Chang noticed three or four men running toward them from the motel, closing fast.

"Go. Hurry!" the man in camouflage said.

The driver stepped hard on the gas, leaving their pursuers panting on the road behind.

"What's your name?" Liu Chang asked. The young man raised a finger to his lips and trained his eyes on the driver, making a vague grunting sound.

A few miles farther up the road, they came to a small truck stop, where Liu Chang asked the driver to let them off. The place, dirty and run-down, apparently doubled as a brothel. They found a relatively quiet mud-brick room at the back, which the proprietor said would cost them 10 yuan a person. Liu Chang nodded agreement. He was anxious to get on with his questions. But the man in camouflage turned to the proprietor. "Do you have any curtains?" he asked.

"Curtains? What do you want curtains for?" he asked, taken aback.

"That's all we need for now," said Liu Chang. "We'll let you know if there's anything else."

As soon as the man stepped out of the room, the man in camouflage launched into a rapid-fire account of what had happened. The explosion had occurred on June 22. When news of the accident spread by word of mouth, relatives of some of the dead miners had traveled from neighboring Shaanxi Province to claim the bodies and arrange for burial. Since their arrival, the mining company's private security had detained them, and forced them to sign pledges of confidentiality in return for cash payments. The company offered each family 25,000 yuan ($3,600 US). "They said if we refused to take the money we would never leave Shahe alive," said the man. "Some caved in, signed the contracts and went home. But we're demanding to collect the bodies."

A sudden movement in the empty lot outside the window caused a dog to start barking, making the man uneasy. "I'll go get some of the others and put together a list of names for you," he said, standing. Given the circumstances, Liu Chang could only watch him leave.

The journalists waited as the light began to fade outside. They saw no sign of the man. Liu Chang finally decided to try the other numbers Mr. Hu had given him. The first two numbers were switched off. The third was outside the service range. But the fourth number rang through. "We're reporters from Beijing," Liu Chang said quickly. "How are things going for you guys over there?"

The voice sounded strained. "My name is Qiu Honggang. I lost my brother in the explosion."

"Is it possible for you to come out and talk with us?" Liu Chang asked.

There was a pause. "Sure," he said finally.

They agreed to meet outside a nearby gas station. Liu Chang waved down a small van, and the reporters shot off down the road like an arrow.

As they approached the station, they could discern four men standing on the side of the road. They raised their heads every now and again, looking around nervously. Liu asked the driver to pull up beside them. "Which of you is Qiu Honggang?" he asked, poking his head out the window. The men did not move. Liu Chang brought out his official press pass and held it out so they could see it. "Get in," he said, sliding the door open.

They drove back in the direction of the truck stop. One of the men, who wore a gray jacket, asked: "Are you guys really journalists? We don't want to be cheated."

"They seem like they're for real," said another of the men, who was wearing a black shirt.

Liu Chang thought nothing of their concerns at that time, but their reasons for the question about real and fake reporters later became clear.

Eyewitness Accounts

Qiu Honggang, the man in the black shirt, came from a village in Langao County in neighboring Shaanxi Province. After learning of the death of his brother, Qiu Hongzheng, on June 23, he traveled immediately to Shahe to claim the body, arrange for cremation, and carry his brother's ashes home for a family burial. "I haven't even been able to see him," he cried when they arrived back at the mud-brick room at the truck stop. "How can I return and face my mother like this?"

"Did any of you experience the blast?" Liu Chang asked. Three of them raised their hands. They were employees at the gold mine, and they had seen everything. Tian Zhengyao, the man in the gray jacket, had been responsible for looking after the mine's cache of explosives.

"Tell him," said the other men, fixing their eyes on Tian. As soon as he opened his mouth, his eyes filled with tears.

Tian said 170 cases of dynamite, each weighing around twenty-four kilograms, were delivered to the mine on June 21 and 22. Instead of storing them above ground, which they usually did, the owner of the mine instructed them to load the shipment into the mineshaft after heavy rain came on June 21. In a five-level mine, with Level Five being the deepest underground, they stacked the explosives on Level Three.

At around one p.m. on June 22, the main electrical line running down into the mine short-circuited. Acrid white smoke rose thinly through the mineshaft. But when the miners down below started to flee, the foreman posted at the entrance ordered them back: "You can't come up! Who said you could come up!"

Tian Zhengyao recalled that the electrical line carried excessive voltage. At around 1:30 p.m., the line caught fire. About thirty minutes later, the fire ignited the cache of explosives on Level Three. A massive explosion rocked the mine, sending out a thick blanket of white smoke that sank through all levels and billowed from the entrance. When the explosion occurred, Tian was working with a crew on Level Five, the deepest part of the mine. They found a way to escape using a secondary passage. Tian then returned to the main entrance to search for his younger brother, Tian Zhengbin.

Another three or four hours elapsed before the smoke cleared enough for Tian Zhengyao and other miners to venture into Level One. Tian groped his way down into the mineshaft. Almost immediately, he came upon a cluster of miners' bodies, eighteen of them bunched together in a group. Some lay curled up on their sides, others huddled on their knees. They had apparently suffocated, their faces frozen in expressions of agony, Tian said. He could not find his brother among them.

Like Tian Zhengyao, thirty-one-year-old He Yongqing also came from Langao County in Shaanxi Province. He had arrived in Shahe in May 2000, looking for part-time work. He generally worked on the night shift, and had been sleeping the afternoon of the explosion. When he heard the sound, he rushed to the entrance, where the whole area was shrouded in white dust. He recalled that another off-duty worker, Zheng Jiubin, had also run into the mineshaft with four other men to drag out whomever they could. All five of these men were eventually found among the dead.

The rain fell even harder that night. At around midnight, the foreman ordered He Yongqing and several other men to start hauling up bodies. The mineshafts remained perfectly intact, he recalled. The bodies had no visible wounds, only blood flowing thinly from the corners of their mouths. He Yongqing soon found the body of his older brother, He Yongchun, and of one of his cousins.

Around four a.m., the foreman called down from the entrance: "Hurry up down there! The sun will be up soon!" By that time, He Yongchun had hauled up twenty-four bodies, and he felt certain that he had seen at least eight others.

Tian Zhengyao stood by and watched as the team of workers brought up the bodies and loaded them into a white Jeep from which they had removed the seats. He could not drive the picture out of his mind. "They were loaded onto the truck like animals and bound together," he cried, "We had no idea where they were being taken." He recalled the Jeep making three trips, leaving the mine and returning, with perhaps nine bodies to a load. He still saw no sign at all of his brother.

They stopped pulling bodies up just before daybreak. By that time, surviving miners and those family members who lived nearby were beginning to gather outside the mine. When the white Jeep had made its last trip, the foremen ordered everyone — survivors, relatives, and bystanders — to pile into the vehicles. The camp had to be cleared out, they said. The trucks left in a caravan. Tian Zhengyao recalled the conversation in his own vehicle.

"Where are we going to stay?" someone asked.

"I don't know," the foreman replied.

"I want to get out and take another look," one woman sobbed.

"No. We've got to vacate," the foreman said.

They went to a traveler's motel adjacent to a local driving school. Company representatives offered them each 1,300 yuan ($190 US), instructing them to take the money and leave Shahe, and not to breathe a word to anyone about what they had seen. They kept anyone who refused to accept the money under the gaze of the company's private security guards.

A List of the Dead

Night began to fall outside the mud-brick room at the back of the truck stop as Liu Chang and Chai Jijun pressed on with their interviews. Suddenly, they saw a face flash past the window. Then it came back, a thuggish face glaring directly into the room. Everyone froze. Chai Jijun shoved his digital camera behind his back, and Liu Chang slid his portable digital recorder under the table.

They waited a few more minutes. Then they all rushed out as a group. Liu Chang hailed another truck, and they drove the men back to the gas station where they had picked them up.

Later that night, Liu Chang called the mobile number for Mr. Hu, their original source. Mr. Hu said security at the motel were still detaining relatives of the victims and survivors, but they could slip out at nine p.m. if the reporters would agree to meet them near the stretch of woods they had passed just before picking up the man in camouflage.

They set out almost immediately, waving down yet another truck. They had barely entered the woods when Liu Chang spotted a group of people standing off in the shadows to one side of the road. He asked the driver to make one entire pass solely to make sure that the company security had not followed them out. Then they swung around and parked the truck by the roadside.

As the cargo trucks rumbled by, one of the persons from the group stepped forward and gave Liu Chang a handwritten letter scratched out on Chinese calligraphy paper. It listed the names of men who had died in the explosion. They also told Liu Chang and Chai Jijun that they had seen for certain several journalists on the scene shortly after the explosion, suggesting that reporters might have been paid off to suppress the story. But Liu Chang could not be sure of the accuracy of their statements — they might actually have seen local government investigators. The first priority, in any case, was to determine the actual facts about the disaster itself.

Back at the hotel, the two journalists looked carefully over the handwritten document as detailed below:

Concerning the serious explosion at Yixingsai Gold Mine in the town of Shahe, Fanzhi County, Shanxi Province

Attn: State Administration of Work Safety

At 2:30 p.m., on June 22, 2002, a serious explosion occurred at the Yixingsai Gold Mine, located in the town of Shahe in Fanzhi County, Shanxi Province.

1. Time and place of disaster:
   Yixingsai Gold Mine, Shahe Town, Fanzhi County, Shanxi Province, June 22, 2002.
2. Cause and circumstances of disaster:

On the morning of June 22, the boss of Yixingsai Gold Mine had workers move 150 cases of explosives inside the mineshaft. At 1:00 p.m. on June 22, workers discovered that the main electrical line running into the mine had short-circuited, sending up smoke. They advised the mine's boss to evacuate workers to avoid casualties. This boss, concerned only with reaching production quotas, ordered the men below to continue work. At 2:30 p.m. there was a loud boom. The electrical line ignited the 150 cases of explosives, causing the death of forty-six workers. There were 117 workers on duty that day. Of these, ninety-seven were working in the mineshaft and twenty were working outside. The principle cause of the disaster was human error. The mine's main electrical line was giving off smoke for nearly one full hour, and the boss was aware of this fact. One: the workers had asked to leave the mine. Two: the explosives could not be moved. Three: the electrical line was not replaced in time in the interest of production quotas and profit making. Reckless disregard for the well being of the workers caused a disaster of grave proportions. After the disaster occurred, the boss of the mine called together survivors, family members and witnesses and gave each person 1,300 yuan to stop news of the disaster from spreading. He then ordered them to haul bodies up from the mineshaft. These were taken away by truck to an unknown location. When county officials, city officials, and reporters came to investigate the scene, mine representatives said there were only two dead and four injured.

When the family members of the deceased came to arrange their last rites, the mine boss refused to let them see the bodies, but instead had them detained by company strongmen. Each family was offered 20,000 to 30,000 yuan. We have been here for several days now, and have not seen the bodies or any attempts to further handle the matter. We therefore report the situation to the authorities in hope that higher officials may see to it that this matter is handled and responsible parties are taken to account. Furthermore, we have the following demands in regard to wrongful death compensation:

We must see the bodies of the deceased, cremate them, and return home with the remains.

We seek to hold the responsible parties criminally liable for their actions, according to relevant laws and regulations.

We ask to be compensated not only for the wrongful death of our loved ones, but also for our traveling expenses and loss of pay.

The following is a list of the deceased:

SURNAME	PLACE OF RESIDENCE
Tian Zhengbin	Gujia Village, Guanyuan Town, Langao County
Liu Huancai	Longbanying Village, Guanyuan Town, Langao County
Qiu Hongzheng	Gujia Village, Guanyuan Town, Langao County
Zheng Jiubin	Jixianchapeng Village, Langao County
Yang Liuyun	Jixianchapeng Village, Langao County
Shuai Xingyou	Jixianchapeng Village, Langao County
Zhou Weiping	Jixianchapeng Village, Langao County
Li Fashu	Jixianchapeng Village, Langao County
Guo Yucai	Jixianchapeng Village, Langao County
Cheng Donghai	Cheping Village, Taohe Town, Langao County
Deng Youcheng	Muzhu Village, Siji Town, Langao County
Zhu Zhenjian	Muzhu Village, Siji Town, Langao County
Hu Yuanli	Lejing Village, Hengqi Town, Langao County
Tan Zhoujun	Lejing Village, Hengqi Town, Langao County
Pan Yuyou	Lejing Village, Hengqi Town, Langao County
Song Nianshuang	Lejing Village, Hengqi Town, Langao County
Kong Ande	Baiping Village, Taohe Town, Langao County
He Yongchun	Baiping Village, Taohe Town, Langao County
He Yongxu	Baiping Village, Taohe Town, Langao County
Liu Minghong	Shuang Village, Shimen Town, Langao County

The number of dead counted from Langao County (above): twenty

Below are listed the nine dead from Xunyang County:

Hu Ming	Luzhou Village, Zhaowan Town, Xunyang County
Hu Delin	Hujiazhuang Village, Zhaowan Town, Xunyang County
Guo Xinghan	Luzhou Village, Zhaowan Town, Xunyang County
Zhang Jibao	Luzhou Village, Zhaowan Town, Xunyang County
Wang Jianping	Hujiazhuang Village, Zhaowan Town, Xunyang County
Li Zhengping	Yanwogou Village, Luhe Town, Xunyang County
Wang Zhibin	Renhe Town, Xunyang County
Wang Zhigang	Renhe Town, Xunyang County
Chen Baoyou	Ankanghanbin Region, Shanxi Province

Notice: The above list of the dead was compiled by the family members of the deceased. Some family members separated from us were unable to sign their names.

Family members had signed their names in the margins beside the twenty-nine names. Liu Chang first noticed the discrepancy in numbers as he studied the letter. It said forty-six workers had died in the explosion, but signatures of the families confirmed only twenty-nine of the deaths. Was it possible they misunderstood the figure?

The suggestion by eyewitnesses that journalists had been on the scene in the early hours of the disaster provided an important piece of information that hinted at other media's probable complicity in the cover-up. This certainly resolved the initial bewilderment of the *China Youth Daily* editor, Fan Yongsheng, who asked: "Shouldn't a story like this have made the front pages?" Then, they remembered Tian Zhengyao's immediate query earlier that day: "Are you guys really reporters?" But these questions would have to wait.

After he had read the letter over carefully, Liu Chang called the State Administration of Work Safety in Beijing, the national-level government office that handled work-related disasters and complaints. Officials there said they had learned of the explosion earlier that day, and were already assembling an inspection team.

The next day, June 28, *China Youth Daily* reporters visited the offices of the county government in Fanzhi. They were told at first that no one was available for an interview. By the time they had settled into a local hotel, however, they received a telephone call informing them that Ding Wenfu, a top county-level party official, had agreed to meet with them.

When they returned to the county office, Ding handed them a copy of the official report filed on the Yixingsai disaster. According to it, they were notified at 5:25 p.m. on June 22 that there had been an explosion at the mine. Party Secretary Wang Jianhua, the county's top leader, personally visited the site and ordered an evacuation. The report said officials from Xinzhou, a prefectural capital with jurisdiction over fourteen of Shanxi's north-central counties, including Fanzhi, also toured the scene. Xinzhou Deputy Mayor Yang Pusheng had asked county officials to submit a report giving a full account of the dead and injured. To this effect, they formed a county subcommittee for disaster inspection in the early hours of June 23, headed up by Wang Yanping, Fanzhi's county governor and second-in-command.

The report said the county dispatched 116 police and emergency vehicles to Yixingsai, sparing no expense, apparently directly contradicting the eyewitness accounts of He Yongqing and others, who had noted the lack of police or officials at the mine on the night of the explosion. When Liu Chang asked about this, Ding Wenfu only answered cryptically: "The circumstances were unclear at the time."

The report continued, stating that the Fanzhi subcommittee briefed prefectural leaders in Xinzhou sometime on June 23. The numbers in that report stood completely at odds with those in the handwritten account from survivors and their relatives: "Of the forty workers on duty at the time of the explosion, two died, four were injured, and thirty-four were safely evacuated," it said.

As they sat down with Ding Wenfu, they received several calls from survivors and relatives detained at the traveler's motel by company security. They pleaded for Liu Chang's help and told him that the security guards were getting rough. They went straight to the motel and marched in through the front door. But the mine's boss and his thugs had already left. As it turned out, provincial leaders, including the deputy governor, were already on their way to Fanzhi. Top county leaders now had no choice but to make a show of action, dispatching police to deal with the crisis. The owner of the Yixingsai mine, his foremen, and security guards had scattered to the four winds.

Liu Chang telephoned the county office later that afternoon hoping to reach Ding Wenfu or other officials. A clerk in the office informed him that the government had secured accommodations for the *China Youth Daily* reporters at a local hotel, and could arrange meetings for them with Ding and other leaders after their registration. Liu Chang understood this ploy immediately. They wanted to corner the reporters and make them an offer under the table, probably an unspecified sum of money in exchange for their cooperation in suppressing the story. But Liu knew better than to reject their hospitality out of hand. They checked in to their hotel suite only long enough to arrange a meeting with local officials. Then they slipped out with their bags, never to return to their room.

Liu Chang filed his first news report that night.

National Attention

The next morning, June 29, Liu Chang's article on the Yixingsai disaster appeared in *China Youth Daily*, called "The jumbled truth of a tragedy." On the basis of signatures from the handwritten letter, Liu Chang reported twenty-nine confirmed dead:

> Under radiant sunlight, this large compound, which sits on the edge of a wide road through the countryside, seems empty and abandoned. In fact, ten people — surviving gold miners and family members — are holding their ground here. On June 28, many others gave their signatures to contracts and walked away with between 25,000 and 60,000 yuan in "damages." But these men and women say they will not leave until they have seen the bodies of their loved ones one last time.
>
> At around 3 p.m. on June 22, a disastrous explosion occurred at the Yixingsai Gold Mine in Shanxi's Fanzhi County. According to a report from the Fanzhi county government issued on June 23, two workers died and four were injured in the explosion. But survivors insist this number is "seriously underreported." When *China Youth Daily* reporters arrived in Fanzhi County, they were spied upon at their hotel room. Whenever they went out to investigate, relatives of those who had died cautioned them: "You are being followed. Look out for yourselves." . . . Everything about this incident is out of the ordinary . . . [1]

Liu's report detailed eyewitness accounts from surviving miners, including Tian Zhengyao and He Yongqing, whom the reporter mentioned by name, in a reporting environment where anonymous sourcing was commonplace. The article also summarized the official disaster report from the Fanzhi county government, emphasizing how it conflicted with onsite accounts. It also mentioned the impending investigation by the State Administration of Work Safety.

As Liu's report became national news, the official inquiry into the Yixingsai disaster was quickly moving ahead. The night before, Shanxi's vice-governor had met with local and regional leaders at the mine and ordered the formation of an inspection team. Xuan Mingren, the vice mayor of Xinzhou City, had complied with this request by assembling a team of more than 100 police officers from Xinzhou and surrounding counties, excluding those from Fanzhi County. Xuan's team began questioning witnesses in Shahe on the morning of June 29, starting with sources from Liu Chang's newspaper report. This led quickly to the arrest of several suspects.

In his second report, filed late June 29, and appearing on June 30, Liu Chang described the appalling conditions in the local mining district and particulars of the ongoing investigation. He also mentioned several suspects who remained at large, including the head of the mining company, Wang Quanquan, and two principal "shareholders":

> Fanzhi County, Shanxi (filed June 29) — *China Youth Daily* reporters arrived at the site of the Yixingsai Gold Mine explosion at 10 a.m. this morning to discover that production in this bustling mining district, in full swing only yesterday, had come to a halt. The few miners remaining lay stretched out in the sun, soaking up the rays. According to our sources, the investigative team formed to look into the tragedy ordered a stop to all mining activity early this morning.
>
> The mountains here are densely dotted with simple, makeshift structures, many of which can be entered only by crawling like a cat on one's hands and knees. Signs over the doors read, "Cafeteria," "Hospital," "Salon," or "Billiards." According to one safety inspection expert on the scene, these structures fall far short of basic safety standards. He points to an exposed circuit box . . .
>
> A police officer with a tablet in one hand takes statements from survivors of the explosion, who say corpses were taken to an unknown location. The owner of the mine, its foreman and two shareholders have all fled. According to one local official, this has hindered progress in the investigation. Shanxi officials urged police this morning to apprehend all of the above suspects within the next three days. That effort is in full swing . . .

By the time the report appeared, media from across the country were already arriving on the scene. Roughly ten news outfits worked there on June

30, including China Central Television (CCTV), the Xinhua News Agency, China National Radio, and Shanxi's *Chinese Business View*. At one point, Shan Baohong, director of Xinhua's Shanxi bureau, remarked to Liu Chang: "You guys from *China Youth Daily* have really been on top of this story. The head honchos in Beijing are putting pressure on us, wondering why we can't beat you to the punch." In the midst of the competition on the ground, this exchange seemed like trifling banter. But it flooded back to Liu Chang months later with greater significance.

Liu Chang learned from police later that afternoon that they had located some of the missing bodies. An eyewitness evacuated from the camp on the night of the explosion told police she remembered the trucks stopping on a remote stretch of road just past the village of Wanyu. Two men had jumped out there, and disappeared into the woods. She took police to the spot, where they located the corpses in a nearby field.

When Liu Chang and Chai Jijun requested that local officials help them view the scene where bodies had been dumped, they waved them off with a warning about their own safety: "You reporters should be more careful. Don't write what you shouldn't write, otherwise you'll piss off the boss or one of his guys. Who can guarantee your safety then?"

The reporters eventually discovered the bodies themselves, aided by eyewitnesses. Only a short walk from where witnesses said the trucks had stopped, they came across two piles of earth littered with charred remains. The stench of rotting flesh overpowered them. Nearby, they found a shallow mass grave with the torso of one corpse fully exposed. Police investigators later concluded that after dumping the bodies, the men had separated them into piles and attempted to set them on fire. Running out of time, they had simply discarded the rest of the bodies close by and covered them hastily with earth.

Before nightfall on June 30, the police found more bodies in four separate abandoned mineshafts. In all, the five dump sites yielded thirty-seven corpses. Police said they believed, on the basis of eyewitness accounts, that they had located all of the bodies.

Liu Chang's third and fourth stories appeared on July 1 and 2. The second of these, "Officials call 6/22 explosion a 'major disaster and cover-up'," reported the latest body count and described the clean-up effort:

> Fanzhi County, Shanxi (filed July 1) — At 7:10 p.m., local police discovered the body of yet another disaster victim in a mineshaft shaft just one kilometer from Yixingsai gold mine. This brings to 37 the total number of bodies found up to now. The explosion at Yixingsai is now being called a "major disaster and cover-up." The State Administration of Work Safety said it would be "firm-fisted" in handling the matter.

> This afternoon, officials from the State Administration of Work Safety arrived in Fanzhi County to carry out a complete clean-up of the Sunjiangou gold mining district. In total, more than 1,000 structures are to be torn down and more than 4,000 miners evacuated by this evening. Under official orders, the disaster site, which had already been closed off, was opened for clean up . . . [2]

By July 3, local officials had not yet begun the process of identifying bodies, nor had they given relatives any indication of when they might be able to see them. Relatives and local officials were all called together for a meeting that morning in the lobby of a local hotel. Journalists from scores of media also attended. Liu Chang read the disgust on the faces of survivors' families as they were served platters of freshly cut watermelon. These people wanted answers, not empty gestures, and they had lost all confidence in the good will of local leaders.

Moments later, Wang Dexue, a high-level Beijing official and director of the State Administration of Work Safety, walked into the room with Shanxi's deputy governor, Jin Shanzhong. One of the relatives ran up to Wang Dexue and dropped to her knees, crying. Another shouted: "Why hasn't the process of identification begun? It's been four days since the bodies were found!"

Wang Dexue turned a menacing gaze on Wang Jianhua, the top county leader, and his second in command, Wang Yanping. "You still haven't arranged for them to see the bodies? What have you been doing?" They said nothing.

Later that morning, Wang Dexue arranged for vans to transport relatives to Shahe's No. 2 Hospital, where the bodies had waited for three days. Police refused to let reporters ride along, but Liu Chang and Chai Jijun flagged down a small truck and followed the caravan.

In the hospital morgue, the coroner sliced open the body bags one by one with a pair of scissors. By this time, the corpses had severely swollen up and badly decomposed, most so unrecognizable that relatives could identify them only by articles of clothing or personal effects.

In the days that followed, police intensified their search for major suspects still on the run. These included Yixingsai gold mine's head, Wang Quanquan; the top foreman; and two major shareholders, Yin Shan and Shu Shibin. Police finally captured Yin Shan on July 8, and Shu Shibin, two weeks later. Finally, on July 25, the case's most-wanted, Wang Quanquan, surrendered to police.

Waiting for the Official Findings

After the arrest of Wang Quanquan, the story cooled off. *China Youth Daily* and other national media awaited the results of the official investigation, which they expected would explain the initial cover-up of the news about the explosion and how county officials might have been involved.

In October, the popular CCTV talk show *Story* invited Liu Chang as a guest for a special aired on Journalist's Day, a professional holiday first held in 2000. Only minutes before he walked onto the set, Liu received an anonymous call from an individual identifying himself as a high-level investigation official. He said reporters from China's official Xinhua News Agency had accepted payoffs in cash and gold ingots in exchange for covering up the Yixingsai disaster.

Liu Chang followed up on the accusation the next day with several other sources inside China's state investigation apparatus. They all confirmed that certain state media had accepted bribes, but refused to offer details. Given the extreme sensitivity of the charges, Liu Chang had no choice but to remain silent about the call. He would have to wait until officials released their findings.

Liu Chang never supposed this would mean a delay of months. In early 2003, he tried pressuring inspection officials directly, but in vain. In a final desperate attempt, he wrote an internal reference, or *neican*, for circulation among top party leaders. They are designed to inform party and government officials about key policy matters deemed too sensitive for the general public. Many newspapers in China have specially designated *neican* desks that gather reports disapproved by the top editors in order to prepare them for circulation as documents for official eyes only. In his own internal reference, Liu Chang urged leaders to disclose all of the results of the investigation, in particular the role journalists and local officials played in the cover-up.

Liu's internal reference caught the attention of a politburo member, who added his own comments and pressured investigators to release their findings. *China Youth Daily* applied its own pressure with an editorial about the public's "right to know" the results of the investigation.

This editorial generated some debate inside *China Youth Daily* as to the appropriateness of demanding the release of the findings. On one side, several editors and reporters felt obligated to look after their compatriots — even if Xinhua reporters had acted unethically, they were still part of the family. On the other side, Liu Chang and others believed that the credibility of the press, as a whole, was at stake, and that the public had a right to know. *China Youth Daily*'s editor-in-chief, Li Xueqian, had even discussed the issue with top Xinhua officials when they crossed paths at a Central Party School training session. The men had agreed that there was no reason for pressing the issue any further — media should stick together. When Liu Chang wrote an account of how the boss of the Yixingsai mine had bribed reporters, the editor-in-chief held the story back.

In the end, the fear of being out-scooped prompted *China Youth Daily* to publish the media corruption story — a graphic illustration of China's increasingly competitive reporting environment. On August 18, 2003, Liu Chang learned that China Central Television's *News Probe*, a popular and highly influential investigative news program, was preparing to air a special program on the Yixingsai disaster. Although he remained uncertain about the specifics of the *News Probe* story, Liu convinced his editors that it would approach the broadcast from a media corruption angle. With the permission of his editors, he submitted a report the same day. It did not deal in-depth with the bribing of journalists, but it did contain a scant one line saying investigators had found that state media had accepted bribes and suppressed the story of the Yixingsai explosion.

Xinhua Comes Clean

It was not until a month later that Xinhua issued its response to the allegations. In an official news release that appeared on September 16, the agency said, without any mention of names, that eleven journalists had "accepted bribes in the form of cash and gold ingots from mining bosses and others, committing economic crimes of great significance."[3]

In the days that followed, calls from the public and other journalists for the release of the full details of the investigation grew. But Xinhua's final revelation on September 27 surprised even Liu Chang. The news agency this time published a list of eleven reporters whom they found to have accepted bribes in Shanxi. It included journalists from Xinhua News Agency, *Shanxi Economic Daily*, *Shanxi Legal Daily*, and *Shanxi Morning News*. Shan Baohong, director of Xinhua's Shanxi bureau, the same journalist who had complained that the *China Youth Daily* reports were putting pressure on him to file his own stories, led the list along with three other Xinhua reporters.[4] Liu recalled how intensely Shan had eventually covered the story, and how he had written compelling editorials voicing outrage at the inhumanity of local officials and owners of the mine.

According to the findings of the investigation, Shan had accepted 20,000 yuan ($2,900 US) from the county's governor, who had handled the matter at the urging of Wang Quanquan, the mine's owner. Xinhua News Agency reporters required, after all, dignified treatment. The Xinhua journalists, including Shan Baohong, a photography editor, and two cub reporters, arrived in Fanzhi on June 23, 2002, and went immediately to the office of the county government. The governor entertained them before visiting the scene of the explosion. He gave Shan and his photography editor each 20,000 yuan. When they asked for a little more for their "little brothers," the governor passed 2,400 yuan and one gold ingot over to each of the cub reporters.

The seven other reporters implicated in the scandal all came from local newspapers: *Shanxi Economic Daily*, *Shanxi Legal Daily*, and *Shanxi Morning News*. They had arrived in Shahe on the night of the explosion and spoken with survivors and relatives. According to the official report, they used their presence merely as a ploy to intimidate the management. Eventually, the group appointed one reporter to negotiate with the boss, Wang Quanquan. At first, Wang had balked at their demands, 30,000 yuan a piece, but eventually acceded to them.

Postscript

Although China has maintained strict control of the media, since the mid-1990s, the state has encouraged the commercialization of media. Part of this process entailed removing state support from more peripheral media while keeping in place key "mouthpieces" such as China Central Television and *People's Daily*. While the party continues to strictly supervise the media, which can also serve as an arm of state power, the media faces increasing pressure to generate advertising revenues. In an environment where state control limits their options, this combination of "power-brokering and profit-mongering" has led some media to routinely abuse their privileges to pad their bottom lines.

This mixture also contributes to what some have called an ethical crisis for Chinese journalism. It takes its most prominent form as "news extortion," or *xinwen qiaozha*, a reference to the writing of hard-hitting articles, or threatening to release them in order to coerce corporations and local governments. When the tactic succeeds, as it frequently does, those extorted take out "advertising contracts" in exchange for the newspaper dropping potentially damaging news stories, while the journalists involved receive a commission. Low salaries throughout the industry compound these problems as does a glut of publications on the market, all competing for a limited advertising pie.

Media describe such practices as rampant and rising. While documented cases remain rare, growing signs that these trends concern leadership have surfaced too. On May 15, 2006, the Xinhua News Agency issued an official release in which the General Administration of Press and Publications (GAPP), China's government monitors for the publishing sector, sternly warned against the practice of news extortion. It outlined four cases, in particular, involving the *China Food Quality News*, the *China Commercial Times*, *Economic Daily*, and *China Industry News*. The GAPP sent the message that nationally circulated publications needed to clean up their regional news bureaus. It called on newspapers to "further normalize the news reporting activities of reporters at their news bureaus" by ratcheting up their internal supervisory mechanisms.

In discussing the present case, Liu Chang remarked that ethical problems of this kind pose one of the biggest dangers facing the press in China. At present, China's own brand of watchdog journalism, or "supervision by public opinion," offers one area in which journalists can pursue investigative reporting and monitor the power of leadership, albeit with many pitfalls and limitations. The abuse of this fragile privilege, first officially acknowledged at the 1987 Party Congress, not only undermines public faith in journalism but also increases calls for curbs on the media's already limited freedoms.

Liu Chang's "gold ingot" case represented one of the earliest and most salient examples of the exploitation of media power by journalists. In fact, two separate offences occurred. In the first case, officials bribed the Xinhua News Agency reporters before they even began to cover the story. By contrast, the actions of the other seven reporters from regional bureaus of central and provincial news media qualify as "news extortion," using the threat of exposure for pay. Media insiders say this kind of behavior happens regularly at regional news bureaus, where chiefs control both business and editorial departments, with the attendant fierce pressure to generate revenues.

A rare case of news extortion reported in the media appeared in November 2004, after a whistle-blower, Tao Zhidong, came forward in *China Newsweekly* magazine to expose the practice at his former newspaper, Hubei's *Edong Evening News*. China Central Television's *News Probe* investigative program aired a segment on the case in February 2005, interviewing a local education official the newspaper had blackmailed:

> *News Probe* Narrator: After he received calls from four principals [about visits they had had from *Edong Evening News* reporters], Jiang Enhua realized the seriousness of the problem and joined the principals for a visit to the hotel room where the reporters were staying.
> Jiang Enhua (school official): "At the time, one of the reporters gave me a look at the report they had already written."
> Chai Jing (CCTV reporter): "What did it say?"
> Jiang Enhua: "Of course it was pretty critical, airing out our dirty laundry, saying we were charging fees illegally. He asked what would we do if it came out. If our cards were shown."
> Chai Jing: "If he was just doing his job, why should he ask you that?"
> Jiang Enhua: "He wanted our opinion about whether the report should be published. Could we take the heat if it went to press, and what were we prepared to do if it didn't? That kind of thing."[5]

The reporter Jiang had spoken with was Tao Zhidong, the eventual whistle-blower who claimed the newspaper's management had encouraged this practice. Eight local schools finally paid the reporters 55,000 yuan in cash for a soft advertisement. Each earned a commission. Tao Zhidong told *China Newsweekly* that the role of reporters intertwined so inextricably with the paper's revenue goals that the most popular greeting in the newsroom became, "So, how's business lately?"[6]

Notes

1. Liu Chang. "*Can ju zhen xiang pu shuo mi li*" (The jumbled truth of a tragedy). *China Youth Daily*, June 29.
2. Liu Chang. 2002. "*Shanxi Fanzhi jin kuang shi gu bei ren ding wei 'te da shi gu': yin man bu bao*" (Shanxi Fanzhi goldmine accident ruled a "major accident" was covered up). *China Youth Daily*, July 1.

3. Xinhua News Agency. 2003. "*Shanxi Fanzhi teda baozha shigu zeren ren shou dao chuli*" (Those responsible for major explosion accident at Fanzhi receive punishment). *People's Daily*, September 16.
4. Xinhua News Agency. 2003. "*Yinman kuangnan zhenxiang shoushou xianjin: 11 ming jizhe bei cha*" (Accepting cash to cover up a mining explosion: 11 reporters are investigated). *Yangcheng Evening News*, September 23.
5. *News Probe*, China Central Television. 2005. "*Shi heng de meijie*" (Media out of control). February 4. Transcript available on the blog of *News Probe* anchor Chai Jing, http://www.chaijing.com/bbs/thread-489-1-1.html.
6. *China Newsweek*. 2004. "*Meiti fubai shiwu lian diaocha: yi fen wanbao de xinwen lesuo luxiantu*" (Investigation into the media food chain of corruption: a map of extortion at one evening newspaper), November 24.

7 *Corruption Reporting*
Mapping Li Zhen's Rise to Power

When the name Li Zhen appeared in a routine official news release from Xinhua News Agency on December 17, 2001, few members of the public knew who this official was. A relatively low-level cadre from Hebei Province who had been "expelled from the party and relieved of his position" following investigation by "top supervisory bodies," he had been "placed under arrest in accordance with the law" for accepting bribes and unlawfully possessing various public and private property, said the release.

The Xinhua news release covered Li Zhen and the crimes of which he was accused only in scant detail:

> Li Zhen was born in May 1962. Investigations have revealed that he accepted bribes amounting to 8.68 million yuan and was illegally in possession of public and private property, including valuables with an estimated value of 10.5 million yuan.[1]

The only thing out of sorts about the case, judging from a superficial reading of the original Xinhua release, was the sheer magnitude of Li Zhen's ill-gotten fortune. China's media focused primarily on the 10.5 million yuan, or 1.5 million dollars, in bribes and property Li Zhen had amassed, which according to some calculations reached a new high water mark for official corruption in China.

Police in Hebei had in fact taken Li Zhen into custody almost two years earlier, in March 2000, and a small burst of press coverage had followed. *Hebei Daily*, the official mouthpiece of high-ranking party leaders in the province, simply reported at that time that Li Zhen had been arrested for "exploiting his position, accepting huge amounts of bribes."[2]

Following up on scanty mainland press coverage that gave few details or context, Hong Kong's *Ming Pao*, not subject to mainland Chinese media restrictions, reported in July 2000 that the arrest of Li Zhen and several associated political figures represented the "biggest political earthquake to hit Hebei in the era of economic reforms."[3] The arrests, said the newspaper, comprised part of a concerted Chinese Communist Party (CCP) campaign to demonstrate its determination to fight corruption. The report also suggested the existence of an extended web of corruption in Hebei Province, possibly implicating more high-level officials:

> We understand that Hebei's Provincial Tax Bureau Chief Li Zhen and two other vice directors are accused of accepting bribes, tax evasion, and money laundering both in China and overseas, in addition to other economic crimes. They were placed under administration detention months ago and subjected to investigation, and their cases alone are said to involve more than ten million yuan. One source told us that the assistant of former [Hebei] party secretary Cheng Weigao was also implicated in the case, and was being investigated by the authorities . . .
>
> Our reporter inquired about the case with the former office of the above-mentioned accused, and although the employee who answered the telephone was unwilling to discuss the case in detail, they did confirm that these officials "were in trouble." An official in the general office of the Hebei provincial government said that deputy governor Cong Fukui "has been in trouble for some time already"; an official in the Cangzhou city government said explicitly that "[former Cangzhou] Secretary Bo Shaoquan has been taken away by discipline inspection authorities . . ."; an official in the provincial transportation department said that [provincial official] Zhang Jian was traveling on business and they had no idea when he would return; an official in the provincial tax bureau said that Li Zhen "is no longer our director."

When news of Li Zhen resurfaced in China's press in December 2001, there was still precious little to go on. The shocking numbers in the official news release on Li Zhen's expulsion from the party did not stand out enough to commend the story to editors at *Lifeweek* magazine when they sat down that month to brainstorm feature stories for the next year. Founded in 1995, Beijing-based *Lifeweek*, one of China's leading weekly news magazines, by its own admission strove to be an opinion leader and "faithful recorder of events," to introduce its readership to new concepts and trends in China and overseas.

Li Zhen's relatively low position in the official hierarchy deterred interest in the story as a feature. As chairman of the Hebei office of the National Tax Bureau, he ranked a full step below provincial level. As a general rule, corruption stories of high-level officials, generally those at the provincial level or above, drew the greatest interest. Judged by this standard, a report about a provincial tax official would not likely send copies flying off newsstands.

As a result, Li Honggu, *Lifeweek*'s deputy editor-in-chief, dismissed the idea when it came up during the December editorial brainstorming meeting. Would anyone really be interested in this person's story?

Glimmers of Newsworthiness

Still, sufficient questions remained after the brief spurt of official Li Zhen news coverage in December 2001 to pique the interest of an astute reader. While the release from Xinhua offered little in the way of details, a separate story from the

China News Service, the country's number two official news agency, was somewhat more forthcoming. The first four paragraphs matched Xinhua's version almost verbatim, but additional facts followed about the nature of Li Zhen's crimes:

> According to an [official] investigation, from 1995 to 1999 Li Zhen assisted a certain manager Wang of a certain Beijing company in contracting for a building project, and received three million yuan in bribes from Wang. At the end of 1992, Li Zhen went through a certain Zhang, then director of the Hebei branch office of China Eastern Leasing Company, to assist Wu Qingwu (now in custody) in getting a loan from China Eastern Leasing in the amount of 20 million yuan, and after this Li Zhen received 150,000 U.S. dollars and 100,000 yuan from Wu Qingwu. In April 1994, Li Zhen received 500,000 yuan and a home worth one million yuan from a certain Qin after helping this Qin obtain loans and contract for building projects.

This section uncharacteristically mentioned, by full name, another central figure, Wu Qingwu, in contrast to routine press announcements of this kind, which generally included the full name of the accused and with only surnames for the others. Did the news service err, or had it made the mistake intentionally? Who was Wu Qingwu, and why was he important?

As *Lifeweek* prepared its December 31, 2001 issue featuring people from government, business, and academia who had significantly impacted China during the year, it found that Li Zhen's name continued to come to light. The magazine's top "person of the year," Liu Liying, a senior anti-corruption official in the CCP's Central Discipline Inspection Commission, had pursued a number of high-profile corruption cases that year and had been dubbed "a flag in the anti-corruption struggle."[4]

As it prepared its story on Liu, the magazine sought a different perspective from another senior corruption investigator. The official avoided the usual pre-packaged attacks on provincial corruption during the interview, and made a bee-line for the topic of Li Zhen. He said assistants in contemporary Chinese politics too closely resembled the eunuchs of China's imperial past who, despite their status as mere servants, gained incredible power by virtue of their proximity to the emperor. The supervisory official said the organizational committee had selected Li Zhen for the shortlist of candidates for vice-chairman of the Central National Tax Bureau in Beijing prior to his arrest. He had fallen only a few votes short of his next major promotion.

The analysis of corruption cases following the profile of corruption fighter Liu Liying reflected the growing interest of *Lifeweek* editors in the Li Zhen story. The first piece introduced the case against the former deputy governor of Hebei Province, Cong Fukui, but at the beginning resembled a preamble to Li Zhen's case:

> In Jiang Shan's professional experience, Li Zhen stands out as an exception. Head of the Shijiazhuang news desk of the Hebei office of [the official] Xinhua News Agency, Jiang Shan has been a journalist for more than 20 years. On December 22, Jiang Shan, off on an excursion to Hainan, spoke to our reporter by long-distance telephone, and summed it up this way: "Since 1975, counting from secretary Liu Zihou . . . to the present secretary Wang Xudong, I have interviewed six provincial party secretaries in Hebei." Successfully carrying out these interviews has always required going through their assistants, and reporters have found contacts with most assistants quite smooth. But Li Zhen, said Jiang Shan, "is summed up uniformly, not just by me but by many journalists covering politics . . . at the provincial level, with a single word: egotistical."
>
> Of course when reporters contacted Li Zhen to make arrangements and see the provincial party secretary, it was for the sake of an interview and in order to write an article. Jiang Shan said: "When leaders from prefecture-level cities wanted to see the secretary, they had to make arrangements just like the journalists — the difference was that this required arrangements that were a whole lot richer.[5]

Here already, in an article about a separate corruption case, stirred a much bigger story about a cunning, young political player who was able to exploit the shortcomings of China's political system to amass both power and riches.

The *Lifeweek* profile also mentioned an editorial published on the Internet site Qianlong.com only days after the Xinhua news release that raised further questions about the Li Zhen case and the possible involvement of more senior leaders. Chu Ruigeng, a columnist for the official *Hebei Daily*, wrote the editorial, and other websites, including the popular Sina.com, quickly cited it.[6]

Chu learned of Li Zhen's arrest by watching China Central Television's (CCTV) evening newscast on December 17. "I couldn't control my anger and emotion [as I watched]," the columnist wrote. Chu's editorial, the first of five on the Li Zhen case, written not for *Hebei Daily* but independently, suggested indignantly the responsibility of another important official who had not yet faced punishment:

> Today people have to ask: were responsible comrades in the Hebei Provincial Committee sleeping when the question of the appointment of the cur, Li Zhen, came up? Did no one step up to oppose it? This was in fact not the case. Some comrades voiced firm opposition, both in writing and in person . . . but the provincial party secretary would hear nothing of it, and even said: "I say someone's good [for the job] and always someone stands up to gainsay me!"

It did not take much digging to find out that Chu was in fact referring to Cheng Weigao, former party secretary and at that time chairman of the Standing Committee of the Hebei Provincial People's Congress. His editorial also hinted that Li's appointment as a provincial assistant had been the subject of fierce debate among top provincial leaders. Was it possible that Li was taking the fall for the misdeeds of the former party secretary? Li Honggu also found it puzzling that Chu emphasized in his editorial Li Zhen's former role as assistant to Cheng Weigao when his subsequent post as chairman of the National Tax Bureau in Hebei formally gave him more clout.

As 2002 approached, Li Zhen would simply not go away. His name cropped up everywhere. That January, Li Honggu traveled to south China's Guangxi Autonomous Region to cover yet another corruption story. Li found that his government sources in this remote region of China were as familiar with Li Zhen as his sources in the capital. Clearly, while the name Li Zhen meant nothing to ordinary Chinese, his dealings were legendary in circles of power.

Had *Lifeweek* been too hasty in turning down a cover story about Li Zhen? Li Honggu began gathering everything he could find about Cheng Weigao's former assistant.

Searching through news archives, Li Honggu found two stories of interest. The first was an article from the *Voice*, a Hebei magazine that had run for just a few issues, which looked back on Li Zhen's formative years, saying he came from an "average family." The bulk of the reporting consisted of interviews in Li's hometown of Zhangjiakou, particularly with teachers at his alma mater, Cigoubao Teacher's College. The second, which appeared in *Hebei Legal News*, was written by Jiang Shan, the Hebei journalist for Xinhua News Agency mentioned in the above article on the Cong Fukui case. When Li Honggu asked Jiang Shan for more information about Li Zhen, the reporter summed the young cadre up by saying he had "a vicious heart and ambitions for China's vice premiership."

Li Zhen's story now thoroughly intrigued Li Honggu while a preliminary picture of the fallen official began to take shape.

Li Zhen grew up in an "average" Chinese family and attained only a secondary-school education. He started his ascent to power from the position of provincial assistant, and had leveraged it to amass further influence. He nearly succeeded in becoming vice-chairman of the Central National Tax Bureau in Beijing, but he ultimately aspired to the post of vice-premier. Obviously, his rise had been unexpectedly interrupted. He now faced a potential death sentence on corruption charges.

Looking beyond the bare facts of his crimes, one could see Li Zhen as an operator of Machiavellian intelligence. Like a chess prodigy, he had learned the ins and outs of China's political game, and had used this knowledge to build his career. Perhaps this really would make a great story.

Li Zhen Makes the Editorial Calendar

Li Honggu finally embraced the idea. The question of when to run the story now emerged along with how much time they would devote to it. Through a source in China's central prosecutor's office in Beijing, the Supreme People's Procuratorate, *Lifeweek* learned that Li Zhen's case would go to trial sometime in May or June 2002. The editors penciled the story in for the first issue after the May 1 holiday.

Li Honggu assembled a three-person investigative team comprising himself and two young reporters, Jin Yan and Zhu Wenyi. Based on what they already knew, the key moment for Li Zhen came with his appointment as Cheng Weigao's assistant. From learning this information, two crucial questions followed. First, how had Li Zhen taken a job in the party secretary's office? Second, how much power had he actually wielded as an assistant, generally merely a clerical position?

But they first faced the more immediate problem of how to reach sources that could answer those questions. This proved more difficult than they had first expected.

Although no longer acting party secretary of Hebei, Li Zhen's former superior, Cheng Weigao, remained a powerful figure in the party. Official sources in Hebei were reluctant to cooperate, and as soon as they started to prepare the story, several of Li Honggu's sources in Beijing changed their minds, too. Cooperation, they said, would be "inconvenient."

Li Honggu trained his focus on Hebei, sending reporter Zhu Wenyi to Zhangjiakou to speak with Li Zhen's family members as well as his former instructors at Cigoubao Teacher's College. Jin Yan, meanwhile, would travel to Hebei's capital city of Shijiazhuang to talk to officials from the provincial-level prosecutor's office there, as well as local People's Congress members whom several of *Lifeweek*'s routine official sources had introduced. She would also attempt to interview Hebei's vice-governor, with the principal aim of reaching sources as close as possible to the Li Zhen case. Li Honggu would speak with his own contacts in Shijazhuang, and rendezvous with Jin Yan afterward.

Lifeweek's sources in Shijiazhuang had revealed important information in the past. Most held prominent positions at the provincial level and could direct the reporters to those more familiar with Li Zhen's case. But the degree to which Li Zhen's influence lingered in the city despite his arrest and impending trial surprised the team members. One of the magazine's most valuable Hebei sources on previous cases had been Rong Huiyong, assistant to one of the province's vice-governors. He regularly rubbed elbows with top leaders, and had worked in close proximity to Li Zhen. This time, however, Rong would not cooperate.

Lifeweek's list contained other sources, but all required painstaking follow-up, and most were of little or no help. Of the sixteen sources they approached in Shijiazhuang, only Zhou Guojun, the lawyer representing Yang Yiming, Li Zhen's successor as assistant, agreed to an interview. Yang Yiming was also facing corruption charges related to the Li Zhen case. Prosecutors refused to discuss the case they were building against Li. They provided solely details on his lifestyle, which gave a two-dimensional picture of Li's flawed character.

Zhu Wenyi in Zhangjiakou had more positive news. She had arranged interviews with two of Li Zhen's former instructors at Cigoubao Teacher's College, as well as the vice-mayor of Chengde City, Li Zhen's classmate. Best of all, however, she had arranged an interview with Li Zhen's older sister, Li Ming.

Li Ming Praises Her Brother

When Li Honggu's team arrived at Li Ming's residence for the interview, the immensity of the home surpassed their imaginations. Li Ming led them to the sitting room, where photographs testifying to the family's social and political standing covered the walls. One of Li Zhen's brothers, Li Yongjun, was also there, as was Li Zhen's mother. Li Ming clung tenaciously to her role as family spokeswoman, and she would sharply cut off the others when they spoke out of turn.

As the interview began, Li Ming explained that her husband, formerly a high-level provincial transportation official, was serving a three-year sentence for corruption. She herself had been confined for 108 days for her suspected involvement.

She spoke far more than the reporters could have dreamed. She voiced her grief at the family's fall, and expressed the hope that they might one day recover their previous stature. She said again and again that both the family and her disgraced brother deserved the respect and admiration of the public. She made no effort to rationalize Li Zhen's behavior. In fact, she pointed to his actions as the surest proof of his extraordinary talent.

Li Ming confirmed the reporters' suspicion that the Li family had political contacts in the capital. Their father, who had passed away several years earlier, had served in the People's Liberation Army. An old comrade in arms, "Uncle Yang," now held a high-level government position in Beijing. Of all the sons, Li Zhen had been the only one clever enough to use this asset, Li Ming said. Uncle Yang had accepted Li Zhen as a surrogate son. Finally, she revealed a fact that answered one of their key questions. Hebei's party secretary, Cheng Weigao, had favored Li Zhen as his assistant and gone to great lengths to protect him, she said, because he needed to make use of Li Zhen's Beijing contacts.

The talkative Li Ming soon touched on the issue of Li Zhen's divorce from his first wife, Yang Lili. Other family members wanted to talk about Yang, and started to tell their own stories. Li Ming cut them off quickly and brought the interview to a close. Leading the reporters to the door, the brother whispered that the story of the divorce left much more to tell. He agreed to meet the reporters the next day, but his enthusiasm had cooled by morning. He only referred them to Li Zhen's secretary, Ji Zhanfeng. "He can fill you in on the details," he said.

The reporters went immediately to Ji Zhanfeng's apartment, asking at the gatehouse on the first floor. Ji Zhanfeng was home, the guard said, but he had not seen him come out for several days. Li Honggu called Ji's number, but no one answered. They knocked at the door and heard nothing. Later that evening, Li Honggu returned to the apartment. A light glowed in Ji's window, but there was still no answer. Clearly, Ji Zhanfeng was laying low.

They were starting to fill out *Lifeweek*'s sketch of Li Zhen. The next challenge involved finding sources who could verify the details Li Ming and other family members provided. They first talked to Jiang Shan, the reporter from Xinhua News Agency. They hoped he could tell them which party leaders had opposed Li Zhen's appointment as assistant to Cheng Weigao. Chu Ruigeng, the *Hebei Daily* writer who had written about the infighting in his Internet column, had already refused to cooperate. Jiang Shan told them directly that they needed to speak with the official, Liu Shanxiang, former secretary of the provincial Discipline Inspection Commission, which investigated charges of official corruption.

Jiang stopped short of providing a contact for Liu Shanxiang, but eventually another source whose father was a well-connected official gave them the pager number for Liu's assistant. The source even exceeded their expectations by providing them with the telephone number for Li Zhen's ex-wife, Yang Lili. The assistant's continued use of a pager, by this time long out of favor in China, puzzled the reporters. Li Honggu knew from personal experience that pager users usually screened calls. He was surprised when the assistant, Feng, called back to arrange a meeting. Feng wanted first to know more about their story and whether they had proper credentials. The meeting with Feng went well, and he called the next day with directions to Liu Shanxiang's home.

It was May 10. Their deadline loomed, only three days away.

Knowing Liu Shanxiang was an elderly official, the reporters thought it considerate to bring him a basket of fruit and flowers, a simple gesture of respect in China. When they met Liu and realized how lucid and youthful he had remained, their gesture seemed slightly inappropriate. But Liu was extremely good-natured, and as their three-hour interview progressed, the fragments of Li Zhen's story came together.

Liu had served as Zhangjiakou's municipal party secretary when Li Zhen began his political rise there, and he offered them a view of Li from a vantage point within Hebei's power structure. He knew well both Li's background and his actions as an official. He had objected strongly to Li's appointment as assistant to Cheng. In fact, he had conducted his own investigation of Li.

Liu Shanxiang confirmed many of Li Ming's details about her brother. He also solved the mystery of Wu Qingwu, the figure curiously mentioned by name in the original Li Zhen news release from Xinhua News Agency. Wu, he said, was Li Zhen's predecessor as former party secretary Cheng Weigao's assistant.

With their deadline looming, the reporters had two sources remaining at the top of their list to consult: Li Zhen's ex-wife, Yang Lili, and his former superior, Cheng Weigao.

According to several sources, Yang Lili had warned Li Zhen before their divorce that she would expose evidence that would send him to prison if he ever tried to lift a finger against her second husband, a former city official in Shijiazhuang. Yang answered Li Honggu's first call, but refused an interview. He could not reach her from that point on.

The decision regarding whether to contact Cheng Weigao was a dilemma. Cheng was crucial to the story, and his perspective would have been valuable. But he also wielded formidable political power. If they alerted Cheng to the investigation, he might do everything within his power to stop it and compromise their search for key documents, including the original indictments against Li Zhen and others. In the end, Li Honggu decided it posed too great a risk to contact the former party secretary.

Two days before their deadline, as Li Honggu busily wrote the story, Jin Yan looked for the indictments and other documents. He secured an interview transcript with Wu Qingwu, Li Zhen's predecessor, which appeared in a Hebei internal reference, a *neibu cankao*, or "internal [government] reference," produced by the Hebei Bureau of Xinhua News Agency. The document proved instrumental for the article.

Neibu cankao, generally referred to as *neican*, have been a feature of Chinese political life since the founding of the People's Republic in 1949. Their essential role involves presenting party and government officials with facts and commentary on key issues deemed too sensitive for the news page. Many Chinese media produce *neican* internally. If an editor regards a story as too risky to publish, he can decide to send it to the *neican* desk, where a specially designated *neican* editor will prepare it for circulation to a specified group of officials. Internal references differ in periodicity and volume of content, as well as degree of classification, ranging from "top secret" (*juemi*) to "confidential" (*mimi*). Unauthorized distribution can amount to a serious violation of secrecy laws, but some *neican* selections of a "confidential" nature circulate rather widely outside official circles. In some cases, it is actually possible to subscribe to them. Nevertheless, the more widely circulated *neican* remain quite dangerous to handle, and journalists must use them with maximum caution.

In the end, the reporters obtained two *neican* documents of direct relevance to Li Zhen's case. In addition to the interview with Wu Qingwu, later for their second article on Li Zhen, they used a *neican* interview with the fallen official himself, in which he spoke in very personal terms about his official dealings in the past. *Lifeweek* reporters needed to find the Li Zhen and Wu Qingwu interviews, since they provided the most direct access possible to their versions of the stories. At that time, police held Li and Wu in custody as they awaited trial.

Li Honggu did not shy away from extracting text from the *neican* interviews. He used at least thirteen direct quotes from the Wu Qingwu *neican* in the first Li Zhen story, and, in his own words, viewed the information as "hard evidence" on par with court papers. Li Honggu also quoted extensively from the *neican* interview in the follow-up story on Li Zhen. But the risks in using these crucial yet classified sources cannot be overemphasized. Qiao Yunhua, the Xinhua News Agency reporter who had done the Li Zhen interview, later contacted Li Honggu and demanded to know who had provided the *neican*. He also said discipline inspection officials were looking into the matter. Li Honggu stood willing to protect his "Deep Throat" to the bitter end, he said, but after that he heard no further news of an investigation.

The two *neican* interviews and other documents gave a rather detailed sketch of Li Zhen's maneuverings as an assistant to Cheng Weigao. They then knew that Li Zhen's first major move had been to strike a deal with Wu Qingwu, Cheng Weigao's assistant at that time, who wished to leave public office and enter the private sector. Li Zhen gave his word he would favor Wu's business interests once he assumed his post. He would make sure Wu had public money at his disposal. Wu, in turn, would share his profits. In one case, Li Zhen obtained a large foreign exchange loan, which he had then passed through a middleman at a state-owned enterprise, skimming 20 million yuan off the top. He then gave this money to Wu Qingwu as a business loan. The tacit alliance between Li Zhen and Wu Qingwu received the blessing of their superior, party secretary Cheng Weigao, but they finalized it outside the organizational committee, the proper channel for appointments. Li Zhen later made the same deal with his own successor, Yang Yiming.

Li Zhen's Web of Connections

The first Li Zhen story, "Li Zhen: the power of an assistant," hit newsstands on May 20, 2002. Li Honggu had determined to write something different from the usual demonization of fallen officials, and the *Lifeweek* story avoided a simple enumeration of Li's crimes. Instead, it raised fundamental questions, even if it did not articulate them directly, about the forces driving political advancement in China, and about a system ripe for abuse by shrewd political players. Specifically, it explained how Li Zhen had used his high-level Beijing contact, "Uncle Yang," to leverage his position within Hebei. From the outset, the feature story sought to draw a road map of how power moved between Hebei and Beijing:

> In terms of geography, Zhangjiakou, Shijiazhuang and Beijing form a perfect triangle. But the principle is not necessarily true, where Zhangjiakou and Shijiazhuang are concerned, that the "shortest distance between two points is a straight line," for you must pass through Beijing . . . Passing through Beijing is the most effective road between Zhangjiakou and Shijiazhuang. And for Li Zhen, this was not just about transportation options.

> Around the age of 25, Li Zhen left Zhangjiakou and stayed for some time in Beijing. He explained to a colleague in Zhangjiakou that he was "going to Beijing to conduct some business" . . . This trip to Beijing truly changed the course of Li Zhen's life, and this change made a deep impression on colleagues who knew Li Zhen . . . Li Zhen's Beijing "resource" is said to be at a senior level, and even now when insiders speak about this it remains a point of mystery. The most reliable sources, Li Zhen's family members, say this [contact] is someone they call "Uncle Yang."
>
> The changes that came after [Li Zhen's trip to Beijing] firmed up the assessment of his abilities offered by his colleagues. At the age of 28, Li Zhen became an assistant to an important Hebei leader, and later, at around 30 years of age, he became "Hebei's top assistant" [to the party secretary of the province].
>
> [The article provides figures here on bribes accepted by Li Zhen, sourced from the Central Discipline Inspection Commission] . . . These eye-raising numbers of Renminbi [currency] have not been the focus among people in Hebei who have paid attention to the Li Zhen case. Rather, his position in the power structure is a subject widely debated. One top-level leader from Hebei province revealed in an interview with our reporters: "Even the advancement of provincial-level leaders relied on Li Zhen's influence behind the scenes."[7]

With the appearance of the *Lifeweek* feature and successive reports of other media, Li Zhen became a widely discussed figure. This buzz encouraged Li Honggu's team to pursue the topic in more detail, revisiting those questions unanswered in the first story. They still had not found out for certain, for example, why the provincial party secretary, Cheng Weigao, had appointed Li as his assistant, and whether Li Zhen's power had actually surpassed Cheng's.

The reporters' first stop was insider Liu Shanxiang, the elderly former discipline inspection official who had proven so helpful for the first story. They drew up a list of nine officials Liu had mentioned in connection with Li Zhen. Reaching them meant going back to Liu Shanxiang through his assistant, Feng Lixin. When they met Feng for dinner, he protested that the May 20 feature story was "far too truthful" and had drawn too much attention to him. Afraid of retribution from Cheng Weigao's circle, he was now reluctant to cooperate.

Feng said they found other assistants similarly apprehensive, and continued refusals bore out the truth — no one wished to speak to the issue. The first story had erected an obstacle in front of them; they found it impossible to confirm certain details from their first round of reporting. Some important ones pertained to the business dealings of Cheng Weigao, a much bigger story.

Finally, a source that had backed away from cooperation on the first story helped them out of their predicament. He provided a list of telephone numbers for members of the standing provincial party committee. They instantly noticed two names that Liu Shanxiang had not mentioned. One was Wang Youhui, a former vice secretary of the Hebei provincial committee and assistant secretary to the National People's Congress. The other was Li Wenshan, a former vice secretary of the provincial party committee and chairman of the Chinese People's Political Consultative Conference (CPPCC).

Wang Youhui's assistant responded with extreme caution, but agreed to speak to his boss after they had provided a portfolio of *Lifeweek* corruption coverage. Wang accepted the interview faster than they could have hoped.

Meeting with Li Wenshan required some deception. The official was a cultural connoisseur, and had published a collection of literary essays. Jin Yan requested an interview saying he was working on a culture-related feature. Li accepted. But when Jin Yan arrived at Li's home, the reporter cut right to the chase. "Actually, I'd like to talk to you about Li Zhen," he said, going straight to his list of questions. Li Wenshan did not falter, and the interview proceeded without a hitch.

Both Wang Youhui and Li Wenshan corroborated and clarified details about Cheng Weigao.

Next, they approached Chen Yujie and Li Zhanshu, officials who had worked closely with Cheng but reportedly had been transferred to Beijing at his request. To track them down, the reporters once again tried Liu Shanxiang's assistant, Feng Lixin. They hoped Liu, the elderly official, could lead them to the former Cheng insiders and help them clarify several discrepancies. Reluctantly, Feng arranged a meeting at their hotel room. For two hours, the elderly official went over the inconsistencies patiently. He refused, however, to introduce them to Chen Yujie and Li Zhanshu. The best he could do, he said, was to give them Chen's telephone number.

They had no time to waste — their deadline was drawing near. Li Honggu scribbled out a list of questions and sent Jin Yan rushing off to catch a train to Beijing. Jin arranged a meeting with Chen, and arrived at her home at around ten p.m. Although at first reluctant to dabble in affairs back in Hebei, she began to trust them more when she realized that Jin primarily wanted to check facts relating to her own role.

This last round of reporting gave them a much fuller picture of how Li Zhen had amassed power and safeguarded his political standing in Hebei. Despite having made numerous enemies, including the director of the organizational committee and a high-ranking discipline inspection official, Li established himself firmly in Cheng Weigao's circle, enjoying the secretary's unconditional support, which emboldened him to continue to seize wealth and power. Before long, his power grew decisive and he turned into, in a very real sense, "Hebei's other party secretary."

In China, patronage from the right parties can make or break one's official career. So long as Li Zhen stayed under Cheng's umbrella of protection, opposing political players had no way of preventing his advancement. Li Zhen's expanding influence was built upon this relationship.

Li himself changed the terms of the equation. In order to ensure his continued upward climb, Li Zhen sought a position as assistant director of the National Tax Bureau's branch office in Hebei. He reasoned that he could still progress through the network of the National Tax Bureau even if he lost ground in the provincial power game. But the move had the unanticipated effect of placing Li outside Cheng Weigao's protective reach. His enemies launched an investigation through the tax bureau network. Li Zhen had dug his own grave.

Pouring through the "hard evidence" they had gathered prior to the first feature deadline, the reporters found the Hebei internal reference containing the Wu Qingwu interview the most useful. Many of the details derived from official sources had apparently also originated from this *neican*. In principle, only provincial officials had access to the *neican*. However, in fact, it had circulated more broadly.

They learned of the existence of another Xinhua *neican* containing a face-to-face interview with Li Zhen from his jail cell, in which he very frankly discussed his dealings as an official. With their second deadline looming, the most urgent task became getting their hands on this promising source. After some digging, they located an official source willing to hand it over.

Li Honggu again tried to reach Li Zhen's ex-wife. He sent Jin Yan and another reporter to her home in Shijiazhuang with a copy of the first feature story and a letter explaining that they needed help verifying details about her past. Li Honggu later joined Jin Yan for a visit to Yang's home. Her husband answered the door, but refused to let them inside.

Even without the details of Li Zhen's divorce, they now had enough to proceed. The second feature story ran in the July 15 issue of *Lifeweek*, one month after the opening of Li Zhen's trial. It took a behind-the-scenes look at Li Zhen's dealings with such figures as Wu Qingwu, Yang Yiming (Li's successor as assistant), and the tobacco tycoon Li Guoting. Documentary evidence, including the two *neican* and the indictments against Li Zhen, Wu Qingwu, and Yang Yiming, proved central to this story.

Most importantly, the feature did not present Li Zhen as a wicked stereotype of official corruption, but intimated that Li represented simply the worst product of a corrupt and corrupting political environment. At one point in the article, a source within Hebei's organizational committee, the body responsible for making official appointments within the party, exposed the opacity of its procedures and their vulnerability to abuse:

> A top leader in the province's organizational committee at the time [of Li Zhen's tenure as assistant to Cheng Weigao] told our reporter: "Although there are no clearly documented regulations on this [making of direct leadership selections by officials], there are relevant [unwritten] rules, and the assistants of important leaders are recommended by the general office [of the provincial party] and examined by the organizational committee, not directly selected by leaders themselves. In the beginning, when Wu Qingwu [was assistant to Cheng Weigao], this [principle] was followed, but when it came [later] to decisions made by the triangle of Wu Qingwu, Li Zhen and their leader [Cheng Weigao], this broke through the longstanding way of doing things in Hebei province." The "mutual give and take" of Wu Qingwu and Li Zhen was clearly unexpected in the environment of the time, and it attracted a lot of attention.
>
> Liu Shanxiang [former head of the discipline inspection commission in Hebei] recalled that on three separate occasions he had contacted Li Zhen's superior [Cheng Weigao] concerning whether Li Zhen was qualified and capable of serving as his assistant. The last time concerned the question of a 50 million yuan loan, and this question was later confirmed in the indictment [against Li Zhen]. But in answer to Liu's request, Li Zhen sent back instructions to Liu's assistant, and the instructions said: "Each time adjustments are made concerning personnel at my side, people must always wag their tongues. This does not deserve an answer!" The distinguishing mark of this so-called "response" was the fact that an official document concerning the question of Li Zhen was ultimately handled and returned by Li Zhen himself.[8]

The article began with a personal touch, describing the scene as Li Zhen's family members awaited his trial on June 21, 2002. It closed with a rare candid moment drawn from the secret *neican* interview with Li Zhen from his jail cell, in which the disgraced official confessed that his appetite for wealth and power had grown in proportion to his time in politics:

> It seems that for Li Zhen the pattern he managed to create was not what he envisioned as the ultimate destination. Responding to a question from a Xinhua News Agency reporter, he summed up by saying: "Had the investigation against me occurred five years earlier, things would not have been so serious; but if it had come five years from now, things would definitely have been much worse." The Xinhua reporter's question had been: "Did your appetite [for money and power] grow in direct proportion to your time spent as an official?" Clearly, Li Zhen had answered with an emphatic affirmative.

Li Zhen's former superior, Cheng Weigao, had so far remained relatively untouched by the political storm in Hebei, and he stood as a potentially dangerous wild card for the magazine. In light of this consideration, the feature story avoided direct mention of Cheng, but the implications were clear enough to displease the Hebei's former party secretary, as they soon learned.

Cheng Weigao Is Not Amused

Not long after the second feature appeared, official pressure on *Lifeweek* intensified. At that point, the discipline inspection officials were supposedly searching for the source of the leaked *neican* documents. In the end, however, no investigation materialized.

A request from the Central Propaganda Department followed, which asked to review all reporting materials for the two stories, including a list of sources. In response, *Lifeweek* forwarded a list of high-ranking officials with blacked-out surnames. These officials, Li Honggu knew, would be above scrutiny by the publicity department. He gave them no information regarding the magazine's lower-level sources. The bureau, naturally, disliked *Lifeweek*'s handling of the matter, but took no further action.

The magazine soon learned that former Hebei Party Secretary Cheng Weigao was the person applying pressure. Cheng had composed a long-winded critique of the reports, highlighting fifteen of what he labeled as factual inaccuracies. He put this letter in the hands of Chinese President Hu Jintao, Politburo Standing Committee member Zeng Qinghong, and Ding Guangen, the propaganda chief.

The propaganda chief eventually summoned Wang Jixian, the general manager of *Lifeweek* publisher, Joint Publishing. Wang learned at this meeting that the Central Discipline Inspection Commission had been quietly investigating Cheng Weigao for several months, which coincided with the magazine's reporting on the Li Zhen story. It helped even further explain the reticence of sources in Hebei. "What do you expect us to do about this?" the propaganda chief asked Wang. "It's impossible to say Cheng Weigao is blameless, but neither is criticizing him an option right now. Your reports have placed us in a tough position," he said.

The propaganda department eventually washed its hands of the issue and advised Cheng Weigao to voice his objections directly to the publishers. In late 2002, Cheng summoned *Lifeweek*'s editor-in-chief Zhu Wei, Joint Publishing Deputy General Manager Pan Zhenping, and Li Honggu to Shijiazhuang and gave them each a copy of his critique, asking them to read it through and consider the "errors." They could decide among themselves how they would rectify these, he said. After he had arranged for dinner delivery, he left the men alone to sift through his report. They found only one area in which a question of accuracy arose, however, concerning Li Zhen's reasons for leaving Cheng's service and seeking a post within the tax bureau.

When Cheng returned, he pressed Li Honggu to reveal his sources for the stories. Li stood by the accuracy of both reports. The only issue in question, he said, was the reason for Li's interest in taking up a post within the tax bureau. Cheng explained that Li had been removed as head of the province's general office, albeit without an official announcement. Hungering for a new post, Li had presented Cheng with his wish list. He wanted to be made party secretary of Baoding City, but Cheng told him that the best he could hope for was a vice-mayorship. "We argued about this for an entire evening," Cheng told them.

"Li Zhen once remarked that he was able to control you. Was this true?" Li Honggu asked. Cheng grew quiet at first. Then he extended an unexpected offer. If Li Honggu agreed to stay with him in Shijiazhuang for one or two weeks, he would explain the entire story at length. Of course, this would have to wait until he had concluded his official business at the upcoming session of the National People's Congress. He would contact them at a suitable time.

In the end, a second meeting turned out to be impossible. Soon after the political meetings, news came that Cheng had been stripped of his party membership. When Li Honggu left a message with Cheng about meeting up in early May, the answer came through his assistant — discipline inspectors had instructed him to avoid all contact with news media.

While Li Honggu never had the opportunity to hear Cheng Weigao's own account of the story, the brief meeting in Shijiazhuang did yield one final fact. Li Zhen had surely counted on Cheng's support to build his sphere of influence in Hebei. But Cheng had relied, at least equally, on his ostensible subordinate. Having transferred to Hebei from a post in another province, Cheng found himself embroiled in a power struggle with local officials, his most notorious rival being the former party secretary, Xing Chongzhi. Above all else, Cheng needed to develop his own political clique with Li Zhen, who boasted both regional contacts and allies in Beijing, a core acquisition.

The chessboard of Hebei politics required establishing and maintaining one's political team. Li Zhen had recognized this game for what it was. He saw an opening and seized it. If it had not been for other variables, he might well have succeeded.

Postscript

Chinese newspapers abound with stories about the Communist Party's struggle to eradicate corruption within its own ranks. Media are considered important weapons in the war against corruption, but they must stay vigilant to make sure that their coverage remains within the bounds of the permissible.

Most reports on corruption follow a predictable, officially encouraged pattern of ritual demonization in which authors attack disgraced officials for their personal character flaws, often blowing them out of proportion; for example, the following passage from a July 14, 2003 article from the official China News Service, printed in several newspapers across China, describes the monstrous depravity of Li Zhen:

> Li Zhen paid no mind to traffic signals, but roared straight through whether the light was red or green. More experienced traffic cops, who knew his car by sight, never dared stop him. A fresh recruit, not knowing better, once pulled Li over, but the official rolled his window down, spat directly in his face and peeled off down the road.

The news service had this much to say about his behavior in the office:

> Li ruled the National Tax Bureau like a tyrant. To make it clear to everyone just how special he was, he assigned himself no fewer than three assistants, two female assistants and one bodyguard. He even went so far as to reserve an entire elevator for his personal use. Whenever anyone, from the deputy director on down, had business with Li, they had first to report it to the security post in the lobby. Otherwise, he would simply refuse to see them.[9]

How did Li Zhen end up like this? How had he escaped censure? Such questions, leading as they do to uncomfortable truths about China's political system, seem to be best left unasked.

When Li Honggu organized his team for a feature story on Li Zhen, he resolved to avoid ritual demonization. "As soon as a political figure falls from his post, the rationalizing mechanism of the State ideology kicks into action, expending great effort to show the fallen official is congenitally flawed and no reflection on the system," Li Honggu wrote in September 2004, looking back on the Li Zhen story. "The media are enthusiastic participants in this process. One thing we were trying hard to find out [at *Lifeweek*] was how the process of official preferment actually worked behind the scenes in China."[10]

The *Lifeweek* stories are known for their complex treatment of the fallen official. They situate Li Zhen within a wider network of political connections, teasing out the invisible forces that drive politics and the process of political advancement in China, which is not to say the stories are without precedent in China. For an earlier example, one might turn to Liu Binyan's "People or monsters," an acclaimed work of literary reportage first appearing in People's Literature in 1979, dealing with local corruption in Heilongjiang Province. But the official pattern persists, particularly in news coverage, and the *Lifeweek* features stand out as a rare exception.

In Li Honggu's case, reporters could not have painted a more or less complete picture of Li Zhen without access to two very relevant documents available only in classified internal materials called *neibu cankao* — a pair of interviews with Wu Qingwu, Li Zhen's predecessor as Cheng Weigao's assistant, and with Li Zhen himself.

News media at various levels prepare *neibu cankao*, or *neican*, or special "internal" news reports for the exclusive perusal of officials. Central party news outlets such as Xinhua News Agency or *People's Daily* produce *neican* on a regular basis and publish them in a magazine format. Other media may issue them on a more informal basis as needed, as for example, when editors spike a story but regard it as a must-read for officials.

As with other documents, *neican* fall into three levels of classification — *juemi* (top-secret), *jimi* (secret), and *mimi* (confidential). Xinhua News Agency compiles the most exclusive *neican*, the top secret National Trends, and passes them on to the standing members of the Politburo. While National Trends stays out of reach to all but a few, some *neican* of a "confidential" nature circulate rather widely outside official circles. Bureaucrats as well as Chinese journalists widely subscribe to Internal Reference Selections, a "confidential" *neican* distributed by Xinhua News Agency, looking at them for possible story leads. Presumably, this *neican* also generates a large amount of revenue for Xinhua.

Whatever their degree of accessibility, all *neican* remain potentially controversial and risky to handle. Unauthorized sharing can expose individuals to accusations of breaches of secrecy, regardless of the document's classification level. In a high-profile 2003 case, Shanghai Municipal People's Court sentenced Shanghai lawyer Zheng Enchong, who fought for the interests of Shanghai residents evicted from their homes to make way for development projects, to a prison term of three years for faxing an article from Internal Reference Selections to a foreign human rights organization. The Shanghai Court ruled that he had violated state secrecy laws by leaking the "confidential" material from the neican.

Chinese media quoting directly from *neican* must carefully weigh the political variables. The news organization's relative position in the official hierarchy constitutes one variable. While a national-level newspaper might opt to use a provincial-level *neican* — not lightly, to be sure — a provincial newspaper would be tempting fate to do so.

These documents, which stand in a gray area between the official document and the news report, uniquely distinguish the Chinese media landscape. Exclusive and authoritative, they make up an internal network of reporting for those within the political system. The closely held nature of *neican* obviates the need for censorship, making them exceptionally honest sources of information. At the same time, they present huge pitfalls in sourcing and rules of use. Some reporters dare not touch them. Others mine them for story leads. Li Honggu decided to lift whole passages, attributing them generally to "Xinhua."

In an interesting twist on the Li Zhen *neican*, Qiao Yunhua, the Xinhua reporter who interviewed the official in his cell, published a morality tale in late 2004 about a cadre who grew more and more corrupt as he advanced through the system. The book, entitled *Before the Gates of Hell*, was based on Qiao's interviews with Li Zhen, and reportedly sold extremely well in Beijing.[11]

By that time, Li Zhen's own story had ended in the manner of most high-profile corruption cases in China. On August 30, 2002, just three months after the first *Lifeweek* story appeared, Li Zhen was sentenced to death on bribery and corruption charges. The sentence was carried out the following November.

Notes

1. *Sheng Huo Ri Bao* (*Life Times*). 2001. "*Shouhui qianwan tanguan bei pu Hebei*" (Corrupt official who accepted ten million in bribes detained in Hebei), December 18.
2. *Wen Wei Po*. 2000. "*Ji guoshui juzhang shou ju'e huilu bei pu*" (National Tax Bureau chief arrested for accepting huge bribes), April 3.
3. *Ming Pao*. 2000. "*Fu shengzhang shiwei shuli guoshu juzhang shou shencha: Hebei jun gaoguan she 300 yi han an*" (Vice governor, city party secretary and tax bureau chief are investigated: group of Hebei officials involved in 30 billion yuan corruption case), July 21.
4. *Lifeweek*. 2001. "*Liu Liying: fan fu xin shiji*" (Liu Liying: a new century in anti-corruption), December 31.
5. *Lifeweek*. 2001. "*Hebei: Cong Fukui an*" (Hebei: Cong Fukui case), December 31.
6. Chu Ruigeng. 2006. "*Guanyu Li Zhen wenti de wu pian zawen*" (Five essays on the Li Zhen question). Chu Ruigeng's Weblog, comment posted on March 11. Available at http://blog.sina.com.cn/s/blog_48c9519d010002no.html.
7. *Lifeweek*. 2002. "*Li Zhen: mishu quanli*" (Li Zhen: the power of an assistant), May 20.
8. Li Honggu, Jin Yan, and Zhu Wenyi. 2002. "*Hebei han guan quan li chang*" (The playing field of Hebei"s corrupt officials). *Lifeweek*, July 15.
9. China News Service. "*Zheng zhi ming xing jiu zhe yang duo luo: 'Hebei di yi mi' da an de bei hou*" (So this is how degenerate political stars are: behind the scenes of the case against "Hebei's first assistant"), July 14.
10. Li Honggu case study on *Lifeweek*'s series of reports on the Li Zhen case. Hong Kong: Journalism and Media Studies Centre at the University of Hong Kong. On file with the China Media Project.
11. Melinda Liu. 2004. "The Proxy War; corruption scandals are a battleground for jousting among the nation's top leadership." *Newsweek International*, November.

8 *Disaster Reporting*

Where Does the Danger Come From?

Around mid-November, 2002, a patient was treated for a severe form of pneumonia in the city of Foshan, southwest of Guangzhou.[1] In the weeks that followed, rumors proliferated about a new and dangerous disease. In the absence of reliable information, panic spread. On January 2, 2003, residents rushed to local pharmacies, reportedly exhausting the antibiotics stocks in Heyuan, a city about 160 kilometers northeast of Guangzhou, in a single afternoon. On January 17, customers picked stores and pharmacies in and around Guangzhou clean of antibiotics as well as other popular home health remedies.

On January 21, unbeknownst to the general public, experts from Guangdong's health office made an official inspection visit to the city of Zhongshan, just south of Guangzhou. They studied several cases of an atypical pneumonia, and concluded that they were highly contagious and of unknown origin. Several days later, a patient, Huang Xingchu, transferred from Heyuan to Guangzhou's Central Military Hospital and died within a few days. Doctors and nurses who had cared for Huang, both in Heyuan and in Guangzhou, began displaying symptoms of the disease.[2]

Severe Acute Respiratory Syndrome, or SARS, had already begun its relentless advance, but China kept its public in the dark. On February 8, as China's Lunar New Year celebrations were coming to a close, text messages swamped the mobile telephone network in Guangzhou, saying a deadly disease had struck the city — first, avian flu, then, anthrax. By February 10, people had emptied antibiotics supplies from every pharmacy from Guangzhou south to the manufacturing hub of Shenzhen. Similarly, they swept up all the cooking vinegar, used in China both as a condiment and an organic disinfectant. Where vinegar remained available, it sold for up to 100 times the usual price.

In this atmosphere of thickening panic, Guangzhou city leaders finally decided to call a press conference.[3] They announced on February 11 that health experts had confirmed cases of atypical pneumonia in Guangdong. The mysterious outbreak in the southern province prompted some coverage in national media, but with minimal interest.

Some journalists had hoped that Guangzhou's press conference would herald a more open approach to dealing with this mounting public health threat. But in fact, only three days earlier, provincial leaders had banned all news coverage of the outbreak. In their view, the political priority of ensuring stability and stifling the spread of sensational rumors overrode all other considerations.

As events quietly unfolded in Guangzhou, the Beijing-based editorial staff of *Caijing*, one of China's leading business and current affairs magazines, trickled back into the office after the week-long holiday. They initially chatted idly about the hysteria that had overtaken southern China. But when Guangzhou leaders and provincial health officials called press conferences, the editors started to treat the story somewhat more seriously.

Since its launch in April 1998, *Caijing* had been focusing on business news. However the magazine continued to prowl for broad public interest topics with a potential economic or business impact. It had already published a series of reports, for example, on the collapse of the public health system in China's rural areas. Only a few months earlier, they had covered a public health crisis in the city of Nanjing.

By the time *Caijing*'s editors gathered for their first post-holiday brainstorming session, SARS had shot to the top of the agenda. The magazine's editor-in-chief, Hu Shuli, argued that the potential for a SARS epidemic made it a critical piece of hard news. Furthermore, it also raised concerns about China's institutional preparedness for dealing with a major health crisis. The response in Guangdong had already provoked serious questions. Why, for example, had leaders in Guangzhou called a press conference only after hysteria had swept through the city?

Hu Shuli put *Caijing*'s deputy editor-in-chief, Lin Libo, in charge of their first series of SARS reports. With the editorial deadline for the February 20 issue looming, Lin could not possibly send reporters to Guangzhou. He decided, instead, to hire a Guangzhou-based stringer to write a review of the main stages of the outbreak to date.

When *Caijing*'s Beijing-based medical reporter, Zhu Xiaochao, tried to reach national health officials about SARS, she found them singularly unhelpful. They returned again and again to the argument that China's Frontier Health and Quarantine Law had not listed SARS, as though the absence of a disease from the text of a national law somehow justified inaction.[4] One of *Caijing*'s key approaches to handling the story — namely China's lack of institutional readiness — had already begun to coalesce.

The February 20 issue of *Caijing* focused secondarily on SARS, although Zhu Xiaochao's report, which dealt with serious flaws in China's system for the detection of and response to infectious diseases, nevertheless appeared prominently in the magazine. A separate piece from journalist Wei Yi, giving a complete timeline of SARS through the February 12 run on local stocks of salt and rice by frightened Guangzhou residents, accompanied the story.[5] Zhu's article, "Going public after the hysteria," opened with the government press conferences in Guangzhou, and moved quickly onto public doubts about the handling of the crisis:

> On February 11, the Guangzhou city government and the Guangdong Provincial Health Office held press conferences in the morning and afternoon respectively, and reported that an atypical pneumonia of unknown origin and cause had affected some areas of Guangdong. By this time, this mystery illness had already invaded the province for more than a month, and during the few days following the Spring Festival related rumors sent a wave of commotion through society.
>
> As early as January 2, the city of Heyuan in Guangdong province had discovered an unrecognized strain of pneumonia and made a report of this to the provincial health office, and the city also experienced a run on major pharmacies by [frightened] city residents.
>
> As to why health officials did not report the disease situation until February, the provincial health commissioner Huang Qingdao said, "Atypical pneumonia is not designated in [relevant] laws as an infectious disease that must be reported, so we felt there was no need to make this public. Now, because the social impact is substantial, we have decided to make [the report] public." . . . On the question of epidemic disease warning, "the Frontier Health and Quarantine Law already states explicitly what diseases should be reported and how, and all reports will be made according to these stipulations."
>
> Huang Jionglie, head of the Guangzhou health office, has said that "for a city like Guangzhou with a population of ten million, a disease affecting just over 100 people is a very small ratio," and so, "as of now the environment in the city of Guangzhou is safe."
>
> The public has greeted the government press conferences with an attitude of welcome, but there are criticisms too. Following the press conferences, National People's Congress delegate Huang Deming delivered a special proposal to the provincial government. He said that none of the diseases that have cropped up in recent years such as mad cow disease and avian influenza fall within the scope of the Frontier Health and Quarantine Law of 1989, and asked whether, according to the position of Guangdong's provincial health office, newly discovered severe infectious diseases that did not fall within the purview of the Frontier Health and Quarantine Law could be concealed as a matter of course. This demonstrates that our country has serious legislative deficiencies where warning on serious disease threats is concerned.[6]

In the weeks that followed the February 20 issue, the SARS story seemed to have evaporated. There was a collective sense of relief that SARS had passed and a major epidemic had been averted. *Caijing* published only one article on SARS in its March 5 issue, but that only dealt with the allegedly suspect actions of Shanghai Roche Pharmaceutical, a division of Hoffmann-La Roche, maker of the antiviral drug Tamiflu. The story claimed that Roche held a promotional event on February

9 at a Guangzhou hotel during which its representatives advertised the benefits of Tamiflu to local journalists, in violation of Chinese laws.[7]

SARS had almost entirely left Hu Shuli's thoughts by early March, when she invited several friends from Guangdong over to her home for dinner.[8] When Hu remarked on how officials in Guangdong seemed to have handled the SARS outbreak with competence and openness, her guests were surprised. "What? SARS is still going on. It's just that no one is allowed to report on it!" they said.

Hu's next shock came shortly after the March session of the annual National People's Congress. As soon as *Caijing*'s newly posted Hong Kong correspondent, Cao Haili, arrived in Hong Kong she e-mailed back to Beijing describing Hong Kong as a city in a heightened state of alarm over SARS, and that people on the streets were wearing protective masks.

On March 26, Hu Shuli saw a report on the World Health Organization (WHO) website stating that officials in Guangdong had reported 792 SARS cases on February 28. Two weeks before that, they had reported 305 cases. Even these official numbers suggested the epidemic was progressing rapidly. Further, SARS was already grabbing international news headlines. Clearly, this topic still deserved *Caijing*'s full attention. Hu shifted reporters back to the story.

Shortly afterwards, health reporter Zhu Xiaochao met again with national health officials. *Caijing* learned that World Health Organization experts had already arrived in Beijing, and had submitted a formal request to investigate the epidemic in Guangdong. Zhu could sense from the constant busy tones at government offices and the complaints of the WHO experts that government leaders were dragging their feet, bringing tensions to a head.

Eventually, Zhu Xiaochao's article, "WHO officials visit Guangzhou," appeared in the April 5 issue of *Caijing*. As it went off to the printing house on April 2, the WHO trip still remained in question. However, as soon as Zhu had confirmed the story, managing editor Wang Shuo ordered a quick change to the headline to give it a sense of urgency:

> On March 22, World Health Organization experts . . . flew to Beijing.
>
> Right now, a contagious disease called Severe Acute Respiratory Syndrome (SARS) is putting Southeast Asia under threat, with Hong Kong at the center, and spreading around the globe, with ten countries on three continents already reporting more than 1,000 cases in total. Many observers believe that this epidemic is related to a disease that began spreading in China's Guangdong province in November of last year. The first task of the WHO expert team is to determine whether or not the two epidemics are connected . . . [9]

Zhu's article summarized in detail the numbers of SARS-infected people provided separately by the central government, the various regional governments at different times in March, and by the WHO team of experts on March 26. The report also briefly addressed the views of both domestic and international researchers regarding the question of the disease's origin. Chinese government specialists announced formally on April 4, just as the new *Caijing* issue came out, that they had isolated the common bacterium, Chlamydia, as the disease agent of SARS. However, the *Caijing* report already cast doubt on this conclusion: "The biochemistry department at the University of Hong Kong was the first to arrive at this conclusion [that the origin of the disease was the coronavirus], which received further support by information from disease prevention centers in the United States, Germany, Canada, Vietnam and Singapore. 'It seems that [the disease agent] is quite possibly the coronavirus,' said WHO expert, John MacKenzie."

Hong Kong correspondent Cao Haili contributed "Hong Kong in the midst of an epidemic" to the same issue. The story examined the international dimensions of SARS, and clearly discredited government claims that the epidemic had been contained to Guangdong.[10] For an economic perspective on the story, Hu Shuli commissioned an editorial from Andy Xie, then chief economist with Morgan Stanley in Hong Kong. Xie's editorial, "Will Asia slide back into recession?" characterized SARS as the greatest challenge facing Asian economies since the 1997 financial crisis.[11]

Caijing's editors did discuss the possible risks of running the SARS issue. Unlike their counterparts in Guangdong, no propaganda directive muzzled the national media. Yet they remained strangely silent on the story with no official news releases, or *tonggao*, from the official Xinhua News Agency, and only sparse coverage from major regional newspapers. *Beijing Youth Daily*, for example, had run a small news item about the discovery of eight SARS cases in Beijing, but with few details buried in the inside pages. In the absence of an official ban, and in the midst of a curious domestic media silence on SARS, *Caijing* was moving into uncharted territory.

Only days before the April 5 issue hit the stands, Zhang Wenkang, China's leading health official, appeared on China Central Television to disclose that there had been 1,190 confirmed SARS cases up to March 31, and forty-six deaths. The epidemic was no longer confined to Guangzhou, he said, but had been confirmed in Beijing, Shanxi, Hunan, Guangxi, and Sichuan.[12] For Hu Shuli, this public admission exploded like a bomb — and yet, the announcement still had surprisingly little impact on news coverage, causing a small surge in news reports. However, they tended to play down the newly released numbers on the epidemic with emotional tales of heroic health workers turning back the threat. On April 2, officials even announced that Beijing had been removed from the list of areas affected by SARS.[13] Hu Shuli grew increasingly suspicious as she noted the silence of several major newspapers, including the generally outspoken *Southern Weekend*.

In Guangzhou, meanwhile, where an explicit propaganda directive still constrained the media, news stories grew visibly out of touch with the public mood and the very real threat posed by SARS. A report from one local newspaper loudly touted a provincial trade fair, hailing it as a success, tallying record attendance. In fact, according to *Caijing*'s sources, scarcely anyone had bothered to show up.[14]

On April 7, news came that Pekka Aro, an official from the International Labor Organization (ILO), had died of SARS in a Beijing hospital, sending out the clearest sign yet that SARS remained a danger in the capital.

Caijing established finding out the truth about the scale of the SARS epidemic as one of its primary objectives. It required covering a massive geographic area with totally unreliable official numbers, while hospitals already operated under strict orders prohibiting workers from speaking to media. Even with the fragmented information *Caijing* reporters managed to glean from area hospitals, it became clear that the number of SARS cases went substantially beyond official reports. One of the magazine's editors, Zhang Jin, learned from his wife, a health worker, that SARS cases at her Beijing hospital alone occupied three wards. *Caijing* reporter Zhang Liang reported that Beijing's Central University of Finance and Economics had cancelled classes upon fears of the disease spreading among the student population.

To cope with the scale of the SARS story, *Caijing*'s editors organized the reporting staff into three groups. The first group went from hospital to hospital, digging up whatever information they could. The second closely tracked efforts by scientific experts to discover the origins of SARS and improve treatment. The question of the disease's origins had already become politically charged. Li Liming, the director of China's Center for Disease Control and Prevention (CDCP), announced on April 4 that scientists had successfully isolated a variant of the common bacterium Chlamydia, one not transmitted sexually, as the origin of SARS.[15] Few experts outside the CDCP accepted this conclusion, however. Typical treatments for chlamydia had so far proved ineffective in fighting SARS. The third group of *Caijing* reporters explored the relevant legal questions, including China's Quarantine Law. How did China's laws differ from those of other countries? How could a pathogen as powerful as SARS remain a blind spot in the Quarantine Law? How serious would the situation have to become before the government closed this loophole? As the three reporting teams busily gathered information, *Caijing* business editor Ye Weiqiang probed further into the economic repercussions of SARS.

On April 13, as production of the April 20 *Caijing* issue entered high gear, China's government leadership elite were holding high-level meetings on SARS in the capital. Premier Wen Jiabao stressed that tackling SARS was central to China's stable development and the safety of its people, as well as its international image. Hu Shuli sensed an important shift in the central government's position on the epidemic. The righteous tone of heroism and self-sacrifice was dissipating, giving way to a more practical and realistic view of the severity of SARS as a national challenge.

For the moment though, the government had not yet revealed its policy on SARS coverage. As the magazine approached its editorial deadline, several editors had serious doubts about the issue's prospects of ever making it to the newsstand. Was SARS worth the risk? For Hu Shuli, this question ultimately came down to a matter of instinct. In her estimation, the importance of the story as a topic of public interest roughly equaled the political risk. With the scales evenly balanced, she decided in favor of running the story.

In fact, Hu Shuli's professional hunch told her that other domestic media were falling short on SARS coverage more for their failure to grasp its deeper significance than for their fear of the consequences of pursuing it. Still, no signs of a directive from the Central Propaganda Department surfaced, even though media in Guangdong continued to face a local ban. Hu Shuli concluded that media in the capital were suffering from a sickness of their own — an exaggerated sense of propaganda self-discipline. They feared making a move before high-level leaders gave the signal.

However, the real shortage of accurate news and health information also created another problem for the news media. National and local health officials were effectively concealing the true scale of the SARS epidemic, which had lulled the Chinese news media into a false sense of normalcy. Many reporters simply avoided Beijing hospitals, where they might easily have discovered that matters were getting worse.

Caijing's April 20 issue headlined "Where does the danger come from?" sold out at Chinese newsstands. Hu Shuli interpreted robust demand for the magazine as the surest sign that SARS had truly become a topic of urgent public concern, and many regarded the search for the origins of the disease not as an abstract scientific issue, but rather as a matter of life and death. The principal feature story in the issue looked at both its scientific aspects and the institutional response. But it also brought these questions down to a more practical level: "Chlamydia? Or coronavirus? These technical terms, recognizable in the past only by microbiologists and disease specialists, are now familiar to the average person."[16]

Another article, "Beijing is sick," provided a detailed timeline of SARS in the capital.[17] But, one of the most popular stories, "SARS promotes administrative transparency," explored the legal and bureaucratic aspects of the war against SARS.[18] "As April came, the focus of world concern over SARS in China shifted from Guangdong to the capital Beijing. In the warm, light breeze [of spring], in the midst of blossoming life, doubts and rumors are proliferating," the article began. One section of it explained the origins and shortcomings of China's Frontier Health and Quarantine Law, and raised questions about the government's sluggishness in addressing the absence of SARS on the law's list of "quarantinable" infectious diseases:[19]

> Zhang Shicheng, deputy director of the national legislation office of the NPC Standing Committee's legislative work committee, took part in the drafting of the Frontier Health and Quarantine Law, and he introduced [to *Caijing*] how the legislative process worked at the time. Drafting work began in 1986 and 1987, and included stipulations on government responsibilities in reporting, publicizing and controlling epidemic situations. "The hepatitis outbreak in Shanghai in 1988 spurred the passing of the law [ahead of schedule] in 1989," Zhang Shicheng said.
>
> The Frontier Health and Quarantine Law provides the legal basis for government responsibility and measures [in dealing with disease epidemics]. And so the question of whether newly occurring diseases like SARS are or are not listed as infectious diseases [in the law], and what level of priority they are designated, is of great importance — it determines whether or not governments are legally obligated to make reports or public announcements [on a disease situation], bring situations under control or eliminate infectious diseases, and it determines whether or not governments have the power to implement a whole series of measures to tackle a given disease, including quarantine of the sick, public announcement of affected areas, closing off affected areas and mobilizing medical personnel. It also determines whether relevant [government] personnel who failed to treat seriously the spread of SARS should face administrative punishment or criminal responsibility.
>
> The Frontier Health and Quarantine Law stipulates that the State Council and State Council ministries dealing with health issues have power of determination, and "the State Council can, as circumstances warrant, add or remove priority infectious diseases [from the list specified in the legislation]."
>
> Zhang Shicheng explained to our reporter: "At the time, in order to add flexibility [to the legislation], it was stipulated that infectious diseases could be added or removed." But he emphasized that "regardless of whether [diseases] are added or removed, all [changes] 'must be announced publicly,' and this announcement, moreover, must be in the form of open publication, not through internal [government] documents. If changes are announced through the news media, these must be media with a definite degree of influence."
>
> He stressed particularly that, "For the addition or removal of infectious diseases that are a threat to the well-being of the population, [changes] must be publicly announced through media with a national reach."
>
> Singapore announced on March 24 that it had made a decree on infectious diseases, ordering that anyone who has come into contact with atypical pneumonia

be quarantined for seven to ten days, with violators subject to severe penalties. The Taiwan region announced as early as March 27 that it had designated SARS as a category-four infectious disease and had according to the law suspended all visits by government personnel to mainland China, Hong Kong, Vietnam and other areas. Also on March 27, Hong Kong announced that it had entered SARS onto the list of infectious diseases accompanying its health statute.

It was on April 8 that China legally designated SARS as an infectious disease in a document distributed internally. But it was almost seven days before this was formally announced to the public.[20]

The section of the article that followed, "Time lapse," offered a well-documented portrait of the confusion within the Chinese government's ranks. An official in China's Ministry of Health told *Caijing* on April 8 that it would formally announce the inclusion of SARS within the Frontier Health and Quarantine Law early the next morning through its official website. On the afternoon of April 11, they still saw no sign of it. However, the *Caijing* reporter found a local news report from Shanghai stating that "yesterday [the reporter] learned from Shanghai's Disease Prevention Office that in order to further strengthen SARS prevention work, the Ministry of Health has stipulated that SARS be added to the list of infectious diseases included in the Frontier Health and Quarantine Law and [that the disease be] handled accordingly, and various local governments have been ordered to carry out prevention work in accordance with the law." The first official public announcement emerged finally on April 14, printed in the *People's Daily*, with the full text appearing on the Ministry of Health website that afternoon. When the *Caijing* reporter asked the ministry to explain these inconsistencies, the answer was "I don't know."[21]

April 20, 2003, the date of the "Where does the danger come from?" issue of *Caijing*, also marked one of the key turning points in the battle against SARS. Facing intense pressure from high-ranking leaders, China's Health Minister Zhang Wenkang and Beijing Mayor Meng Xuenong publicly announced that they were stepping down. These high-profile resignations — which were in fact removals — signaled the central government's determination to deal with the epidemic more seriously and openly.

By the time the government released its first report on SARS after the April 20 issue, the full extent of the epidemic had come into sharper focus. It stated that SARS had spread even to regions as remote as Inner Mongolia and provinces in the far northwest. Suddenly, Chinese journalists were allowed to cover nearly everything. The number and variety of potential SARS stories staggered the imagination. *Caijing* had to make serious choices. "There is a saying in Beijing that there are more reporters than news stories," Hu Shuli later quipped. "But that time around, the news really had us outnumbered."

Access to central sources no longer caused the biggest problem. The focus at *Caijing* shifted to defining the crucial stories. At this point, Hu Shuli mobilized as much of her staff as she could to report on SARS. As they planned the next issue, using SARS once again as the cover story, they felt that its impact on China's rural and migrant populations would grow into one of the most pressing issues. China's weak rural health infrastructure would transform fighting SARS in the countryside into a major struggle.

On April 23, China's State Council established a new Beijing headquarters for the effort against SARS, and announced a two billion yuan ($289 million US) fund to provide medical assistance in poor rural areas.[22] This news validated the editors' choice of a cover story on rural disease prevention. She asked a veteran reporter, Lou Yi, to prepare for a reporting trip to Shanxi Province. When several of the editors expressed reservations about Lou going there alone, Hu Shuli cut the conversation short with a snap decision. "I'll go with Lou Yi myself," she said.

Westward Bound

On April 24, Hu Shuli and Lou Yi departed for Shanxi's capital city of Taiyuan. Hu toted along a large supply of protective gear — masks, cotton balls soaked in isopropyl alcohol, and antibacterial ozone lamps. She also packed a pair of white medical frocks.

When they arrived in Taiyuan, they met with reporter Li Qiyan, a native of Shanxi who had flown in from Beijing especially to help with the reporting. The three set themselves up in a community center that also served as the local headquarters of the anti-SARS effort. Medical staff there told them that a suspected SARS-carrier from Qingxu County, located on the outskirts of Taiyuan, had fled the quarantine, going home before medical personnel could convince him to stay. The *Caijing* team traveled to Qingxu to report on conditions there.

When they returned to Taiyuan, they planned to speak to officials at Shanxi People's Hospital, one of the province's leading medical facilities. Security densely surrounded the hospital, but Hu Shuli managed to slip in unnoticed by wearing one of the medical frocks she had brought along for the trip. Next, they spoke with top provincial leaders, including the vice- governor, and with local officials from the Center for Disease Control and Prevention.

On April 26, Hu Shuli hurried back to Beijing. The deadline for the next issue was closing in fast.

The May 5 issue, "SARS invades the west," marked the first time since the founding of the magazine, seven years earlier, that *Caijing* had run two consecutive cover stories on the same topic. For the first time also, a series of reports on a single topic occupied more than half of the total editorial content. The first feature story in the issue, "Shanxi's epidemic zone," a collaboration between Hu Shuli, Lou Yi, and Li Qiyan, discussed the challenges facing China's hinterlands as they fought to prevent the spread of SARS despite a crippled health infrastructure:

> When Xie Mou, retired female worker from Taiyuan City, returned home [to Shanxi] from Beijing, she sensed that something was not right. Her chest felt tight and she was feverish. She wasted no time, going straight to the clinic at Shanxi People's Hospital in Taiyuan.
>
> Xie Mou's brother had recently passed away in Beijing. He had gone to Beijing for colon cancer treatment and died instead at You'an Hospital. His death certificate read: "Feverish, reason unknown." Now Xie Mou too was "feverish, reason unknown."
>
> This was March 23. Eight days earlier, the World Health Organization had designated as SARS an 'atypical pneumonia' that had been discovered in China's Guangdong province, Hong Kong and a number of countries in Asia, and had determined that this was an epidemic posing a serious threat to countries around the globe . . . In Beijing, many people were hearing rumors that atypical pneumonia had already quietly entered Beijing, and that You'an Hospital was one of the treatment centers.
>
> If Xie Mou had a nose for news, she might at least have informed doctors at the People's Hospital about her brother's suspicious illness. Given sufficient knowledge, it is entirely possible she might have recognized her own serious symptoms. If.
>
> Unfortunately, she was in Shanxi, in Taiyuan. She did not understand English. She could not access the Internet. She did not even have the opportunity to hear "rumors." And so "if" was not to be. She thought her fever was just a common cold, and she did not talk about her brother's mysterious cause of death. She was admitted for observation in the emergency room at People's Hospital. She died three days later, and only just before she died was she diagnosed with SARS.[23]

Due to the limited number of staff reporters, *Caijing* engaged freelance journalists to write stories on SARS in Sichuan and Gansu Provinces, further strengthening its emphasis on western China and its challenges. Another article, "Migrant workers under the shadow of SARS," addressed the dangers of disease proliferation facing China's migrant working population.[24] *Caijing* also called on international experts: a Harvard University professor and authority on health policy and management, William Hsiao, wrote of the urgent need to improve China's disease prevention and response system:

> Why China?
>
> Since a long time past, China's public health and medical systems have faced a rather deep-level crisis. International comparison reveals that in spending on public health, China sits at the very bottom worldwide. I began researching China's public health situation in 1981, making a comparative analysis with more than 30 other countries. My research has shown that even Africa's poorest nations spend more per capita on public health than China by a factor of two . . . [25]

During China's usually hectic May 1 holiday, the streets of Beijing stayed quiet and empty. On May 2, Hu Shuli convened an editorial meeting in the open air setting of the city's Beihai Park, a session staff later referred to as the "Beihai Conference." As they decided how to handle the next round of SARS coverage, Hu Shuli voiced her concern that the magazine's biweekly format could not adequately handle the task. The staff had already grown accustomed to her: "Oh, if only we were a daily!" complaint. But some of the editors expressed a different misgiving that SARS coverage was shoving aside *Caijing*'s bread-and-butter economic coverage. Fatigue was setting in. "I said I'd had enough after that issue [on May 5]," one editor, Zhang Jin, remembered saying. "But Hu Shuli was absolutely adamant. She said the story wasn't finished and it was impossible to say what would happen next, and what the economic consequences would be."

Caijing decided to address both of its concerns by publishing a series of weekly special editions dealing exclusively with SARS. In total, the magazine put out four of them, produced by a ten-person editorial team. *Caijing* continued to cover SARS aggressively through the middle of June, when they lined up a powerful roster of writers to comment on the crisis. These included the acclaimed Chinese economist Wu Jinglian; the ancient Chinese literature scholar Wang Yuanhua; the legal scholar Jiang Ping; and, finally, Zhou Ruijin, the former editor-in-chief of the official *People's Daily* newspaper. In this series, which appeared under the title "SARS must change China," the contributors reflected on the impact of SARS from the vantage point of their respective fields.[26] They shared the general consensus that SARS presented a historic opportunity for China to learn from its experience and move more confidently toward reform.

"At the time, I saw SARS as a treasure trove of news stories. I thought that, if done well, these stories might provide an impetus for institutional reforms in China, that they could become a turning point," Hu later said. "The resignation of [Health Minister] Zhang Wenkang and [Beijing Mayor] Meng Xuenong on April 20, and the leadership's calm resolve to step up and face the challenge seemed to highlight this possibility. If we could reflect deeply on the costs incurred by the epidemic, then perhaps this might push institutional reforms."[27]

But Hu Shuli's hopes for deeper national reflection on the lessons of SARS ended suddenly that June. The first blow came with the arrest of Shanghai's wealthiest entrepreneur, Zhou Zhengyi, on charges of illegally acquiring bank loans and state land.[28] Soon after came the apprehension of Liu Jinbao, the then chief executive officer of Bank of China (Hong Kong) Limited. On June 13, just a week before the release of *Caijing*'s next SARS issue, the Central Propaganda Department decided in a series of closed meetings between June 13 and July 6 that it would tighten the reins on the media.[29]

The time for transparency had passed. The window of opportunity that had opened with a pair of high-level resignations on April 20 suddenly slammed shut.

Party leaders made it clear through a cluster of disciplinary actions against domestic media that they had no desire to reflect truthfully on the events of the past six months.

Postscript

When an 8.0-magnitude earthquake struck western Sichuan Province on May 12, 2008, China's media responded swiftly and purposefully. Li Datong, a veteran journalist and former editor-in-chief of *Freezing Point*, wrote from Beijing about his surprise that he could access information on the earthquake almost immediately: "After I felt my building shake I went online to see if there was any official report on what had happened. To my surprise, the epicenter of the quake and its size had already been announced, and there were even preliminary casualty estimates."[30]

China's relatively transparent handling of the Sichuan earthquake in the early stages sharply departed from its approach to disaster stories in the past, when party leaders suppressed news in order to "preserve stability" or "snuff out rumors." In contrast, in 1975, Typhoon Nina leapt inland to Henan Province from the Taiwan Strait. Floodwaters destroyed the Banqiao Dam, sending a massive tidal wave rushing downstream, killing roughly 25,000 people. The government mobilized thousands of People's Liberation Army soldiers to deal with the crisis, but China's official newspapers never even reported it. The same silence followed the Tangshan earthquake the next year, in which an estimated 240,000 people perished.

In 1988, a hepatitis outbreak that qualified among the largest public health crises of the twentieth century gripped Shanghai and its surrounding areas. At the epidemic's peak, about 10,000 new hepatitis A cases were reported each day, affecting an estimated 310,000 people in Shanghai and another 100,000 in neighboring cities. But during the three months that the epidemic raged on, as Shanghai's hospitals overflowed with patients, the city's leading newspaper, *Wenhui Daily*, ran only nineteen small news items about the disease.

Given China's continued legacy of suppressing news about disaster reporting, the leadership's more open approach to coverage of the 2008 Sichuan earthquake came as a welcome surprise. Chinese news practices themselves became a major international news story. The *Washington Post* reported that China's "normally timid news media" had followed the earthquake with "unprecedented openness and intensity."[31] The Associated Press described the coverage during the first few days of the crisis as follows: "Bodies buried under mounds of rubble, bloodied survivors pulled from debris, weeping family members begging for information — the stark images are blanketing Chinese newspapers and television broadcasts. The country's media are mounting an aggressive effort to cover the worst earthquake in decades, marking a major departure from China's past tendency to conceal crises."[32]

In many fashions, China's 2003 SARS epidemic paved the way for the response to the Sichuan earthquake that struck five years later. SARS did not, of course, instantly fix China's regime of information controls in the way many observers, both inside and outside China, had hoped, and officials continued to suppress important stories. One of the most notable post-SARS examples concerned a major chemical spill in November 2005 that dumped 100 tons of the carcinogen benzene into the Songhua River, poisoning the water supply for the northern Chinese city of Harbin and Russian cities and towns downstream. Government efforts to conceal the November 13 disaster at the beginning, not making it public until ten days later, infuriated the local population.[33]

However a series of tragedies in recent years, including SARS and the Songhua River spill, has prompted China's leaders, particularly at the national level, to reconsider the handling of information during disasters. Increasingly, officials recognize that a more open approach can improve the effectiveness of disaster response and raise public confidence. They recognize also that news is almost impossible to control in the Internet age, when individuals can post personal eyewitness accounts as well as photographs and videos across a range of new media, increasing at the same time the political cost of control itself.

China's Government Information Release Ordinance, national legislation that took effect on May 1, 2008, almost two weeks before the Sichuan earthquake, strongly indicated China's growing commitment to openness rather than secrecy as the primary principle governing the handling of information. The ordinance obligates governments at all levels to make public a whole range of designated information categories. It mandates that government offices maintain accessible logs of available information, and allows citizens to apply for its release. Many scholars and journalists believe the legislation could be crucial in putting pressure on local governments to become more open. Others, however, doubt whether the central government has the resolve necessary to make this happen.

Upon the implementation of the Government Information Release Ordinance, what *China Newsweekly* called a "rush" of formal release requests occurred.[34] A Shanghai lawyer, Yan Yiming, for example, filed applications with both the Anhui Provincial Health Department and the Fuyang city government, demanding an explanation for not issuing timely information on the 2008 outbreak of hand, foot, and mouth disease. It remains uncertain whether and how local and national officials will handle such requests. But their sudden outpouring under this new national legislation makes it clear that China's public actively and increasingly thirsts for information, and ultimately participation, that party leaders will have to grapple with more and more.

In the midst of the government's new attempts at openness, however, control remains the ultimate general principle guiding the management of media and information in China. This became abundantly clear during the government's handling of the May 2008 Sichuan earthquake, when it paired a relatively open approach to media with persistent directives on coverage from the Central Propaganda Department. At the end of May, more than two weeks after the earthquake, commercial and state media still actively stayed on the scene — an important break with the past — but with instructions not to report critically, for example, on shoddy school construction that had resulted in the deaths of thousands of school children.[35]

In April 2008, Chinese President Hu Jintao delivered a message on media policy that signaled ongoing information control even as it pledged more transparency in handling disaster stories than before. President Hu said that for "public incidents" in the future, defined as natural disasters, production accidents, and epidemic situations, reporters from China Central Television and the official Xinhua News Agency, at the very least, must be allowed to report from the scene. President Hu also urged media to report stories "at the first available moment" and to "increase the transparency of news" (meaning events should not be covered up).[36] Even if party leaders remain true to their word, however, it does not rule out the possibility that state media like Xinhua will simply monopolize news coverage of future disasters, and that more professionally-oriented commercial and party media, such as *Caijing*, *Southern Metropolis Daily*, or *China Youth Daily*, will be instructed to stick to the party line, using only the official news agency story.

The 2003 SARS case in many ways signaled the beginning of the present-day debate over access to information in China. It forced party leaders to come to grips with the extraordinary costs of secrecy. Like SARS, the 2008 earthquake offered a major test of China's transparency in handling major disaster stories. And like SARS, it offered glimpses of progress as well as clear illustrations of how far China must go before the media report disaster stories freely and openly.

Notes

1. *Nanfang Daily*. 2003. "*Congrong yingdue ding daju — Guangdong kangji fei dianxing feiyan shilu*" (A record of Guangdong's fight against atypical pneumonia), February 20. Available at http://news.sina.com.cn/c/2003-02-20/1129915672.shtml.
2. *Economic Observer*. 2003. "*SARS zhiyi yuanqi nanyue diaocha*" (An investigation of the emergence of SARS in southern Guangdong), May 10. Available at http://www.tsinghua.edu.cn/docsn/shxx/site/chinac/liudb/sars/lanmu/qingkuang/diaocha.htm.
3. *Nanfang Daily*. "*Congrong yingdue ding daju.*"
4. Frontier Health and Quarantine Law of the People's Republic of China, adopted at the 18th Meeting of the Standing Committee of the Sixth National People's Congress, promulgated by Order No. 46 of the President of the People's Republic of China on December 2, 1986, and effective as of May 1, 1987. This law, designed to prevent the spread of diseases into and out of the country and protect human health, went into effect on May 1, 1987.
5. *Caijing*. 2003. "'*Feidianxing feiyan*' *shijian huifang*" (Playback of the "atypical pneumonia incident"), February 20.
6. *Caijing*. 2003. "*Gongkai zai konghuang zhi hou*" (Going public after the hysteria), February 20.

7. *Caijing*. 2003. "*Yiyaoshang zaoyu Guangdong zhiyi*" (A pharmaceutical company is touched by the Guangdong epidemic), March 5.
8. These are the National People's Congress (NPC) and the Chinese People's Political Consultative Conference (CPPCC), for which plenary sessions are held for two weeks in March each year. The NPC is China's highest legislative body, although it had traditionally done very little legislating, serving as mostly a rubber-stamp congress. In theory the CPPCC exists to represent the interests of various mass organizations and non-CPC parties in state affairs.
9. *Caijing*. 2003. "*Weisheng zuzhi zhuanjia qu Guangdong*" (WHO expert team goes to Guangdong), April 5.
10. Cao Haili. 2003. "*Yi zhong Xianggang*" (Hong Kong in the midst of an epidemic). *Caijing*, April 5.
11. Andy Xie. 2003. "*Yazhou hui zai ci shuai tui ma?*" (Will Asia slide back into recession?). *Caijing*, April 5.
12. *China Daily*. 2003. "*Minister, epidemic under control*," April 3.
13. *Beijing Evening News*. 2003. "*You xiao kongzhi 'fei dian xing fei yan'*" ("Atypical pneumonia" effectively under control), April 3.
14. *Yangcheng Evening News*. 2003. "*Dongguan juban guoji gongye bolanhui*" (Dongguan holds international industry fair), April 1.
15. *People's Daily*. 2003. "*Weisheng buzhang Zhang Wenkang jiu feidanxing feiyan fangzhi qingkuang da jizhe wen*" (Health Minister Zhang Wenkang answers reporters questions concerning atypical pneumonia), April 5. Available at http://www.people.com.cn/GB/paper464/8877/828486.html.
16. Zhu Xiaochao and Cao Haili. 2003. "*Weixian laizi hefang?*" (Where does the danger come from?). *Caijing*, April 20.
17. Lou Yi. 2003. "*Beijing bing le*" (Beijing is sick). *Caijing*, April 20.
18. Li Yong and Wu Xiaoliang. 2003. "*SARS cui cu xing zheng*" (SARS promotes administrative transparency). *Caijing*, April 20.
19. Frontier Health and Quarantine Law of the People's Republic of China, adopted at the 18th Meeting of the Standing Committee of the Sixth National People's Congress, promulgated by Order No. 46 of the President of the People's Republic of China on December 2, 1986, and effective as of May 1, 1987.
20. Li Yong and Wu Xiaoliang. 2003. "*SARS cui cu xing zheng*" (SARS promotes administrative transparency). *Caijing*, April 20.
21. Hu Shuli and Kang Weiping. 2004. Case study on SARS reporting. Hong Kong: Journalism and Media Studies Centre at the University of Hong Kong. On file with the China Media Project.
22. China News Service. 2003. "*Guowuyuan jueding chengli fangzhi feidian zhijunbu*" (State council sets up SARS headquarters, forms 2 billion yuan fund), April 23. Available at http://news.sina.com.cn/c/2003-04-23/18581013049.shtml.
23. Hu Shuli, Lou Yi, and Liu Qiyan. "*Yi qu Shanxi*" (Shanxi's epidemic zone). *Caijing*, May 5.
24. Zhao Xiaojian and Hu Yifan. 2003. "*Nong min gong zai SARS yin xing zhong*" (Migrant workers under the shadow of SARS). *Caijing*, May 5.
25. W. Hsiao. 2003. "*Chongjian zhongguo gonggong weisheng yiliao xitong*" (Rebuilding China's public health and medical systems). *Caijing*, May 5.
26. *Caijing*. 2003. "*SARS bi xu gai bian zhongguo*" (SARS must change China), June 20. Available at http://magazine.*Caijing*.com.cn/2003-06-20/110069084.html.
27. Hu Shuli and Kang Weiping. 2004. Case study on SARS reporting.

28. Zhou Zhengyi was sentenced to three years in prison in June 2004. Some political observers have suggested Chinese President Hu Jintao orchestrated the arrests to embarrass Zhou and other figures close to former President Jiang Zemin.
29. Hu Shuli and Kang Weiping. 2004. Case study on SARS reporting.
30. Li Datong. 2008. "China and the earthquake." OpenDemocracy, June 2. Available at http://www.opendemocracy.net/article/governments/china-and-the-earthquake.
31. Maureen Fan. 2008. "Chinese media take firm stand on openness about earthquake." *Washington Post*, May 18.
32. Associated Press. 2008. "China media unusually aggressive in covering quake." May 14.
33. Philip Pan. 2005. "In visit to Harbin, Chinese leader silent on spill coverup." *Washington Post*, November 27.
34. Gao Tiejun. 2008. "*Gongmin 'xinxi gongkai shenqing' qi rechao/guanzhu de doushi lao wenti*" (A flood of "information requests" turn to old problems). *China Newsweekly*, May 21. Available at http://npc.people.com.cn/GB/28320/122662/122663/7275323.html.
35. Tom Mitchell. 2008. "Beijing reins in quake coverage." *Financial Times*, June 1.
36. Wang Duo. 2008. "*Lao lao ba wo xin wen xuan chuan gong zuo de zhu dong quan*" (Firmly grasping the initiative in news and propaganda work). *China Journalist*, July. Available at http://xwjz.eastday.com/eastday/xwjz/node271090/node271092/ula3694447.html/.

9 *The Origins of Investigative Journalism*

The Emergence of China's Watchdog Reporting

By Li-Fung Cho

China's media consumers are increasingly able to access news stories exposing government corruption and examining the social costs of the nation's market-based economic reforms. Some China observers laud this development as a sign of growing press freedom in China. Others dismiss these developments, arguing that China's new watchdog journalism functions at most as a watchdog on a government leash, a newer and more sophisticated tool for legitimizing and maintaining Chinese Communist Party (CCP) control. In fact, China's version of watchdog reporting is a complex phenomenon that resists simplistic analysis based on the dichotomy of "freedom versus control."

China's watchdog journalism grows out of what the Chinese calls *yulun jiandu*, or "supervision by public opinion." The phrase describes a government program peculiar to China, a mechanism by which the government uses the press as a tool for social and political control that provides an official framework for the coverage of controversial topics. In initiating and mandating this procedure, however, China's government has effectively opened up space for the press to pursue investigative journalism without prior official sanction. *Yulun jiandu* has created a public channel for the press to expose official malfeasance and social ills, and reflect the public interest with the cautious blessing of the CCP.

The program has resulted in the transformation of Chinese investigative reporters into public actors in a newfound world of muckraking journalism. These developments have spurred an incremental shift in the definition of the relationship between the state, the press, and society in China, and one that has implications for the future development of press autonomy. As such, the party-state in China has a dual and seemingly paradoxical role in both promoting and stifling watchdog journalism.

Since its establishment, the People's Republic of China has defined the role of its press primarily as a propaganda mouthpiece of the party leadership. In the more open era of the 1980s, as economic reforms were taking root, the party envisioned another place for the media — that of documenting, reporting, and reflecting the views of ordinary Chinese citizens in order to monitor the effectiveness of CCP policies.[1]

The use of the term *yulun jiandu*, which translates literally as "supervision by public opinion," encapsulates the departure from the image of the press as a simple mouthpiece. It is used more or less interchangeably with the term *meiti jiandu*, or "media supervision," which works bi-directionally as a means for the Chinese public to voice opinions and grievances and as a mechanism for the party-state to assess the public perception of government policies.[2]

The mandate of *yulun jiandu* arose in part from the new social and political realities resulting from China's economic reform policies, which created tremendous growth but at the same time resulted in a surge in corruption and abuse of power. Social inequalities felt keenly by the general populace increasingly marked the path of economic development. They, in turn, led to heightened reader demand for critical reporting on widespread official malfeasance. The CCP recognized that it needed to address the growing problem of official corruption, which steadily eroded popular support and tolerance for the regime. The concept of *yulun jiandu* originated within this political context.

In his political report to the CCP's Thirteenth Congress in 1987, then Premier Zhao Ziyang used *yulun jiandu* to stress the importance of the media in monitoring the party and government, marking the first time an official used the term in a high-level party document. Each Party Congress report has used it since, a sign of the concept's continuing importance.

From the time of its official debut, however, the term *yulun jiandu* has undergone several changes in meaning at the highest levels of the leadership. In Section Five of Zhao Ziyang's 1987 political report, under the heading of creating a systematic channel of communication between the party and society, Zhao set out three principles for China's media: (1) the press should exercise oversight over the work and conduct of public officials, an idea expressed by the phrase "supervision by public opinion," or *yulun jiandu*; (2) the press should inform the public of important events; and (3) the press should reflect public debates on important issues.[3]

Several key points in Zhao's 1987 report bear emphasizing. First, Zhao endorsed the media's watchdog role as part of a larger political movement to stem official corruption. He stressed, in particular, that the press should monitor party-state power, as opposed to corporate malfeasance or basic social ills. Zhao's emphasis on the scrutiny of party-state power located his interpretation of *yulun jiandu* closest to the notion of the watchdog press as found in classical liberal press theory. Second, it should be noted that Zhao, in effect, supported the concept of the public's right to know when he sought to use the press to increase government transparency, and to open up channels of communication between the party and the general public.[4] Zhao's call for the media to represent the voices and discontent of the masses also effectively paved the way for the press to serve as a public channel to expose the shortcomings of the party-state. Zhao Ziyang's vision of *yulun jiandu* transformed Chinese journalists into public actors.

Zhao's formulation of *yulun jiandu* significantly marked the first time in the history of the CCP that its leadership promoted a public role for the press in checking official power in the public interest. The idea that the media could examine party-state corruption without prior official sanction dramatically departed from its traditional role as a propaganda mouthpiece.

Zhao Ziyang's liberal conception of *yulun jiandu* would prove to be short-lived. In 1989, Qin Benli, the editor of Shanghai's reformist *World Economic Herald*, responded to Zhao's call by intensifying the investigation and criticism of official government policies and the administration.[5] Qin took Zhao's words as "rhetorical ammunition," moving beyond the official agenda to advocate for political and economic reform. But the reliance of Qin and other like-minded reformist journalists on Zhao's language turned out to be misguided. Less than one year after Zhao had emphasized the media's watchdog role, and only weeks before the June Fourth crackdown on pro-democracy demonstrators in Beijing, Qin was removed from his post, and the *World Economic Herald* was forcibly disbanded for its aggressive reporting.[6] In the aftermath, Zhao Ziyang was blamed for contributing to the unrest by "guiding the media in the wrong direction," and allowing journalists to go too far in their criticism of the government.[7]

The events of June 4, 1989, derailed the effort to promote a new role for the media as monitors of official power in the public interest. In the midst of the political uncertainty that followed the crackdown, new policies emerged that aimed at stifling the watchdog function of the media. Jiang Zemin, Zhao Ziyang's successor as party secretary, reversed attempts to liberalize the press. In November 1989, Jiang re-asserted the party's dominance over *yulun jiandu*, saying it must "guide and direct" public opinion toward stable economic and social progress under the party's leadership.[8]

According to Jiang's formulation, *yulun jiandu* must, first and foremost, serve the state agenda. This shift from emphasizing the watchdog role of *yulun jiandu*, or "supervision by public opinion," to *yulun daoxiang*, or "guidance of public opinion," reflected a basic departure from Zhao's liberal media policies. Politburo member, Li Ruihuan, in charge of ideological activities at that time, went even further than Jiang, stressing that the Chinese press must, above all, establish positive propaganda about the party as its priority.[9]

In 1992, when Jiang Zemin incorporated *yulun jiandu* into his first political report to the CCP congress, he associated it specifically with other forms of party supervision, including administrative supervision and legal supervision, and emphasized press monitoring as an integral part of the party's internal supervisory mechanism at every level.[10] In this respect, the report underscored *yulun jiandu*'s close link to the entrenched party structure, further distancing its function at that time from Zhao Ziyang's original concept of using the media's watchdog role to create a communication channel between the party and society.

But regardless of the shift in rhetoric surrounding the term, the central leadership in the Jiang Zemin era did mandate *yulun jiandu*, and this alone provided more aggressive news media outlets with the leverage they needed to continue to push the boundaries. Part of the impetus came again from the nagging social and political problems stemming from economic reform. Some media scholars attributed the government's renewed emphasis on *yulun jiandu* to such problems as massive layoffs at unprofitable state-owned enterprises, the dislocation of farmers, and unfettered abuse of taxation powers by local governments. Local corruption took an enormous economic and political toll. Official corruption and the social disruption resulting from reform threatened to undermine not only the Chinese economy but also the stability of the political order.

In order to promote public trust in leadership, the central government not only tolerated but actively encouraged *yulun jiandu* as a means of combating local corruption and other social ills. In 1992, for example, *People's Daily*, the official state newspaper, with the support of China's parliament, organized a national news reporting campaign involving twenty media organizations aimed at exposing poor quality products.[11] Jiang Zemin's second political report, to the Fifteenth Party Congress in 1997, reflected this initiative and emphasized that the power of the press to exercise its watchdog function comes from the people.[12] In 1998, shortly after Jiang's speech, Premier Zhu Rongji made a high-profile visit to *Focus*, a popular investigative news program on China Central Television. Zhu reiterated the watchdog function of the media and introduced the concept that the news media should be a "mouthpiece of the people."[13]

High-profile visits to *Focus* by leaders such as Zhu Rongji and Li Peng (1997) did not, however, signal a reversal in the universal party media policy of "guidance of public opinion," or *yulun daoxiang*. Despite renewed calls for the press to exercise its watchdog function, "guidance" continued to take precedence over "supervision."[14] The media could exercise its watchdog role only at the behest of the party. Jiang Zemin restated this stance during an interview with the American investigative news program *60 Minutes* in the year 2000, in which he asserted "China's press has freedom. This freedom, however, must obey and serve the interest of protecting the state and the public."[15] The CCP continues to see the press as a tool with which it can curb local corruption and exert social and political control.[16]

When Jiang Zemin used the term *yulun jiandu* again in his political report to the Sixteenth Party Congress, at which he handed the reins over to his successor, Hu Jintao, the public seemed to come back into the picture for the first time since the 1980s. "We should conscientiously implement the system of making government affairs known to the public. We should tighten organizational and democratic supervision and give play to supervisory function of the media," Jiang said.[17]

But Jiang also stressed in his report the importance of "maintaining social stability" through the "strengthening of ideological and political work," a term that generally signaled a tightening of press controls to journalists.[18] Jiang's report also emphasized that "they (the press) cannot use public opinion to exercise supervision on their own. We must tighten supervision by the party."[19] This was by far the clearest indication from the party that China's *yulun jiandu* should not be seen to correspond to the Western press theory of the "Fourth Estate," which implied that the press has powers independent of the government to criticize state policies.

In 2004, the government finally characterized *yulun jiandu* as "an official form of party supervision stipulated in the Internal Supervision Regulations of the Communist Party of China."[20] Numerous newspaper articles appeared at that time in *China Daily* and *People's Daily*, both official mouthpieces of the government, reaffirming the government's commitment to *yulun jiandu* as a method of weeding out party corruption at the local level.[21]

Hu Jintao's political report, his first, to the Seventeenth Party Congress in 2007 again emphasized the need for *yulun jiandu*, and like his predecessor, Jiang Zemin, Hu stressed that journalists should not view *yulun jiandu* as a right or entitlement independent of the party. Insofar as the media operated as a form of supervision, it was to be "connected to the party-state system of policing and controlling society, not apart from it."[22] Hu's words were: "We will implement the inner-party oversight regulations, strengthen democratic oversight and give scope to the oversight role of public opinion, pooling forces of oversight from all sides to make it more effective."[23]

Local Protectionism Remains a Formidable Barrier

While in theory *yulun jiandu* constitutes one of a number of mechanisms by which the central government can monitor local government corruption and abuse of power, local protectionism by entrenched party officials remains one of the biggest obstacles to its effectiveness. In China, local officials exercise powerful control over regional political, legal, and administrative institutions, and they can and do use this power to suppress negative coverage. Liang Jianzeng, executive producer of China Central Television's *Focus*, described just how difficult he finds carrying out watchdog reporting, even with the full support of leaders in Beijing and high demand from an estimated 300 million television viewers:

> Local governments often try to obstruct our investigation because they fear it will only bring additional administrative supervision from the Central Government. They often build alliances based on mutual interests. They worry that ratting out a colleague will boomerang back to strike them down.[24]

Local governments control the licensing of their media and also designate candidates for senior management positions at press organizations within their geographic jurisdictions, thus giving regional leaders a substantial degree of influence over them. Despite the central government's call for media at all levels to serve a watchdog function, their investigative power depends principally on the degree of autonomy their local party-state overseers give them.

Local protectionism often prevents media from writing critical reports on their "own turf," while it is common for local governments to impose news blackouts when negative news stories such as mine accidents occur locally.[25] Fear of exposure of official negligence or corruption to party superiors, and a concern for the potential impact on local economic development and outside investment from negative news coverage, motivate these cover-ups.

Given the restrictions on watchdog reporting, some media have pursued news stories outside their own formal administrative regions, a practice known as *yidi jiandu* or "extra-regional media supervision."[26]

Yidi jiandu Drives an Expansion of Watchdog Reporting

China's party press structure has traditionally confined local media to coverage within their geographic boundaries. A newspaper like Guangdong's official *Nanfang Daily* typically limits its coverage to provincial affairs in Guangdong, while a metropolitan newspaper in the province's largest city, Guangzhou, reports mainly on local events. Economic and social change in reform China have somewhat eroded these boundaries. The decentralized and increasingly trans-provincial character of China's economy — exemplified by the heightened mobility of labor, goods, and services — has thus rendered irrelevant many of the regional restrictions that formerly governed China's press system.[27]

China's economic reform policies require regional governments to maintain a high degree of economic autonomy, thus contributing to growing conflicts of interest between local officials and leaders in the central government on such issues as taxation and environmental protection. This, in turn, has created "gaps" or "opportunities" that enterprising investigative journalists can exploit.[28] *Yidi jiandu*, or "extra-regional media supervision," emerged in China's press at the same time as entrenched regional officials who prevented reporting by local media persistently frustrated the central government mandate for watchdog reporting about cases of official malfeasance.

Yidi jiandu leverages the political and administrative gaps that develop when competing power interests come into play. Chinese journalists have described three basic types of gaps enabling watchdog reporting: (1) The geographic gap, or *da kongjian cha*, by which an "out-of-town" reporter not subject to the direct administrative control of regional government officials enjoys much greater reporting freedom than does a local one; (2) the self-interest gap, or *da liyi cha*, by which local government officials willingly tolerate or avert their eyes from reporting on problems in *other* provinces by media under their jurisdiction, as it makes them less likely to focus on local problems; and (3) the information gap, or *da zixun cha*, by which local officials have a harder time "tracking" the activities of out-of-town journalists, thus giving them more time to publish stories before political pressure to prevent publication occurs.

One early example of *yidi jiandu* concerned the 1997 investigative report by Guangdong's *Southern Weekend* on a traffic accident that occurred in Henan Province, in which an eleven-year-old boy was killed and his father seriously injured. The driver responsible for the hit-and-run was Zhang Jinzhu, a senior police official. When local Henan media reported the traffic incident, they refrained from releasing the complete details in light of Zhang's powerful local standing. *Southern Weekend*'s in-depth investigations, conducted surreptitiously, contributed to a huge nationwide public outcry against police misdeeds and abuse of power. Zuo Fang, an editor at *Southern Weekend* at that time, said during an interview that, "once we have uncovered and reported cases of this kind, local authorities do not dare to cover them up."[29]

While *yidi jiandu* can offer Chinese media an effective tactic, policies regarding the practice vary immensely, and depend upon the individual power relationships between central and provincial leaders, and among various provinces.

Watchdog reporting, or *yulun jiandu*, faces persistent challenges in China — and yet it remains for many Chinese journalists an important institution within which professionalism can develop. The ever-present tension between the development of the press as a public monitor of official power and its continuing role as an extension of the party-state defines the emergence and development of *yulun jiandu* in China. Watchdog journalism in China differs markedly from the generally accepted model of press autonomy represented by classical liberal press theory.[30] Furthermore, the capacity for watchdog reporting in China to influence public opinion or bring about solutions to social problems owes much to the media's ongoing position as an arm of the party-state.[31]

In sharp contrast to the Western liberal ideal of independent and even adversarial state-press relations, China's press system advocates a "constructive" approach. Media are in most cases best seen as cooperating and collaborating with the party-state toward shared goals such as opposition to local corruption and abuse of power. The interaction between the press and the state stays contentious but interdependent as opposed to naturally adversarial.

Still, the emergence of watchdog journalism in China has had some role in redefining the state-press power relationship. Media do have the potential to influence public opinion in ways that force the party-state to respond to popular views.[32] While *yulun jiandu* remains subject to the guidance and interference of the party, watchdog journalists continue to contest the boundaries of acceptable coverage, and view important stories as attempts to negotiate and redefine state-press relations.[33]

Notes

1. Sun Xupei and Elizabeth C. Michel. 2001. *An Orchestra of Voices: Making the Argument for Greater Speech and Press Freedom in the People's Republic of China*. Westport, Conn.: Praeger, 2001.
2. Interview with Sun Xupei. 2005. *On the conception of yulun jiandu*. Hong Kong: Journalism and Media Studies Centre at the University of Hong Kong. Interview transcripts on file with the China Media Project.
3. Zhao Ziyang. 1987. "Advance along the road of Socialism with Chinese characteristics" (*Yanzhe you Zhongguo tece de Shehui Zhuyi daolu qianjin*). Report to the Thirteenth Party Congress of the Communist Party of China, October 25.
4. Wu Guoguang. 1997. *Zhao Ziyang and Political Reform* (*Zhao Ziyang yu zhengzhi gaige*). Hong Kong: Pacific Century Publishers.
5. Robin Porter, and Royal Institute of International Affairs, eds. 1992. *Reporting the News from China*, 2nd ed. London: Royal Institute of International Affairs; Yu Xu. 1991. "The press and social change: a case study of the 'World Economic Herald' in China's political reform." Doctoral dissertation, University of Iowa., U.M.I., 1994.
6. Hsiao Chingchang and Yang Meirong. 1990. "Don't force us to lie: the case of the 'World Economic Herald'." In *Voices of China: The Interplay of Politics and Journalism*, ed. Chin-chuan Lee. New York: Guilford Press, 111–21; Allison Liu Jernow. 1993. *Don't Force Us to Lie: The Struggle of Chinese Journalists in the Reform Era*. New York: Committee to Protect Journalists; Yu, "The press and social change."
7. "A timetable of events" (Da shi ji). *Biweekly discussion* (*Ban yue tan*), May 6, 1989. Cited in Qian Gang. 2006. "Guidance, supervision, reform, freedom: plotting the direction of Chinese media through an analysis of the all-important buzzword." Paper presented at the annual meeting of the Association for Education in Journalism and Mass Communication, San Francisco.
8. Jiang Zemin. 1990. "Issues in the party's journalism work." In *Selections from Documents on Journalism*, ed. Journalism Research Institute of Xinhua News Agency. Beijing: Xinhua Press.
9. Li Ruihuang. 1990. *Guidelines That Insist on Giving Priority to Positive Propaganda* [a] (*Jianchi zhengmian xuenchuan weizhu de fangzhen*), ed. Xinhua she xinwen yanjiu suo, Xinwen Gongzuo Renxian Shuenbian Beijing: Xinhua chuban she.
10. Jiang Zemin. 1992. "Accelerate the pace of reform, openness and modern construction, capture the greater victory of Socialism with Chinese characteristics" (*Jiakuai gaige kaifang he xiandaihua jianshe bufa, duocu you Zhongguo tece Shehui Zhuyi shiye de gengda shengli*). Report to the Fourteenth National Congress of the Communist Party of China. Beijing: Fourteenth National Congress of the Communist Party of China, October 12.
11. *Journalism Front*. 1992. "Promoting quality consciousness among the population," 6–7.
12. Jiang Zemin. 1997. "Hold high the great banner of Deng Xiaoping Theory for an all-round advancement of the cause of building Socialism with Chinese characteristics into the 21st century" (Gaoju Deng Xiaoping Lilun weida jizhi, ba jianshe you Zhongguo tece Shehui Zhuyi shiye quanmian tuixiang ershiyi shiji). Report to the Fifteenth National Congress of the Communist Party of China. Beijing: Fifteenth National Congress of the Communist Party of China.
13. Interview with ibid.
14. Qian Gang. "Guidance, supervision, reform."
15. Interview with Mike Wallace on CBS, *60 Minutes*, August 15, 2000. Cited in Laurence J. Brahm. *China's Century: The Awakening of the Next Economic Powerhouse*. Singapore: Wiley, 2001, 365.

16. Anne S. Cheung. 2006. "Public opinion supervision: a case study of media freedom in China." ExpressO Preprint Series 1717.
17. Jiang Zemin. 2002. "Build a well-off society in an all-round way and create a new situation in building Socialism with Chinese characteristics" (*Quanmian jianshe xiaokang shehui, kaichuang Zhongguo tece Shehui Zhuyi shiye xinjumian*). Report to the Sixteenth National Congress of the Communist Party of China, November 8. Official English translation available at http://english.cpc.people.com.cn/66739/4496615.html#.
18. Qian Gang. "Guidance, supervision, reform."
19. National People's Congress and the National Committee of the Chinese People's Political Consultative Conference.
20. "Internal supervision regulations of the Communist Party of China" (Draft) (Zhongguo Gongchandang dangnei jiandu tiaoli (Shixing)). Official English translation available at http://cpc.people.com.cn/GB/33838/2539945.html, 2004.
21. *People's Daily*. 2004. "China to enhance supervision reportage by public opinion," August 5; Xinhua. 2006. "Communist Party of China to introduce regulations on internal supervision," June 17; *China Daily*. 2004. "Party fortifies crackdown on corruption," February 18.
22. Y. Hu. 2001. *News and Public Opinion* (*Xinwen yu yulun*). Beijing: Zhongguo Dianshi Chubanshe.
23. Hu Jintao. 2007. "Hold high the great banner of Socialism with Chinese characteristics and strive for new victories in building a moderately-prosperous society in all respects" (*Gaoju Zhongguo tece Shehui Zhuyi weida jizhi, wei duochu quanmian jianshe xiaokang shehui xinshengli er fendou*). Report to the Seventeenth National Congress of the Communist Party of China, October 15. Official English translation available at http://english.cpc.people.com.cn/66102/index.html#.
24. *Southern Weekend*. 2000. "Their proposed bill deals with supervision by public opinion" (他們的提案：与與論監督有關), March 3.
25. Interview with Keqin Wang. 2004. *China Economic Times Investigative Reporter Discusses Investigative Reporting*. Hong Kong: Journalism and Media Studies Centre at the University of Hong Kong. Interview transcript on file with the China Media Project.
26. In China, *yidi jiandu* (异地監督) is also known as *kuadi jiandu* (跨地監督). Various translations of both terms include: "extra-regional media supervision," "inter-regional supervision," "extra-territorial reporting," "cross-region media supervision," and "inter-district media monitoring."
27. Interview with Sun Xupei.
28. Interview with Qian Gang. 2003. "Southern Weekend editor discusses editorial transformations of Southern Weekend from 1995 to 1998." Hong Kong: Journalism and Media Studies Centre at the University of Hong Kong. Interview transcript on file with the China Media Project.
29. M. Sheridan. 1998. "Chinese editors in deadly duel with corruption." *Sunday Times*, April 12.
30. Benjamin L. Liebman. "Watchdog or demagogue? The media in the Chinese legal system." *Columbia Law Review* 105, no. 1 (2002): 157.
31. Interview with Liping Jin. 2005. China Newsweek editor-in-chief and former producer at China Central Television Focus news programme discusses investigative reporting in China. Hong Kong: Journalism and Media Studies Centre at the University of Hong Kong. Interview transcript on file with the China Media Project.
32. Liebman. "Watchdog or demagogue?"
33. Cheung. "Public opinion supervision."

Bibliography

Brahm, Laurence J. 2001. *China's Century: The Awakening of the Next Economic Powerhouse*. Singapore: Wiley.

Cheung, Anne S. 2006. "Public opinion supervision: a case study of media freedom in China." *ExpressO Preprint Series* 1717.

China Daily. 2004. "Party fortifies crackdown on corruption." February 18.

Hsiao, Ching-Chang, and Mei-Rong Yang. 1990. "Don't force us to lie: the case of the World Economic Herald." In *Voices of China: The Interplay of Politics and Journalism*, ed. Chin-chuan Lee. 111–21. New York: Guilford Press.

Hu, Jintao. 2007. Hold high the great banner of Socialism with Chinese characteristics and strive for new victories in building a moderately prosperous society in all respects (*Gaoju Zhongguo tece Shehui Zhuyi weida jizhi, wei duochu quanmian jianshe xiaokang shehui xinshengli er fendou*). Report to the Seventeenth National Congress of the Communist Party of China, October 15.

Hu, Y. 2001. *News and Public Opinion* (*Xinwen yu yulun*). Beijing: Zhongguo Dianshi Chubanshe.

Internal Report. 2003. (*Neibu tongxun*), 13.

Internal supervision regulations of the Communist Party of China. Draft 2004. (Zhongguo Gongchandang dangnei jiandu tiaoli. Shixing). Available at http://cpc.people.com.cn/GB/33838/2539945.html.

Jernow, Allison Liu. 1993. *Don't Force Us to Lie: The Struggle of Chinese Journalists in the Reform Era*. New York: Committee to Protect Journalists.

Jiang, Zemin. 2002. Build a well-off society in an all-round way and create a new situation in building Socialism with Chinese characteristics (*Quanmian jianshe xiaokang shehui, kaichuang Zhongguo tece Shehui Zhuyi shiye xinjumian*). Report to the Sixteenth National Congress of the Communist Party of China, November 8.

———. 1992. Accelerate the pace of reform, openness and modern construction, capture the greater victory of Socialism with Chinese characteristics (*Jiakuai gaige kaifang he xiandaihua jianshe bufa, duocu you Zhongguo tece Shehui Zhuyi shiye e gengda shengli*). Report to the Fourteenth National Congress of the Communist Party of China. Beijing: Fourteenth National Congress of the Communist Party of China, October 12.

———. 1997. Hold high the great banner of Deng Xiaoping Theory for an all-round advancement of the cause of building Socialism with Chinese characteristics into the 21st century (*Gaoju Deng Xiaoping Lilun weida jizhi, ba jianshe you Zhongguo tece Shehui Zhuyi shiye quanmian tuixiang ershiyi shiji*). Report to the Fifteenth National Congress of the Communist Party of China. Beijing: Fifteenth National Congress of the Communist Party of China.

———. 1990. "Issues in the Party's Journalism Work." In *Selections from Documents on Journalism*, ed. Journalism Research Institute of Xinhua News Agency, 189–200. Beijing: Xinhua Press.

Jin, Liping. 2005. China Newsweek editor-in-chief and former producer at China Central Television Focus news programme discusses investigative reporting in China. Hong Kong: Journalism and Media Studies Centre at the University of Hong Kong. Interview transcript on file with China Media Project.

Journalism Front. 1992. "Promoting quality consciousness among the population."

Li, Cheng. 2006. "Think national, blame local: central-provincial dynamics in the Hu era." *China Leadership Monitor*, no. 17 (Winter).

Li, Linda Chelan. 1998. *Centre and Provinces — China 1978–1993: Power as Non-Zero-Sum*. New York: Oxford University Press.

Li, Ruihuang. 1990. *Guidelines That Insist on Giving Priority to Positive Propaganda [a] Jianchi zhengmian xuenchuan weizhu de fangzhen*, ed. Xinhua she xinwen yanjiu suo, *Xinwen Gongzuo Renxian Shuenbian*. Beijing: Xinhua chuban she.

Liebman, Benjamin L. 2005. "Watchdog or demagogue? The media in the Chinese legal system." *Columbia Law Review*, 105 (January): 157.

Lu, Ye. 2005. Fudan University journalism professor discusses extra-regional watchdog reporting in China. Hong Kong: Journalism and Media Studies Centre at the University of Hong Kong. Interview transcripts on file with China Media Project.

People's Daily. 2004. "China to enhance supervision reportage by public opinion." August 5, 2004.

Porter, Robin, and Royal Institute of International Affairs, ed. 1992. *Reporting the News from China*, 2nd ed. London: Royal Institute of International Affairs.

Qian, Gang. 2006. "Guidance, supervision, reform, freedom: plotting the direction of Chinese media through an analysis of the all-important buzzword." Paper presented at the annual meeting of the Association for Education in Journalism and Mass Communication, San Francisco.

———. 2003. Southern Weekend editor discusses editorial transformations of Southern Weekend from 1995 to 1998. Hong Kong: Journalism and Media Studies Centre at the University of Hong Kong. Interview transcript on file with China Media Project.

Sheridan, M. 1998. "Chinese editors in deadly duel with corruption." *Sunday Times*, April 12.

Smith, Craig S. 1998. "Seeds of disaster: how China managed to lose $25 billion on its grain program." *Wall Street Journal*, July 2.

Sun, Jie. 2004. China Central Television Focus news program producer discusses supervision by public opinion. Hong Kong: Journalism and Media Studies Centre at the University of Hong Kong. Interview transcript on file with China Media Project.

Sun, Xupei. 2005. On the conception of *yulun jiandu*. Hong Kong: Journalism and Media Studies Centre at the University of Hong Kong. Interview transcripts on file with China Media Project.

Sun, Xupei and Elizabeth C. Michel. 2001. *An Orchestra of Voices: Making the Argument for Greater Speech and Press Freedom in the People's Republic of China*. Westport, Conn.: Praeger.

Wang, Hui, and Theodore Huters. 2003. *China's New Order: Society, Politics, and Economy in Transition China's New Order: Society, Politics, and Economy in Transition.* Cambridge, Mass.: Harvard University Press.

Wang, Keqin. 2004. China Economic Times investigative reporter discusses investigative reporting. Hong Kong: Journalism and Media Studies Centre at the University of Hong Kong. Interview transcript on file with China Media Project.

Wei, Yongzheng. 2007. "'Supervision by public opinion' mentioned for the fifth time in Party Secretary Hu report" (Huzhong shuji baogao diwuci ti yulun jiandu). Comment posted at http://blog.people.com.cn/blog/log/showlog.jspe?log_id=1192589422297750&site_id=23113&static=1. (Accessed October 31, 2007).

Wu, Guoguang. 1997. *Zhao Ziyang and Political Reform (Zhao Ziyang yu zhengzhi gaige)*. Chu ban. ed, *Tou Shi Zhongguo Cong Shu*, 5. Xianggang: Taiping Yang Shi Ji Yan Jiu Suo.

Xinhua News. 2003. "National People's Congress and the National Committee of the Chinese People's Political Consultative Conference." March 14.

———. 2006. "Communist Party of China to introduce regulations on internal supervision." June 17.

Yu, Xu. 1991. "The press, and social change: a case study of the World Economic Herald in China's political reform." Ph.D. dissertation, University of Iowa.

Zhao, Ziyang. 1987. Advance along the road of Socialism with Chinese characteristics (*Yanzhe you Zhongguo tece de Shehui Zhuyi daolu qianjin*). Report to the Thirteenth Party Congress of the Communist Party of China, October 5.

Index